Estimating Risk

For Bernice

Estimating Risk

A Management Approach

ANDY GARLICK

GOWER

Published by
Gower Publishing Limited
Gower House
Croft Road
Aldershot
Hampshire
GU11 3HR
England

Gower Publishing Company
Suite 420
101 Cherry Street
Burlington
VT 05401-4405
USA

Andy Garlick has asserted his moral right under the Copyright, Designs and Patents Act, 1988, to be identified as the author of this work.

British Library Cataloguing in Publication Data
Garlick, Andy
   Estimating risk : a management approach
   1. Risk management
   I. Title
   658.1'55

   ISBN-13: 9780566087769

Library of Congress Control Number: 2007927945

Printed and bound in Great Britain by TJ International Ltd, Padstow, Cornwall.

Contents

List of Figures ix
List of Tables xiii
Preface xv

PART I   RISK MANAGEMENT OVERVIEW   1

1   Risk in Context   3

Risk management   3
Quantitative risk analysis   4
Estimating risk   6

2   A Brief Introduction to Risk Management   9

Taking stock   9
Risk vocabulary   10
The risk management process   16
Risk assessment   17
Information systems   29

3   Quantitative Risk Estimates   33

Taking stock   33
Representing uncertainty quantitatively   34
Risk models   38
Dependence between cost and sales   40
Modelling correlation   41
The core concepts   44
Real risk models   47
Risk registers and risk models   53
Summary   54

4   Using Risk Models   57

Moving forward   57
ABCo and its business plan: talking about risk   57
The waste management PPP   60
The bidder perspective   61
The subcontractor perspective   72
The client perspective   73
Negotiating   74
Managing the job   74
Summary   76

PART II   RISK MODELS   **79**

5   Reliability and Other Binary Models   **81**

Overview of reliability modelling   81
Fault and event trees   84
Summary   91

6   Cost and Other Additive Models   **93**

The ABCo model   93
The waste management PPP   99
Summary   115

7   Time and Programme   **117**

Schedule risk analysis   118
Contingencies   123
Summary   126

8   General Models   **129**

Influence diagrams   130
Bayesian networks   132
Decision trees   134
Summary   135

PART III DECISIONS AND RISK   **137**

9   Public Sector Decisions   **139**

The Green Book   139
Procurement and risk transfer   144
Summary   147

10   Private Sector Decisions   **149**

What investors expect and what they get   149
What managers do   152
Can risk transfer be value for money?   154

11   Safety Decisions   **157**

A brief history of safety risk modelling and its use   157
Risk based regulation – a rational dream   160
The awakening   163
What does it mean for business risk modellers?   168

PART IV   TECHNIQUES   **171**

12   Probability   **173**

Random processes and random variables   173
Probability distributions   175
Mean, variance and percentiles   179
Some more useful distributions   180
Multiple events, conditional probabilities and independence   184

Joint probability distributions and correlation   186
Functions of several random variables   188
Some approximations   189
Is probability relevant   192

13   Monte Carlo   195

The Monte Carlo concept   195
How to do Monte Carlo simulations   197
Modelling dependence   198
Visualisation and importance   200
Sampling and estimation   207
Summary   213

14   Other Methods   215

Exact methods   215
The direct method   217
Discrete probability distributions and Bayesian networks 218
When Monte Carlo does not work   219
Summary   222

15   Decision Analysis   223

Decision theory   223
Multi-attribute decisions   229
Decision trees   230
Summary   234

Index   *235*
About the Author   *241*

List of Figures

Figure P.1	The structure of the book	xvii
Figure I.1	The structure of Part I	1
Figure 2.1	Chapter 2 overview	9
Figure 2.2	The two dimensions of risk	12
Figure 2.3	The (risk) management process	16
Figure 2.4	Focusing in	17
Figure 2.5	Range of consequences of a single risk	24
Figure 2.6	Alternative perspectives on the risk assessment process	25
Figure 2.7	Risk and reward	29
Figure 3.1	Chapter 3 overview	34
Figure 3.2	A bell curve	35
Figure 3.3	An S-curve	36
Figure 3.4	Bell curves and S-curves compared	37
Figure 3.5	ABCo profit spread	39
Figure 3.6	ABCo profit spread with dependence	42
Figure 3.7	Consequences of ABCo risks for profit and loss account and balance sheet	50
Figure 3.8	ABCo distribution of project delay	51
Figure 3.9	ABCo final model results	52
Figure 4.1	Chapter 4 overview	58
Figure 4.2	Bidder organisational structure	63
Figure 4.3	Initial sensitivity chart	67
Figure 4.4	Initial risk provisions	68
Figure 4.5	Improved sensitivity chart	69
Figure 4.6	Improved risk provisions	70
Figure 4.7	Distribution of return	71
Figure 4.8	Baselines and risk	75
Figure 5.1	Manuscript loss event tree	85
Figure 5.2	Laptop fault tree	86
Figure 5.3	Internet fault tree	87
Figure 5.4	Partial quantification of the event tree	88
Figure 5.5	Housekeeping fault tree	88

Figure 6.1	Comparison of the direct method and Monte Carlo for operations	96
Figure 6.2	Comparison of the direct method and Monte Carlo for overheads	97
Figure 6.3	ABCo complete model results	98
Figure 6.4	The PPP risk model	102
Figure 6.5	Relationship between actual costs and main contractor costs	110
Figure 6.6	Risk provisions for risks spread over time	112
Figure 6.7	Distribution of maximum overspend	113
Figure 6.8	Risk provisions for point risks	114
Figure 6.9	Comparison of revealed and exact provisions for point risks	114
Figure 7.1	ABCo production facility schedule	119
Figure 7.2	Distribution of project duration	120
Figure 7.3	Updated ABCo production facility schedule	121
Figure 7.4	Updated distribution of project delay	122
Figure 7.5	The effect of realistic review processes	122
Figure 7.6	The effect of ineffective risk release	124
Figure 7.7	A project organisation	125
Figure 8.1	Waste management PPP influence diagram	131
Figure 8.2	Cryptosporidiosis influence diagram	132
Figure 8.3	Influence diagram for site development	133
Figure 8.4	Increase in confidence with tests	133
Figure 8.5	Site development decision tree	134
Figure 10.1	Utility and worry	151
Figure 10.2	Stakeholder expectations on risk	152
Figure 11.1	fN-curves and S-curves	159
Figure 11.2	Comparison of standard and single lead junction	161
Figure 11.3	Train collision event tree	162
Figure 11.4	Train collision fN-curves	162
Figure 12.1	Decays in 100 experiments lasting 100 hours each	179
Figure 12.2	P5, P20, P80 and P95 for symmetrical and skewed triangle distributions	182
Figure 12.3	Use of triangle distributions in a 50 per cent probability risk	185
Figure 12.4	Principle of Chebyshev's inequality	190
Figure 12.5	Using Chebyshev's inequality as an approximation	191
Figure 12.6	Demonstration of Central Limit Theorem for skewed triangles	192
Figure 13.1	Summing triangle distributions – probability density	198
Figure 13.2	Summing triangle distributions – S-curves	199
Figure 13.3	Correlation and rank correlation	200
Figure 13.4	The effect of correlation on scatter	201
Figure 13.5	Sensitivity chart for simple risk model	202

Figure 13.6   Variation sensitivity chart for simple risk model   203

Figure 13.7   Scatter charts for individual risks   204

Figure 13.8   Correlation chart for simple risk model   205

Figure 13.9   Tornado chart for simple risk model   205

Figure 13.10   Variation sensitivity chart for project risk model   206

Figure 13.11   Correlation chart for project risk model   206

Figure 13.12   Scatter chart for project risk model   208

Figure 13.13   Standard deviation of percentile estimators   211

Figure 13.14   Convergence of estimators   212

Figure 14.1   Distribution of time to completion   216

Figure 14.2   Results of the direct method for point risks   219

Figure 15.1   Comparison of two options   224

Figure 15.2   Decision chart for simple decision   225

Figure 15.3   Decision tree for site development   231

Figure 15.4   Decision chart and the value of information   233

List of Tables

Table 2.1	ABCo risk workshop output	18
Table 2.2	ABCo risk register	20
Table 2.3	ABCo likelihood and consequence categories	22
Table 2.4	ABCo risk prioritisation matrix	22
Table 2.5	ABCo qualitative risk profile	23
Table 2.6	ABCo risk prioritisation matrix with typical values	27
Table 3.1	Core concept summary	47
Table 3.2	ABCo target financial performance (in £m)	48
Table 3.3	ABCo downside scenario financial performance (in £m)	49
Table 4.1	Initial bid summary (in £m)	68
Table 4.2	Improved bid summary	70
Table 4.3	Financial parameters	71
Table 6.1	ABCo operational risks	94
Table 6.2	ABCo cost risks	96
Table 6.3	ABCo profit and loss risk model description	98
Table 6.4	Simplified funding table	101
Table 6.5	Risk model inputs	103
Table 6.6	Risk model profiles	105
Table 6.7	Risk model output sheet	106
Table 7.1	A possible contingency management system	126
Table 9.1	Recommended maximum adjustments for optimism bias	140
Table 9.2	Initial IT system evaluation	142
Table 9.3	Updated IT system evaluation	142
Table 10.1	Percentage reference table	153
Table 10.2	Factors which improve value for money in procurement	155
Table 10.3	Factors which detract from value for money	156
Table 12.1	Distribution gallery	181
Table 12.2	Conditional probabilities for rain	186
Table 13.1	Simple risk model	202
Table 13.2	Project risk model	205
Table 14.1	Simple point risk model for the direct method	218
Table 15.1	Decision table for simple example	224

Engineers dealing with Arrow's clouds

Can Anybody Help?

Our knowledge of the way things work,
Sets us a challenge we just cannot shirk.
And Arrow sees in his mind's eye,
Large clouds of vagueness, trailing by.

Engineers sit with furrowed brow,
'How can we write our Standards now?'
But having thought and talked a lot,
'Big Safety Factors hit the spot!'

'Engineers,' says Gordon over lunch,
'Are such an optimistic bunch.
To estimate the money spent,
We'll add in sixty-six per cent!'

The people say 'that isn't funny!
He ought to realise it's *our* money?
We know engineers from before –
They'll spend it all, and then some more!'

So Gordon phones in from his car,
A wheeze to help PSBR.
'We'll do the job with PFI,
And sod' em all at *Private Eye*!'

The Chairman of the Board was brisk,
'Now it seems we've got all the risk!
It's not a time to act like misers,
We need a shed load of advisors.'

'Is anyone prepared to try
To grasp these clouds as they float by?'

Preface

The role of risk management has grown dramatically in many organisations over the last 10 to 20 years. As a 'risk enthusiast' – as someone, to my shock and surprise, once called me – I am delighted, but it still seems that the disciplines and techniques of risk management have yet to settle into their true role. I can pick out three reasons contributing to why this is the case. Firstly, risk management has grown out of a broad range of disciplines, some of which are very technical or specialist in nature, and the way these different fields are brought together has yet to be optimised. Secondly, risk management as a discipline has not been able to develop in a way which recognises that managers and organisations have always done it (or should have). Thirdly, and following from the first two points, we need to be clearer about the risk management capabilities needed by both managers and their specialist risk advisors.

What makes risk interesting is that it is concerned with future uncertainty, while risk management is about trying to change the future for the better. In the words of Nobel-prize winning economist Kenneth Arrow [(1992), 'I know a hawk from a handsaw', in Szenberg (ed.), *Eminent Economists: their Life and Philosophies*, (Cambridge University Press), 42–50], 'our knowledge of the way things work, in society or in nature, comes trailing clouds of vagueness', so it is not surprising that some aspects of risk management are difficult, while others evoke disagreement, disquiet or incomprehension. In particular, when you represent the future with numerical measures, the clouds of vagueness can make life tricky – as well as interesting. Yet risk management tries to present itself as a settled and accepted engineering technique, complete with standards and other indications of an established practice. As a result of this, challenges are glossed over and progress is held up.

People want concrete, objective processes they can apply, check and then get down the pub. They want to sleep well at night having done the right thing. As an example, engineers build in safety factors to their structural designs. But this kind of approach is too blunt an instrument for dealing with future uncertainty. We need to come to terms with subjective assessments of the implications of the clouds of vagueness. There is no single right thing and we have to reckon on losing some sleep.

So one of the most unsettled areas of risk management in organisations is quantitative risk analysis. There is little consensus on when it is useful, what it means, how it can be used, how it should be done and whether it is right. Instead 'doing a Monte Carlo' is regarded as a form of magic, practised by an initiated priesthood on hapless managers, generally with the aim of persuading them that the risk is less than they might have thought. Much of it is not understood and admittedly some of it is nonsense. This does not mean risk management is not worth doing, but we do need to improve what we do.

As a result, this book is addressed at managers and their risk advisors alike, with the specific aim of helping to arrive at a more settled way of dealing with risk using numbers.

Why do I think this is useful? Because only with a quantitative approach to future uncertainty can we compare issues on a common scale to see which are important and which are relatively trivial. We can improve our decision-making process. I think this is essential to ensure we use our scarce resources in the best way. It also seems to me to be sensible to put business forecasting into the same sort of quantitative language that accountants use to report the past. Imagine the company results presentation at which the FD says, 'we made quite a lot of money last year.' Of course, it is more difficult to say how much money you will make next year, even within a range, but it is certainly worth trying.

To create a 'management approach', I have tried to:

- set everything against an organisational or business background where management is the main influence on risk;
- relate everything back to the decisions that managers have to make to promote the success of their organisation;
- identify what managers need to do in their organisations to promote the effective use of these techniques.

Because all managers need to be risk managers, they have to be able to understand something of the techniques described in this book. The question is, how much? By setting this in a plan-do-review format, the way risk analysis fits in with existing processes should be clearer.

This does not mean it is a management manual. Some of the material is definitely for specialists only, but my intention is to relate the theoretical back to the practical. It is also not a step-by-step guide. Instead it indicates the sorts of things you could be trying to do. There are no process charts and no spreadsheet formulas.

The book gives my personal view as a practitioner, not an academic. It is based on my experiences working in the field and consulting on risk over many years, but it has no pretensions of being comprehensive. There are not many references; just a few I think are interesting. You can Google as well as I can. Almost everything is explained by way of examples. Almost everything is glossed with my personal prejudices.

I have aimed to put forward a rigorous but minimal approach which attempts to lift the veil and clarify what can and cannot be achieved. In spite of being a risk enthusiast, I am not in favour of doing a project schedule risk analysis only because it is 'best practice' or 'that's what we do round here'. My aim is not just to demystify, but also to reduce the amount of nonsense, to focus on activities which have practical benefits rather than those that are process requirements with no discernable benefit. I am convinced that the way to bring quantitative risk analysis more into the mainstream of management thinking is partly by introducing new concepts for managers to work with, but mainly by cutting out the unhelpful chaff.

I have tried to introduce a touch of humour. I find a lot of wry amusement in the way people deal with the world in general and risk in particular. In the course of this book I poke fun at almost everyone. I am also very critical of situations where I think failure to follow a sensible line is wasting our resources. Some readers might find this an arrogant and patronising mixture of stupidity and ignorance. They are right of course, so this book is not the last word, but I hope that it makes a contribution, alongside everyone else's ideas, to move us forward. I shall welcome – and respond to – all comments by email and you can also find some of the material on my website www.riskagenda.com.

To cover the material in the way I want to, the book is split into four sections. Broadly speaking, Part I is directed at managers. It seeks to tell them what they need to know, what to look for and how to use it. By contrast, Parts II, III and IV are intended more as a text book for risk advisors. There is a need to define the knowledge and capabilities of the people I characterised earlier as a priesthood. They often fall short of having what I regard as the basic level of competence for doing

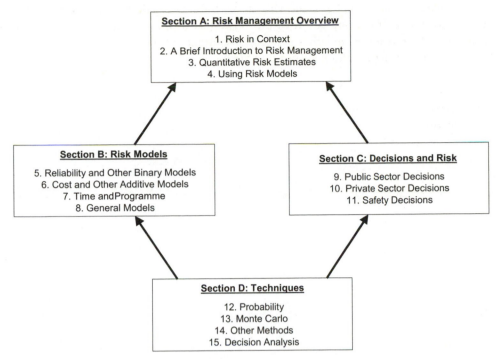

Figure P.1   The structure of the book

this kind of work: there are no professional standards for risk modellers. Although I cannot remedy that situation, this book aims to provide some useful tools for the trade.

Part II describes various types of quantitative risk models. My intention is to emphasise that these are all variants of the same thing. Part III discusses how the risk models can be used to help make decisions. This is the *raison d'etre* for the models. Unless there is the possibility that you are going to decide to do something differently, there is no point in developing them. Finally Part IV supports the two technical sections with descriptions of the underlying techniques. Figure P.1 shows a little more detail.

As you can see, this structure is not sequential. It is designed to be dipped into as you follow up on specific topics. As a result, some things are repeated and no doubt many things have been missed.

In spite of it being a personal view, I could not have written this book on my own.

Firstly, and perhaps surprisingly, a big thanks to Microsoft, Gates *et al.*, for Excel. It is a wonderful tool for someone who sees the world in numbers and graphs. As you will see, their software has made a major contribution to this book.

Many other people have also helped in the production of this book. They are firstly, of course, all those whom I have worked with professionally over the years, starting with my teachers at school and university, my collaborators on randomised methods for numerical analysis and especially my colleagues and clients during the last 20 years of consulting on safety risk and business risk. I cannot name them all, so will not mention any, but people reading this may well recognise their contribution.

I also owe a great debt to my parents and family for their help and support throughout this period. Special thanks are due to my son Richard for the cartoon, and to my daughter Heather for her constant encouragement to chill out from time to time. Most of all I owe an enormous debt to my wife Bernice, who has dealt with all my foibles on a daily basis for more than 30 years with great love. If I annoy you with this book, just think what she has to put up with. Most recently she has shown great resilience to my prima donna behaviour while doing this first book. I can hear her groaning at the word 'first'.

Andy Garlick
andy.garlick@riskagenda.com
www.riskagenda.com

Risk Management Overview

The first of four sections in the book, Part I provides an overview of risk management, focusing particularly on the role of quantitative techniques in organisational and business risk management. This section is intended to be reasonably self-contained and suitable for the general reader. It is therefore quite explicit in defining jargon and explaining any of the necessary concepts. To illustrate these concepts and view them in realistic situations, examples are drawn from a fictional, yet typical, manufacturing company.

Figure I.1 describes the contents of Part I.

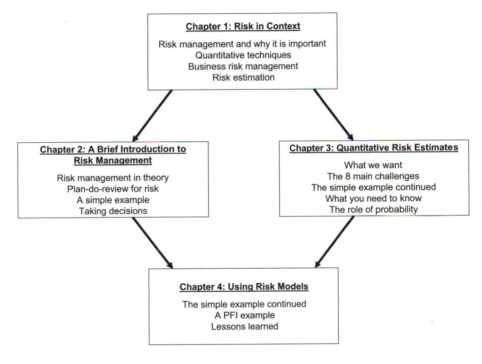

Figure I.1   The structure of Part I

Chapter 1 provides a short introduction to risk and the benefits of visibly incorporating risk awareness within management. It then sets out the context for business risk management, which will be the main topic of the book.

In Chapter 2 we move on to provide a brief overview of the qualitative approach to risk management which has become widely adopted in recent years.

Chapter 3 sets out to introduce quantitative risk estimates. Defining what they are and what insights they can give you to help in the management of your organisation is one of the primary goals of the book.

Finally, Chapter 4 deals with the other main purpose of the book: to clarify the role of quantitative risk estimates and provide guidance on when they can be developed usefully. The ABCo manufacturing company is revisited before a new example involving an imaginary major PFI deal is developed. The section concludes with a review of the main features covered.

Part I is followed by three sections which contain supporting material for what has been presented in the initial section. Explanations of how to develop quantitative risk estimates and how they have been implemented in practice are explored through the remainder of the book.

1 Risk in Context

Risk management

The last 20 years or so have seen a tremendous increase in the awareness of 'risk' and use of 'risk management' in organisations. We see this in the recent initiative to introduce risk management into UK government departments. We see it in new requirements for corporate governance, especially the Turnbull guidance. We see it in structured approaches to risk sharing and the allocation of responsibility in new forms of contract, including PFIs. And we see it in changing ways of regulating safety, which require risks to be demonstrably reduced to levels as low as reasonably practicable.

All these examples are drawn from the UK, but similar trends are seen worldwide. It is as if a whole new industry has been created. Worse, there is a suspicion that this industry was created to service the latest management fad. But risk is turning out to be quite a robust fad. This should not be surprising as it is not a fad at all, but a core management concept which will be with us for as long as we have managers.

It has always been the job of managers in organisations to take decisions and act bearing future uncertainty in mind. This is what risk management is about. At its core is the knowledge that we cannot predict the future with certainty, but we can take steps which will tend to favour preferable outcomes over less attractive ones. There are ways to do this systematically, listing the different possible futures and listing the actions which will tend to prevent the unwanted outcomes and promote the desirable ones. (It is also a good idea to carry out the actions you have listed, a point that is sometimes forgotten.)

So, avoiding formal definitions for the moment, risk is the existence of uncertainty about the future. Risk management is the discipline of making decisions and acting whilst demonstrably taking account of this potential for different future outcomes. The next chapter provides a primer on the accepted wisdom of how it should be done, but it is worth pointing out straight away that this is not conceptually difficult. The problem, if there is one, is the practical difficulty of enumerating and dealing with the many and complex ways in which the future may unfold.

Because it is a core function of managers to work for better futures – what else are they there for? – it goes without saying that risk management is important. Sometimes one is asked to demonstrate the business case for risk management. You get involved in comparing the costs of buying and implementing a dedicated risk database with the cost of all the horrible things which you hope will not happen because you've got the database. I don't think this is a very useful exercise: either you think visible risk management is a good idea or not in the same way as you might think keeping a set of accounts is a good idea or not.

It is worth pointing out that not everything which goes wrong indicates a failure of risk management. It is traditional to lard books about risk management with juicy reminders about nasty things happening to companies. Cautionary tales have been wrung out of Enron, Worldcom, Marks and Spencer, Railtrack, Shell and Barings, amongst others. They are presented as risk management object lessons: if only Ken Lay had made a decent risk register! In fact, these anecdotes remind us of two things: it is difficult to understand fully the range of future outcomes; and if you take risks bad things sometimes happen.

Shell did not see the furore over Brent Spar coming; Mr Lay's problem was not his lack of a risk register: it was just risk materialising. Over the course of several papers at a recent annual forum, the Institute of Risk Management agonised about whether specific incidents were risks materialising randomly in line with their probabilities or avoidable mistakes made by people. Surprise, surprise; in retrospect they were all in the latter group!

You may think that these difficulties make it a waste of time to try to identify the range of possible outcomes and to promote the preferred ones. If so, stop reading. But if not, don't think nothing will ever go wrong again. Sometimes something will happen at random; sometimes something will happen because of a mistake, the consequences of which were totally predictable in retrospect; and some things just can't be helped. We shall discuss the relationship between risk and randomness, and its relevance to risk modelling in organisational environments several times in the course of this book.

Meanwhile readers who would like to know more about the historical background of risk (and be entertained) should read Peter Bernstein's book *Against the Gods: the Remarkable Story of Risk* (1996, John Wiley and Sons).

Quantitative risk analysis

This growth of risk management in organisations has not been primarily concerned with the quantitative nature of risk. It has focused mainly on using the range of identified possible futures to determine risk management actions which can be taken. It sometimes seems to be more in the nature of managing glorified to-do lists. This approach aligns with the adoption of risk management as one of the tools for improved corporate governance following various corporate disasters, including those mentioned previously.

Although good corporate governance practice does not focus on quantitative modelling, there are several areas where the characterisation of risk has been undertaken numerically for some time.

RELIABILITY

Reliability analysis has a history extending back more than half a century. Its aim is to quantify the likelihood that a system such as a train or a weapons launcher or, more recently, software, will operate in the required manner. This requires detailed system modelling and a flavour of this is provided in Chapter 5.

SAFETY RISK

The risk that people might be killed or injured has also been quantified for many years. This applies to hazardous plants, such as nuclear reactors and oil refineries; hazardous systems, such as railways; or any hazardous profession where statistical data is collected, such as fire-fighting. Associated with this research has been the extensive analysis of numbers to help decide whether certain systems or occupations are safe or not. This is described in Chapter 11.

PHYSICAL RISK ANALYSIS

Associated with health and safety risk is a whole area of work aimed at understanding and characterising the risk which arises from natural and man-made phenomena such as earthquakes, infectious diseases, carcinogens, drug side-effects, pollution and so on. This largely academic work has also tried to develop criteria for dealing with these phenomena which recognise societal and personal attitudes to risk. Sophisticated techniques have been developed for characterising environmental risk. Other techniques have been put forward to elicit and understand people's perceptions and preferences when it comes to risk.

FINANCIAL RISK

Seemingly in another universe, the financial community has had a long-standing involvement with risk and its analysis. For centuries it has offered risk-based products like life insurance and more recently has offered their clients risk management products such as hedges and derivatives. Their ability to do this – and specifically their ability to price the growing list of ever more innovative products – is based on their capability to analyse the risks in a trading environment, using, for example, the Value at Risk technique. The financial community has also, to a greater extent than others, integrated their analysis with their corporate governance arrangements in areas such as maintaining appropriate liquidity ratios to guard against the failure of financial institutions.

BUSINESS RISK MANAGEMENT

Putting the history of quantified risk together with the growth of corporate risk management raises an obvious question. Do the quantitative techniques used in other areas of risk analysis have a role in supporting risk management in organisations? For the purposes of this book we shall refer to this as business risk management simply because it is a term which slips off the tongue more easily than organisational risk management. Throughout this book, business risk management means the risk management activities which organisations, whether they think of themselves as businesses or not, carry out to help them secure their objectives.

Up to now the take-up has been fairly patchy. Many projects have a contingency sum in their budget which is determined in part by the assessed chance that the project manager can deliver a task for the amount estimated by the quantity surveyor. On the other hand, few lists of corporate risks are fully quantified. Often this is for good reasons: it would be very difficult to do so because the risks are not articulated in a suitable way and there would be little benefit to be gained anyway. As another example, consider the area of risk management known as business continuity, the risk control measures needed to maintain service delivery when there is a major loss of assets because of fire, flood, terrorist attack, avian flu or good old-fashioned computer crashes. This has created its own industry, which seems to focus on putting protection in place in a way which pays little heed to the ratio of the cost of the protection to the risk it averts.

Furthermore, as well as a slow rate of adoption, much of the quantitative risk work that is done is not done well, is just plain wrong, is misunderstood or is done in a way which does not help as much as it could.

I think that there is a much bigger role for quantitative techniques in business risk management:

- to help managers understand the risks they are taking;
- to help managers be clear that the rewards are commensurate with these risks;

- to help managers work more effectively with their partners on risk management, risk sharing and risk allocation, at the right price.

Which brings us to the title of the book.

Estimating risk

The objective of this book is to explain and clarify the potential role of quantitative risk estimates as part of practical risk management in organisations. The aim is to provide a set of tools which can assist managers to make good decisions and act on them in the light of future uncertainty. This tool set is not just the techniques which can be used, but, perhaps more importantly, a set of concepts which need to be understood both by managers and by risk specialists so that they can work together effectively.

One point is worth making straight away. As far as I am concerned, risk management encompasses all future uncertainty. Sometimes a distinction is drawn between risk and uncertainty. The way the distinction is drawn can differ: it may be the distinction between events we know can happen or have some experience of and those we do not know about; or it may be the difference between events which may or may not happen and those we know will happen, but the consequences are uncertain. I do not find any of these distinctions useful and will not be using them: risk management is about all the causes of future uncertainty to the extent they affect your objectives. This means that we cover upside as well as downside in our definition of risk. Specific upside outcomes are sometimes referred to as opportunities. We will not be using that distinction: with numbers this comes with a change of sign.

Given this, it is important not to underestimate the size of the challenge. Probably the three biggest risks which organisations face are:

- systematic underestimation of the cost and time to carry out virtually any activity you care to name; frustration with this has led the Treasury to introduce optimism bias adjustments to appraisal techniques in advance of proper risk analysis (see Chapter 10);
- systematic underestimation of the management resources and, especially, managerial talent, needed to achieve objectives successfully; how often does the risk professional hear 'are you telling me I won't be able to manage x?' followed by the manager, or more usually their successor, screwing x up;
- the essential unpredictability of the future environment (be it political, economic, social and so on) and the resulting requirements; I do not know how it is possible to enter into a 25-year contract without an agreement to review things every few years in such a way that neither party is unfairly penalised.

These risks are not the traditional future threats that many view as the major risks, such as unsuitable soil conditions, quality failures, hurricanes, fraud and so on. The latter are important, but mean nothing unless put side by side with the three listed above. Those, by comparison, present truly significant challenges to the risk analyst.

This sets the stage for four questions which I shall try to answer in the course of this first part of the book.

- What is quantitative risk estimation, and what do you need to know?
- When should you do it, and when not?

- How should you do it, and how not?
- How do you make the decision?

I come back to these at the end of Part I, to finish Chapter 4.

In dealing with these questions, I am very aware that some of the concepts I expect managers to become familiar with are likely to be challenging at first sight. Managers do not expect to use probabilistic terms in the same way or to the same extent that they are expected to have, for example, basic financial skills. But if formal and quantified risk management is to be part of an organisation's culture, it seems to me that a relatively small amount of effort to climb the risk literacy (or numeracy) ladder is necessary.

I am conscious, too, that I am probably expecting risk advisors to learn some new material. I have less sympathy for them. Making the most of the tools available, avoiding mistakes and helping their clients – the managers – to get the most value from what the quantitative approach has to offer requires a basic level of knowledge which is often not attained by those carrying out this role. I think addressing this will improve the professionalism of the trade.

2 *A Brief Introduction to Risk Management*

Taking stock

The previous chapter explained that the basic disciplines of risk management are very simple:

1. List the risks (that is, the ways in which the future may differ from the baseline prediction).
2. Write an action plan.
3. Implement the action plan.

This is very similar to a plan-do-review approach to management – and we must also remember the review stage during this process. Whilst simple in principle, implementing these disciplines involves a number of complexities. This chapter provides more details of what is involved, whilst remaining relatively approachable and high level. Figure 2.1 provides an overview of the topics we shall cover.

We will start with some specialist risk jargon to give us a way to talk about risk and, more importantly, to ensure the way we talk about it aligns with good practice. We then fit these concepts into a plan-do-review model for risk management.

Whilst this book is not specifically about risk management per se, it is important to understand the overall process before zooming in on risk assessment – a key part of the planning element of plan-do-review. At this point we shall introduce an imaginary manufacturing company, ABCo, to provide examples of the techniques so you can see how they work in practice. This background will set the stage for understanding the quantitative methods for estimating risk described in Chapter 3.

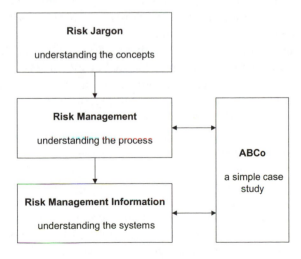

Figure 2.1 **Chapter 2 overview**

The final element of this chapter is a discussion of risk management information systems. These provide important support to risk management and thus play a key role in determining quantitative estimates of risk.

Risk vocabulary

Risk suffers from a plethora of jargon. This is not necessarily helpful to organisations who want to ensure their managers recognise that risk management is part of their job, and always was. The terminology creates the impression that it is a technical speciality for men in white coats. This section tries to provide a minimum vocabulary whilst sticking to accepted practice: see the Risk Management Standards and Guidance box.

Previously accepted practice gives us something of a problem as much of the formal work on business risk management is derived from work done on safety risks and is not optimal for business risk management or, indeed, the 'management approach'. There will be more about this later, but it is certainly not the intention of this book to redefine jargon, though we will introduce one or two usages which go beyond current commonly accepted definitions.

We start off with several interrelated sets of definitions, taken from the Australia/New Zealand standard. (From now on we shall refer to this as 'the Standard'.) The first set concerns itself with the definition of risk itself. We shall then move on to risk assessment before arriving at risk management.

RISK

The definitions in the Risk Defined box gradually take us to the crux of future uncertainty.

The first important point is that risk has something to do with objectives. We do not look at everything that is uncertain about the future, rather just those things which impact the objectives of our organisation. It is therefore essential to know what the objectives of our organisation are. These will range from the measurable (to make £5 million profit next year) to the unmeasurable (to be a good neighbour), from the financial, through non-financial (to increase the number of customers with loyalty cards), to reputational (to be recognised as the world leader in our industry) and from environmental (to be certified to comply with EN14000) to safety ('we've made it our top priority'). Everything with an impact on these objectives is the concern of risk management.

Note that the definition says nothing about adverse impacts. In spite of the usual connotation of the word risk, risk management likes to be concerned with positive consequences as well as negative ones. Often the terms opportunity or opportunities are used for this, whilst uncertain negative impacts are described as threats. Opportunities are in principle subject to risk management in the way described here. In practice, they are often dealt with differently and do not form a major part of any analysis.

The definitions also show that we have to characterise risk in terms of specific events and consider the consequences of these events and their likelihood. Risk has not been measured until we know what the events are, have thought through their consequences and have assigned likelihoods. Risk is an essentially two-dimensional concept. This is illustrated in Figure 2.2, which shows a number of events plotted on a likelihood–consequence chart. Evidently, those events with a high consequence and high likelihood of materialisation are of most concern. These occur at the top right of the chart, such as Event 4. Conversely, we

Risk Management Standards and Guidance

There are a number of standards for risk management. Indeed there is even an international guideline for risk jargon: ISO/IEC Guide 73, *Risk Management – Vocabulary – Guidelines for use in standards*. Its intention is to allow anyone who wants to to produce their own standard for risk management. This is not helpful to those of us who think it should be presented as a set of common concepts and disciplines and would prefer there to be one 'standard'.

Perhaps the best example of a standard is the joint Australia/New Zealand standard AS/NZS 4360: 2004, *Risk Management*, originally published in 1995 and re-published in 2004. It is supported by a handbook, HB 436: 2004, *Risk Management Guidelines*, which incorporates the standard. The guidance runs to 120 pages in total and is a well thought-out overview of the subject. However, this standard is not completely compliant with the standard for vocabulary mentioned in the previous paragraph. There are good reasons for this. These changes are minor but allow the standard to work more coherently.

Another standard of interest was produced by a group of UK organisations. This is the IRM/ AIRMIC/ALARM publication *A Risk Management Standard*, published in 2002. This is much shorter than the AS/NZS standard and is available as a brochure which can, for example, be downloaded from the IRM website (www.theirm.org). This document, which incorporates the vocabulary standard, may become a British or European standard.

These 'standards' are really only guidance or checklists for implementing the common sense processes already described. They do not pretend to provide prescriptive instructions for setting up a risk management system. The two standards are based around different flow charts, neither of which is suited to a management approach, as we shall come to shortly. However, to avoid confusing things with a different set of jargon we shall stick to the Australia/New Zealand vocabulary in the main text.

There is plenty of other guidance on risk management available. Examples in the UK come from the Treasury (see the risk portal at www.hm-treasury.co.uk, which contains links to *The Orange Book: Management of Risk – Principles and Concepts* and the *Risk Management Assessment Framework*), The Housing Corporation (search on risk at www.housingcorp.gov. uk), the Association for Project Management (*Project Risk Analysis and Management Guide* (PRAM), www.apm.org.uk), the Institution of Civil Engineers (*Risk Analysis and Management for Projects* (RAMP), www.ramprisk.com) and the Office of Government Commerce (look for risk in the toolkit section of www.ogc.gov.uk). It is debatable whether it is a good idea to have so many documents addressing the same basic, simple concepts for the different disciplines and environments involved. It is certainly wearisome to at least one risk practitioner!

are not much concerned with those that are of low consequence and are in any case unlikely, such as Event 2.

More interesting are the intermediate group on the diagonal, especially those such as Event 5, which are unlikely, but very significant if they do materialise.

Thinking about this a bit more, it becomes apparent that it is no easy job to develop a complete list of events which can characterise the future in enough detail to cover all outcomes, without becoming unmanageable. The eight events on the chart will not come close to covering all of the risk in even the simplest organisation.

It is also important to think through how you will distinguish between the events themselves and their consequences. It will probably be useful to bring in concepts such as cause and effect, source and category and so on. In practice the uncertain future is a long chain of cause and effect:

- the workman was pushed for time;
- so forgot the waterproofing;

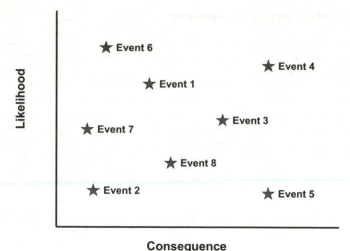

Figure 2.2   The two dimensions of risk

Risk Defined

Risk is the chance of something happening that will have an impact on objectives.

Note 1: A risk is often specified in terms of an *event* or circumstance and the *consequences* which may flow from it.

Note 2: Risk is measured in terms of a combination of the *consequences* of an *event* and their *likelihood*.

Note 3: Risk may have a positive or negative impact.

Event is the occurrence of a particular set of circumstances.

Consequence is the outcome or impact of an *event*.

Likelihood is used as a general description of *probability* or *frequency*.

Probability is a measure of the chance of occurrence expressed as a number between 0 and 1.

Frequency is a measure of the number of occurrences per unit of time.

Source: (2004), *Risk Management*, AS/NZS 4360:2004, 2–5

- so the bridge leaked;
- so the reinforcement corroded;
- so a lump of concrete fell off;
- so the bridge was closed for reinstatement;
- so the performance regime imposed a penalty;
- so the budget was not met;
- so the Operations Director was fired;
- and the company got a reputation for incompetence.

All of these events and consequences could be identified as such in a risk analysis. There is no single, 'correct' way to do it. The trick is to do it the right way for your organisation, consistently and easily.

What about the final component of the definition of risk, chance leading to likelihood, then probability and frequency? The vaguely defined sequence of words in the Risk Defined box gives an indication that this is a problematic area, in spite of the simplicity of Figure 2.2. In fact these are concepts which have the potential to become very complicated very quickly. Few managers have a detailed knowledge of what probability is and yet to understand risk they need to be able to express their view of the future in terms of events and the probability of those events. They need to do this in a way which distinguishes between the probability of the events and the probability of the consequences. They need to do this in a way which distinguishes between the probability of something happening in the next year and the probability of it happening, ever. They need to do it in a way which distinguishes (from the example above) between the probability of getting any penalty and the probability that the penalty will be more than £1 million, and between the lump of concrete falling harmlessly or falling on someone's head.

This is a lot to take on board if probability is not part of your day-to-day thinking.

In the joint Australia/New Zealand standard *Risk Management* (AS/NZS 4360: 2004), probability is defined as a measure 'of the chance of occurrence expressed as a number between 0 and 1'. But you need a lot more to make this meaningful and usable. Probability theory is an extensive body of knowledge. It is also one that has several interpretations, with different people seeing it in different ways. For me, and many others, probability is a profoundly subjective concept. Even when a coin is tossed the assignment of equal probabilities of heads and tails is based on the assumption of an evenly weighted coin.

More relevantly, the probability of the kind of events which constitute the future of a project or organisation are matters of informed, and individual, speculation and not a truth waiting to be calculated. I think it is important to accept this subjectivity. Maintaining the pretence that risk is an objective entity which can be calculated, rather than a subjective quantity to be guessed, wastes peoples time and leads to inefficient formulations and decisions based on assumptions which are not properly appreciated. You will read a lot more about this!

RISK ASSESSMENT

The Risk Assessment Defined box provides a sequence of definitions from the Standard and needs little commentary.

This sequence maps out the bones of a process for deciding what the risks are and assessing their significance. This is the core of risk management and, as I keep saying, there is not a great deal to it – in principle.

Risk Assessment Defined

Risk assessment is the overall process of *risk identification*, *risk analysis* and *risk evaluation*.

Risk identification is the process of determining what, where, when, why and how something could happen.

Risk analysis is a systematic process to understand the nature of and to deduce the level of risk.

Risk evaluation is the process of comparing the level of risk against *risk criteria*.

Risk criteria are the terms of reference by which the significance of risk is assessed.

Source: (2004), *Risk Management*, AS/NZS 4360:2004, 2–5

In practice there is a lot of hard work and some pitfalls. They arise from two main causes which we have already identified: first, there are lots of risks, even for quite simple enterprises (and the important ones might be missed); and second, risk analysis, involving the concepts of likelihood and probability, can be conceptually difficult.

The tools provided to deal with these issues are not as helpful as they are made out to be in my opinion. However, we shall return to this after we have described the complete risk management idea.

RISK MANAGEMENT

The Risk Management Defined box contains another set of definitions from the Standard. Here we have our management fad, stripped down to its official definition, and there are several things to notice. First, the definition of risk management itself does not mention risk. This is perhaps surprising. Indeed, the entire set of definitions underline the point we made earlier that risk management is just management and reflects any manager's responsibilities in their part of the organisation.

Second, the definition shows that there is more to risk management than process. The process is important, but the culture and organisational structure it fits into are key elements, both in defining the process and determining its success.

So, taking these points together, it can be seen that the only real change which formal risk management brings to an organisation is making explicit and visible what was previously done, or was supposed to have been done, anyway. By introducing explicitness and visibility, it is expected that risk will be managed more comprehensively and effectively than would otherwise be the case.

This is an important point to hold on to in what follows. Risk management is not an additional activity to add on to what your organisation is doing already. It is a slightly different way of approaching what you are doing already – different in that there is perhaps more emphasis on being comprehensive and certainly more emphasis on making it visible. It follows that if you are going to introduce the formal risk management discipline, you need to do it in a way which not only fits with your existing people, processes and systems, but also uses your existing people, processes and systems as appropriate. It must be done in a way which avoids doing the same thing twice, once the old way and once the new, 'risk management' way. However, this book is not about introducing risk management or making it work (directly) so we will not pursue this topic further.

Risk Management Defined

Risk management is the culture, process and structures that are directed towards realising potential opportunities whilst managing adverse effects.

Risk management process is the systematic application of management policies, procedures and practices to the tasks of communicating, establishing the context for, identifying, analysing, evaluating, *treating*, *monitoring* and reviewing risk.

Risk treatment is the process of selection and implementation of measures to modify risk.

Monitor is to check, supervise, observe critically or measure the progress of an activity, action or system on a regular basis in order to identify change from the performance level required or expected.

Source: (2004), *Risk Management*, AS/NZS 4360:2004, 2–5

The other definitions add more detail. They emphasise that the risk management process combines risk assessment, risk treatment (see the Residual Risk Defined box), risk monitoring and risk review. This is the plan-do-review loop again. In addition, the list emphasises two further activities within risk management: the importance of setting the context and communication.

Setting the context

The way the objectives of the organisation are reflected in the objectives for risk management sets the context for the entire scheme, whether it is a continuing risk management process or a one-off exercise which is being designed.

Communicating and consulting

Like all management activities, risk management does not happen in a vacuum and the management activities have to be designed and implemented in consultation with the people and organisations affected – the stakeholders – and in communication with them. The importance of this is underlined when it is clear that one party is making decisions which affect another. This is starkest where safety and environmental risk is involved, but most risk decision making affects others in some way.

We chose to provide definitions taken from the Australia/New Zealand standard. The UK Institute of Risk Management standard puts more of a focus on risk reporting. This is really just another way of looking at communication, although one which tends to place the emphasis on the regular production of lists of risks which have been identified for management consumption and the like, rather than active engagement with all stakeholders.

The risk management activities which complement risk analysis are important and useful. Putting them in place in organisations introducing formal risk management can be challenging. Effective ways to do this have yet to be reliably established. Indeed, there are some indications at the time of writing that organisations are becoming rather

---

Residual Risk Defined

There are lots of things which can be done 'to modify risk'. As defined by the Standard, these include:

Risk reduction is an action taken to lessen the likelihood, negative consequences or both, associated with a risk (of which the following are really examples).

Risk avoidance is a decision not to become involved in, or to withdraw from, a risk situation.

Risk control is an existing process, policy, device, practice or other action that acts to minimise negative risk or enhance positive opportunities.

Risk sharing is sharing with another party the burden of loss, or benefit of gain from a particular risk.

Following which there is acceptance of the *residual risk* – 'the risk remaining after the implementation of risk treatment' (all definitions from AS/NZS 4360:2004, 2–5).

There is a well known structure termed the 4 Ts: tolerate (that is, do nothing), treat (that is, do something, such as *risk reduction* or *risk control*), transfer (that is, *risk sharing*, where the party you are sharing with takes it all) or terminate (that is, do something else, *risk avoidance*). There is also a fifth T: take the opportunity!

impatient with the lack of tangible benefits from formal risk management initiatives, in spite of the copious evidence of the devastating effects risks have when they materialise. These problems arise in part from these organisational factors discussed here, especially the failure to recognise that risk management is something they are doing already and must avoid doing twice.

We now focus on the risk management process itself, rather than the organisational issues relating to its successful implementation.

The risk management process

The risk management process is mapped out in standards and guidance documents using the definitions listed in the previous section and a variety of flow charts. The descriptions generally provide a good overview of the tools and disciplines which are associated with risk management. They tend to be strong on statements of the obvious and generic advice, but weak on specific guidance and, in some places, logical coherence. From the point of view of a management approach, their primary weakness is that they do not map well into a classic plan-do-review loop, principally because the definition of risk treatment includes both selection and implementation of measures to modify risk. Selection is part of 'plan' and implementation is 'do'.

With this perspective, a simple risk management process is shown in Figure 2.3.

Figure 2.3 emphasises the broad scope of risk management compared with just risk assessment. It particularly emphasises the importance of implementation. You have to do what you say you will do in your risk assessment. Risk management is an active (or proactive) and continuing activity. The other elements show how context, communication and review have to be part of the formal risk management system, as we have just discussed.

Figure 2.3   The (risk) management process

However we are now going to focus on risk assessment, with a view to zooming in on the quantitative techniques described in the next chapter. This is illustrated in Figure 2.4, which reiterates some aspects of the terminology.

Risk assessment

The Risk Assessment Defined box introduced the concepts of risk identification, risk analysis and risk evaluation against risk criteria. We will briefly describe each of these activities in turn before suggesting a slightly different perspective which I think is more useful for business risk management.

RISK IDENTIFICATION

Risk analysis is crucially dependent on how and what risks are identified. The standard method is generally to engage in some sort of brainstorming session with the intention of promoting comprehensiveness by systematically considering what can go wrong with each element of a project or system. This can be approached in different ways, with several lists of such prompts. These sessions are conducted by a team of people who have insight into the enterprise being considered and whose broad knowledge should enable most risks to be discovered. Positive benefits are gained simply from allowing (or forcing!) people from different functions to sit together, understand the activity and share their perspectives on the risk and opportunities involved in their projects, and what should be done about them.

The ABCo Corporate Risks box introduces a manufacturing company which we shall use as a case study for many of the concepts in this book. At this point ABCo has begun to implement

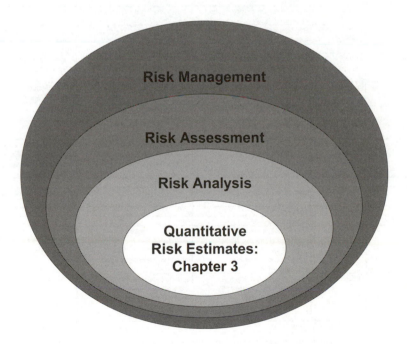

Figure 2.4   Focusing in

a comprehensive approach to risk management. It has just held a workshop session to identify the risks across the company.

It is characteristic of these sessions to produce a large numbers of worries, some well-defined, some less so. They will also produce lists of actions which are expected to control the risks. These sessions tend to be less effective in prioritising the risks in any plausible way or, indeed, in articulating the risks in a coherent manner which would make it clear what

ABCo Corporate Risks

Table 2.1 shows the results of a risk workshop carried out to develop a corporate risk register for ABCo. The context is that the FD has decided to implement integrated risk management as a way of complying with the so-called Turnbull requirements on some aspects of corporate governance. 'Turnbull' is in fact a guidance document on internal control which must be complied with by companies listed on the London Stock Exchange. It has a risk-based philosophy. The latest version can be found on the website of the Financial Reporting Council at www.frc.org.uk.

Table 2.1   ABCo risk workshop output

ID	Category	Title	Risk	Treatment	Comments
1	Marketing and Sales	Product A	Sales of Product A.	Reduce prices.	
2	Marketing and Sales	Product B	Customers may not like Product B.	Offer discounts.	This could damage the ABCo brand.
3	Marketing and Sales	YZCo	YZCo may enter the market before us with a new product superior to Product B.	Undercut them.	
4	Marketing and Sales	Advertising	The budget may not be big enough.		We need to commission Saatchis to do a new TV campaign for Product B.
5	Operations	Overhead costs	It may not be possible to cut overhead costs to the extent planned.	Voluntary severance scheme.	
6	Operations	Liabilities	Adverse outcome of injury court case.	They haven't got a leg to stand on.	
7	Operations	Waste disposal	Site operators will increase their fees.		The Environmental Director met someone in a pub who said he'd sort it, easy.
8	Engineering	Project Beacon	There is a risk that Project Beacon may overrun on time and cost.	Full project risk management. Financial contingency and float.	This would also affect sales of Product B: see Risk 2.
9	Engineering	Widget	There is a risk that the actuating devices on production line A will wear out and halt production.	Buy 40 more in case.	It is understood that a previous widget failure led to an LTA.
10	IT	Project 4star	Late delivery of new system for holistic integrated technology.	Project plan shows delivery on time.	
11	IT	Business continuity		It is essential that we spend squillions on a best practice data security system.	Management consultants have been asked to develop requirements (unbudgeted cost of £500k).
12	HR		Industrial action.		
13	HR		Loss of key staff.		There are very few succession plans in place.
14	Strategic		Substitution.		
15	Strategic		Wrong product mix.		
16	Corporate	Insurance premiums	There is a risk that next year's insurance premiums will be higher than we have budgeted due to hardening of the insurance market.	Consider increased deductibles. Persuade brokers that maximum loss is £10 million.	
17	Corporate	Office rental	There is a risk that the 5-yearly rent review will increase HQ rents beyond budget.	Seek to persuade Executive and Board to move from Park Lane to portacabins vacated by Project Beacon management team.	

ABCo's workshop session lasted half a day and involved the main executive directors, helped by a facilitator. The facilitator was not a very good one – the table tends to reflect what people will put down when left to their own devices. The table shows only a subset of the 70-odd risks identified to give a flavour of the output.

While the corporate risk management exercise was masterminded by the FD, ABCo also has a strong project delivery department which has been implementing project risk management for a number of years. Project risk management has exactly the same underlying philosophy as corporate risk management and, in fact, fits in to provide a further piece of the jigsaw, helping to produce a comprehensive and integrated company-wide system. There is more on project risk management in Chapter 7.

See the Information Recording Home Truths boxes below for more on the format of the table.

the causes, risk events and consequences are. The actions tend to be bright ideas, rather than comprehensive, committed management decisions.

The facilitator of the session, perhaps someone from the risk team, is generally left with the tedious task of developing the risk descriptions properly so that they can be analysed with clarity. This is generally glossed over in the standards and text books, but is bound to be necessary if organisations want to get maximum value out of expensive sessions bringing busy managers together. The facilitator needs the skills to understand the organisational context, the enterprise that is being assessed, the politics of the participants and the ability to synthesise coherence from disjointed discussions. A facilitator who just types up what is said and then claims to be finished is either wasting people's time or producing dross. The ABCo Updated Risk Register box shows how the register might look after investigation and improvement by the risk team.

At this point it is worth thinking about how comprehensive the risk register needs to be. The risk register concept is (arguably) derived from a safety analysis technique called HAZOPS (from hazard and operability studies) which is based on answering an elaborate structure of prompts. This seeks to be comprehensive by using a diagram of the system and analysing each section systematically against a number of relevant keywords and modifiers. Because this is aimed at delivering a safe facility, the process is conducted in a very comprehensive, but time-consuming way. Furthermore each hazard identified must be managed and explicitly closed out.

The HAZOPS process is excellent for leaving no stones unturned, but it is perhaps a bit too time-consuming for most business risk management purposes. A balance has to be drawn between the time spent identifying and treating risk and delivering the project. Clearly it is important to be comprehensive where the most important risks are concerned. Striking this balance will be a matter of judgement and it is up to the team to support the facilitator in getting this right.

An examination of the risk listing provided in Table 2.2 shows that the consequences are of several types. It makes sense to try to measure the consequences on a common scale. The obvious scale to use is a financial one and many risks are easily measured by looking at the overrunning costs of a project, the potential reduction in sales next year and so on. But not all risks can be characterised this way: think of a safety risk which could result in people being killed and injured or a reputational risk which could lead to adverse publicity and the loss of the company's licence to trade (literally, as in the case of Enron, or effectively, as with Coca Cola's bottled water). There are many more potential types of consequence, but for now it is most important to keep in mind the types relevant to your organisation. It is good economic principle that they be traded or valued against each other in some way, however that is much

ABCo Updated Risk Register

The improved version of the ABCo risk register is shown in Table 2.2.

Table 2.2   ABCo risk register

ID	Risk Model Category	Title	Risk	Treatment	L	C	Comments
8	Project Beacon	Project Beacon	There is a risk that Project Beacon may overrun on time and cost.	Full project risk management in place. Monthly Board risk reviews.	A	1	This would also affect sales of Product B, see Risk 2.
5	Overhead initiative	Overhead costs	There is a risk that it may not be possible to cut overhead costs to the extent planned.	Review of objectives and activities of the overhead reduction initiative by a Red Team.	B	1	
10	IT project	Project 4star	There is a risk of cost and time overruns on Project 4star. This will damage our reputation in the City.	IT Director to review requirements and plans with CEO. All activity halted in interim.	A	2	Serious doubts about need for another 4star system. Loss of data during transition could affect our ability to produce annual accounts.
1	Sales	Product A	There is a risk that sales of Product A may fall behind projections.	Streamline operations so that direct costs can be adapted to sales.	A	2	
2	Sales	Product B	There is a risk that sales of Product B may fall behind projections. This will damage consumer confidence in ABCo.	Early delivery of Project Beacon, see Risk 8.	A	1	It is planned that Product B will come onto the market 6 months into the year following completion of Project Beacon.
4	Operations	Advertising	There is a risk that the planned campaign for Product B will cost more than budgeted.	M&S have been advised of the budget available and reminded of company financial control Procedures.	B	2	This is not a risk and will be closed. M&S have been advised of the budget.
6	Operations	Liabilities	There is a risk that there will be an adverse outcome in (a) the injury court case and (b) the industrial tribunal.	HR Director to ensure full rehearsal of hearing with company lawyers.	C	1	It is considered that although the probability of an adverse outcome is low, the award could be high. Industrial tribunal case added later.
7	Operations	Waste disposal	There is a risk that WasteCo will put up their disposal charges over inflation.	Investigate GetridCo charges. Operations Director to reduce waste to 20% of current levels. Investigate new Varnish technology.	B	2	It is essential that any alternative operator is fully compliant with statutory requirements and company standards.
9	Operations	Widget	There is a risk that the actuating devices on production line A will wear out and halt production. This can also lead to serious injuries.	Operations Director to find alternative supplier and agree contingency plan.	C	3	The cost and storage Implications of maintaining standby parts on site are prohibitive.
12	Operations	Pay claim	There is a risk of this year's pay settlement exceeding budget.	Fully briefed and rehearsed negotiating team.	A	3	This risk has replaced 'industrial action' as it is more realistic. In the course of discussions, another risk was recognised and added as Risk 18, Working Time Directive.
18	Operations	Working Time Directive	There is a risk that requirements of the WTD will mean the recruitment of up to 10 extra staff.	Operations to study how WTD requirements can be met with current staffing.	C	1	It is considered low probability that this issue cannot be resolved at mimimal cost.
16	Operations	Insurance premiums	There is a risk that next year's insurance premiums will be higher than we have budgeted for due to hardening of the insurance market.	Consider increased deductibles. Persuade brokers that maximum loss is £10 million.	B	2	
17	Operations	Office rental	There is a risk that the 5-year rent review will increase HQ rents beyond budget.	Seek to persuade Executive and Board to move from Park Lane to portacabins vacated by Project Beacon management team.	A	3	
3	CLOSED	YZCo	There is a risk that YZCo may enter the market before us with a new product superior to Product B.				There is no intelligence to suggest this will happen. Too vague to be included in risk model.
11	CLOSED	Business continuity	There is a risk that our business continuity arrangements are not optimised.	IT Director to carry out business continuity risk analysis with internal team. Initial view in 2 weeks.			It is considered that consultants will not add value to the review as it is company knowledge that is needed. Risk can be closed for this year.

This has been shortened, but does give an indication of how the risks have been dealt with in a consistent way, and the description of treatment measures improved. There is always room for further improvement.

> Remember, the project delivery team at ABCo have been doing risk management for some time, so as well as this corporate register there is a risk register for Project Beacon.
>
> The scoring system of (L) and (C) stands for Likelihood and Consequence, which is explained in Table 2.3 (see the ABCo Prioritisation Scheme box).

more easily said than done. We shall return to this several times. In my experience, it is good practice to flag up risk consequences for at least three areas: financial, because it is the common scale; reputational, because it reflects your long-term business future; and safety, because it has an overarching importance.

RISK ANALYSIS

At this stage the process has apparently leapt ahead of itself in that the risks are well developed, but unprioritised. The risk management team has produced a good first pass statement as to suitable risk treatments. Although in theory the next stage is to carry out a risk analysis to determine the likelihood and consequences of each risk with the 'existing controls', in practice there is often little need for this. Instead what may be needed could be a detailed analysis of a small number of key risks, for example inflation over a 30 year fixed price contract, and an analysis of the risk profile, made up of all the risks.

In other words, most risk assessments are able to put an outline risk management plan in place prior to detailed analysis of likelihood and consequence. It is important to note that the consequence of this is that the scheduled risk treatments are available at an early stage for implementation and monitoring, once they are confirmed by management.

So the key thing for risk analysis is to be able to assign likelihood and consequence to each specific risk. There are two choices: either do it qualitatively; or do it with numbers; that is, quantitatively.

This book is primarily about the latter and we take this up in Chapter 3, but we briefly pause here to describe the former.

Qualitative Risk Analysis

There are two stages to a qualitative risk analysis: first, define a set of qualitative likelihood and consequence bands, and use this to define some significance criteria; second, assign each risk to one or more pairs of likelihood and consequence bands.

The ABCo Prioritisation Scheme box shows a typical set of such bands, and the updated corporate risk register (see Table 2.2) shows how the risks have been assigned to the bands. This might have been done during the workshop, but here we assume it was done by a smaller group outside the session. Workshops are much less beneficial when it comes to estimating risk than for risk identification. It is hard to get large numbers of people to agree on sensible and consistent allocations. They tend to form erroneous preconceptions and forget to use the proper definitions of each category. These problems are multiplied when you try to set numerical estimates as we shall describe later.

As a result the company can now produce the qualitative risk profile by assigning each risk to one of the likelihood categories and one of the consequence categories. We have already seen this in Table 2.2 and so it is straightforward to draw the profile as a series of plots (once for each consequence type), as shown in the ABCo Qualitative Risk Profile box.

This risk profile is a version of the likelihood/consequence chart (see Figure 2.2) shown earlier. It explicitly shows the greater concern for high likelihood, high consequence risks at the top right of the diagram through the differing colours.

The three-by-three structure shown here is very coarse. Most organisations feel the need to move on to a five-by-five scheme at minimum in order to articulate their risks adequately. This is the first step towards full quantitative risk analysis. A second step is to supplement the descriptions in Table 2.3 with numerical ranges of likelihood and consequence. The matrix approach is attractively simple and avoids the need to generate numbers, which people feel

---

ABCo Prioritisation Scheme

The FD is anxious not to reinvent wheels and to keep this process simple. They therefore select an indicative risk prioritisation scheme from the Standard.

Table 2.3   ABCo likelihood and consequence categories

Likelihood

Level	Descriptor	Definition
A	Probable	Can be expected to occur
B	Possible	Not expected to occur
C	Improbable	Conceivable, but highly unlikely to occur

Consequence

Level	Descriptor	Definition
1	Major	Some important objectives cannot be achieved
2	Moderate	Some objectives affected
3	Minor	Minor effects that are easily remedied

Along with these schemes, the standard provides a prioritisation matrix where the red, yellow and green colours indicate the priority attached to putting treatment in place.

Table 2.4   ABCo risk prioritisation matrix

		Consequences		
		Minor 3	Moderate 2	Major 1
Likelihood	Probable A	Yellow	Red	Red
	Possible B	Green	Yellow	Red
	Improbable C	Green	Green	Yellow

Key	Green Low Risk	Yellow Medium Risk	Red High Risk

ABCo Qualitative Risk Profile

Table 2.5   ABCo qualitative risk profile

			Consequences		
			Minor	Moderate	Major
			3	2	1
Likelihood	Probable	A	12. Pay claim 17. Office rental	10. IT project 1. Sales of Product A	8. Project Beacon and 2. Sales of Product B
	Possible	B		4. Advertising 7. Waste disposal 16. Insurance premiums	5. Overhead initiative
	Improbable	C	9. Widgets		18. WTD 6. Liabilities

	Key	Green Low Risk	Yellow Medium Risk	Red High Risk

Red Risk Summary

8 and 2	Delivery of Project Beacon affects sales of new Product B. Full project risk management report next month.
5	Overhead cost reduction initiative will be subject to review by an independent team to ensure credibility of savings.
10	Project 4 star on hold until the requirements and project plan have been confirmed.
1	Operations Director is restructuring production to ensure we can resource additional sales and demobilise if sales are less than anticipated.

This matrix of cells contains the identification number and brief title of each risk. It shows the concentration of red risks, and those of other priorities. Accompanied by the red risk listing, it gives managers a feel for where they have the greatest exposure to risk. It can also be accompanied by another matrix showing how the risk profile will change when all of the additional risk treatments are in place. There are many variants on this theme which can be implemented in software applications – see the later *Risk Management Information Systems* section of this chapter. You would expect to draw up one of these for each risk consequence of importance to your organisation; for example, one for each of financial, safety and reputational risks. This is the financial one.

contain false implications of accuracy. But it is also the case that using matrices in this way can destroy useful information. Furthermore it suffers from the drawback that many risks have a range of consequences with a corresponding range of probabilities. In terms of the jargon we have used, there are several events for one risk and it is necessary to try to choose the one (or even more than one) which is most useful.

Figure 2.5 shows a range of events which might arise from a single risk. They range from a high consequence, low likelihood event to a business-as-usual daily occurrence. You would probably choose the worst case to score, but this would neglect the minor occurrences which might be a more significant issue.

The quantitative approach offers solutions for both these problems because it does not force scoring in bands, and it provides a full representation of the different consequences of a risk. While these are useful properties, I am not trying to argue that qualitative risk analysis is always inferior to the use of numbers. Sometimes one is more appropriate, sometimes the other. However, it is useful to understand the areas of weakness of an approach which apparently avoids the need to come to grips with the more mathematical areas of probability.

RISK EVALUATION

Risk evaluation, as defined in the Standard, is about comparing the output of the risk analysis with risk criteria. The process goes something along these lines: First, you identify what the risk is now. (Or what the risk is under existing controls or under planned controls – this is sometimes known as the inherent risk.) Second, you decide if this is acceptable. (Or tolerable or in line with your risk appetite – see the matrices which have been developed for the ABCo example). If it is acceptable, do nothing. If not, do something so that it is.

So, for example, the risk criterion might be that all red and yellow risks must be treated: we have an appetite only for green risks. A variant of this would be to decide that red risks are intolerable and must be treated; yellow risks should be treated if it is cost effective to do so; and green risks are okay.

The weaknesses of the first approach are rather obvious; those of the second, which is based on a commonly used set of criteria for safety risk management, are less so. But risk management practitioners have been reluctant to articulate the more logical approach explicitly. This process would run by asking:

1. What are the options available to us? (including 'do nothing')
2. What is the risk for each of these? (and other relevant factors)
3. Which is the best of the available options? (when considered against our objectives)

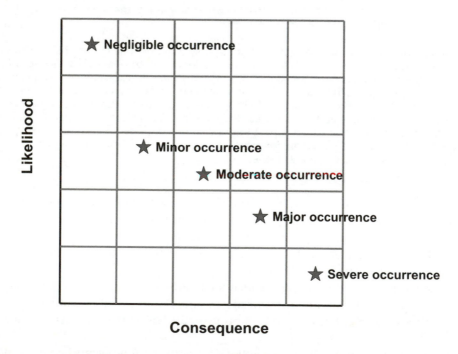

Figure 2.5   Range of consequences of a single risk

Put this way, risk evaluation must focus first on the available options before trying to analyse the risk. There is no point in analysing risk if there are no risk management decisions to be made. It follows that a key objective of the risk management process must be the ability to stimulate the organisation into generating proposals for risk treatment. This is sometimes forgotten when there is a focus on thinking – comprehensively – of all the things which might go wrong.

The two approaches are summarised in Figure 2.6 which compares the risk assessment concept set out in the standards with what I think is the more logical alternative.

The left-hand side of Figure 2.6 suggests the risk is analysed and then evaluated against criteria. Depending on the outcome a decision is made on whether or not the risk is treated. A suitable treatment must then be selected. The right-hand side shows a simpler process (in concept) in which the risk is estimated under each treatment option and a decision is made based on which treatment is optimal. Of course in practice you might expect both ways of looking at this would come to the same thing. For example it might be:

- very unlikely that a risk would be red when optimally treated;
- not worth looking beyond the obvious for a risk that is green;
- necessary to do some analysis for everything in between.

This brings us to the formulation on the left side of Figure 2.6, as outlined previously. Equally it cannot be seriously proposed that all of the treatment options are identified for each risk, as implied by the right-hand side formulation. Common sense will decree what should be done. The Before and After box explains the importance of this distinction.

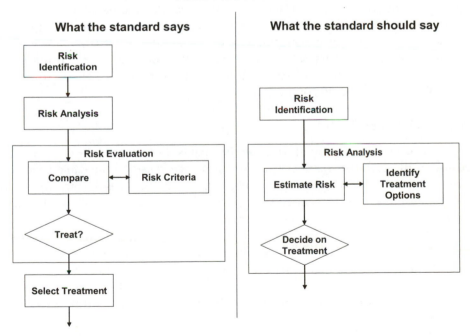

Figure 2.6   Alternative perspectives on the risk assessment process

---

Before and After

Why do I make such a fuss about two ways of looking at things which I admit come down to more or less the same thing? Because the wrong one wastes people's time.

What both the Australia/New Zealand standard and the UK standard miss is the integrated approach to planning which I have sketched in Figure 2.6. This approach recognises that decisions regarding risk are an inherent part of the assessment, not a different activity. The current standards have needlessly separated risk analysis from treatment decisions with something called risk evaluation which applies the organisation's risk criteria, somewhat grandiosely called the risk appetite.

The standard process tends to generate a lot of rather pointless activity aimed at analysing the risk with the 'existing controls', also known as the 'inherent risk', without recognising two things. Firstly, many projects do not have any controls yet. Secondly, it is usually pretty obvious what will be done about most risks whether the controls exist yet or not, so the first step – not the last – is to write this down as the risk treatment.

The result is extensive studies of the risk 'with and without mitigation', 'before and after' or some other such formulation. This is all rather artificial and, in my opinion, a waste of time. To make this more rigorous you could do it using the definitions in the *Residual Risk Defined* box on page 15. The *before* state would be with *risk controls*, whilst the *after* would be when the *risk reduction actions* are included. But this just shifts the issue into the definitions and is still likely to be pointless. Arguably there is no such thing as inherent risk.

Why do people waste their time? Because that what it seems to say in the standards, and that is what people build into expensive software. It reminds me of the naughty child coming home from school and being asked why they had committed some playground offence. 'Because someone told me to …' You have been warned.

You will have noticed a new bit of jargon: *risk estimation*. Risk estimation is simply working out the risk under defined conditions such as a specified treatment option. It is part of risk analysis, but only part. I have chosen the term estimation because it is reminiscent of the word's usage in statistical inference, which recognises that an exact answer is not possible. This contrasts with the objective concept of calculation. You cannot calculate the true risk, just estimate it. This explains the title of the book.

DECISIONS ON TREATMENT

We now come to the key question in risk analysis: what is the best option?

Because of the particular nature of risk this has engendered considerable thought and discussion, driven by the context and how people view risk. Part III is devoted to this topic. However, for business risk management there is a very simple answer which can be used as a starting point from where other considerations can be taken on board.

Implicit in the discussion of the previous section, and illustrated by Figure 2.6, is the idea that the best option is not necessarily that which gives the biggest risk reduction, yet nor is it the first thing you think of that turns a red risk into a green one. There has to be the idea of value for money; that the cost of the treatment is repaid by the value of the risk reduction. Perhaps we must live with a red risk if we cannot think of a way of reducing it; perhaps a cost-free change to an office process could make a green risk even greener.

So the simple answer is to use the financial consequences and adopt the rule that the best option is that with the lowest net cost, taking account of the cost of the risk. But how is the cost of the risk defined, bearing in mind that by definition there is uncertainty in the consequences of the risk? We need a financial value for each cell in the qualitative risk profile which has the property that it is high in the top right and low in the bottom left. And across the top, where the risks are likely to occur, the cost should be of the same order as the consequence. (We have already noted that it is a good practice to add indicative ranges to the categories to help people score risks better.)

The ABCo Valuing Risk box shows how this could be done: each consequence category has been allocated a range and a typical value. Each cell has also been given a typical value: this represents what it would typically be worth spending to avert risks in that cell.

Having done this you could divide the value of each cell by the typical value of its consequence column. This would give you a number between 0 and 1 which would be higher at the top of the matrix and lower at the bottom. Essentially it is a measure of the typical

ABCo Valuing Risk

As the main text reveals, we are aiming to value risk by multiplying consequence by a measure of likelihood called probability. This approach works well in a quantitative framework because the numbers are available. If you are using a qualitative framework it is slightly less clear how to approach this. However, if the categories on the matrix have an indicative quantitative interpretation in terms of a range, it is possible to take a typical probability number and a typical consequence number, multiply them and use that as a measure of the risk. At one time, before the importance of the two-dimensional quality of risk was recognised, risk was sometimes defined as the product of probability and consequence.

For the ABCo matrix you might value each element of the risk matrix in the following way.

Table 2.6 ABCo risk prioritisation matrix with typical values

				Consequences		
				Minor	Moderate	Major
			Range	Less than £100k	£100k-£1m	Over £1m
		Range	Typical	£40k	£400k	£4m
Likelihood	Probable	50%–100%	75%	£30k	£300k	£3m
	Possible	10%–50%	25%	£10k	£100k	£1m
	Improbable	Less than 10%	5%	£2k	£20k	£200k

The numbers in Table 2.6 are actually the mean cost in thousands of pounds, and it is possible to rationalise the red, yellow and green bands in terms of this (green less than £25k, red greater than £250k). You can see how the qualitative approach can drive you into levels of complication and artificiality which are perhaps unnecessary.

It is possible to add the typical risk values to obtain some form of estimate of the total risk. However, this is pushing the qualitative risk analysis approach a bit. However a gross abuse which is sometimes perpetrated is to multiply the labels of the bands (assuming they are 1,2,3 rather than A,B,C). There is no logic to this whatsoever (in fact the bands are often logarithmic so adding would be better). Using matrices is not an adequate excuse for disengaging brain.

likelihood of risks in each cell. Sounds like a useful number. Let's give it a name. How about calling it probability?

Now it's time to stop the charade. To implement a sensible decision approach, even with qualitative matrices, we need to quantify likelihood using the probability element of the risk definition. Good practice qualitative risk management would require that we provide indicative ranges for both probability and consequence. For decision-making purposes we can use typical values for each category and multiply them to get the value of the risks in each cell. For the time being we will call this the mean consequence. The simple decision approach is to select the option with the lowest mean net cost or, equivalently, the highest mean net benefit.

Of course we have leapt ahead here. We noticed that the definition of risk mentioned probability as a measure of likelihood, but did not follow through with an adequate definition of probability itself. We have provided an operational definition here, but in Chapter 3 we shall work through the whole concept properly.

The purpose of this rather contrived discussion has been to emphasise the point that with risk matrices you are drawn into focusing on the red/yellow/green prioritisation of risks and a decision process like the left-hand side of Figure 2.6. The more rational approach on the right side draws you away from matrices and towards quantification. Matrices are a good screening tool to deal with big piles of messy issues; but, they do not help when you are faced with an important decision with big stakes. Arguably, by destroying information, they actually hinder.

Leaving to one side the categories versus numbers debate, we can still ask what the drawbacks are of this simple approach to decision making. The first thing is that it ignores non-financial consequences. We have already said that perhaps the two key non-financial consequences of risk which any organisation will need to take on board are safety and reputation.

So the first observation we can make is to note that we have had to assume all the options are 'safe'. Safety is discussed in Part III, using a basic approach similar to that used here, except that, quite rightly, there is a need to err on the side of safety and there are subsidiary concepts of acceptable levels of risk. To use the jargon, each of the options considered in the organisational risk management context will have safety risk reduced to the lowest reasonably practicable level.

Reputation is less tangible. There is a tendency to label anything really nasty which happens to a company as a reputational risk. The implication is that the company would have been all right if only it had implemented reputational risk management. This is simplistic. All organisations have to take risks, and these risks may materialise. Additionally, some risks may not be reasonably foreseeable. But the reality of risk management is that:

- there are many reasons why your stakeholders lose confidence: if you do not deliver, if you are defrauded, if they do not like your values (for example, how you value risk), if you are secretive;
- your stakeholders will find out what you are up to: your delivery record, your incidents, how you make decisions, your secrets;
- if your stakeholders lose confidence in you, you are in trouble;
- 'in trouble' means that the probability of lots of risks goes up (a lot).

The implication is that you cannot manage risk through the simple approach alone. You need to do it by communicating and understanding all stakeholders and the effect they can have on your organisation. But the simple approach is still a good starting point.

Returning to the financial issues surrounding the simple approach, there are two new concepts to think about: the *risk premium* and *betting the farm*. In general the value of a risk to an individual or organisation is not simply its mean value. There should be a reward for accepting a risk which goes beyond this. This is sometimes known as the risk premium. Figure 2.7 illustrates the point that the higher the risk, the higher the premium. Proposition 2 might be pursued whilst Proposition 1 is not. In the extreme case where one of the potential consequences of the risk is disastrous, such as bankruptcy – betting the farm – it is likely that there is no price at which such a risk might be taken. It is here that the true dimensions of the risk appetite begin to emerge, rather than in the red/yellow/green distinctions of the risk matrix. In other words, for many people and organisations, entrepreneurial as they are, there is no acceptable risk premium for betting the farm.

A more prosaic issue is how we plot portfolios of risks on the chart. Clearly numerical estimates of the risk make this more straightforward, though again qualitative approaches can be attempted.

To sum up, the basic concepts of risk decisions are very simple: seek the lowest mean net cost option. However risk analysts need to be aware of some of the potential complicating issues. Later in the book we will put much more detail on these simple concepts.

Information systems

Our discussion has focused on the risk assessment process at the expense of other aspects of risk management and its implementation. This is not to say these are not important topics. The design of a risk management system so that it can be efficient and effective in implementation for a particular organisation is not a straightforward task. The implementation itself also throws up many challenges. Although not all of these topics are central to this book, there is

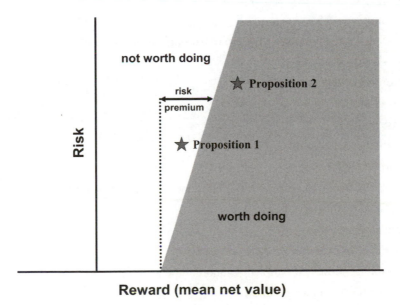

Figure 2.7   Risk and reward

one aspect which affects quantitative risk assessment and that is the systems which are used to store information about risk.

At the core of these systems is the risk register which is a list of the risks and all the relevant information – the tables earlier in this chapter. These are often implemented as spreadsheets which contain the main fields necessary to describe the risk. However for anything other than the most basic risk management requirement, a spreadsheet quickly becomes unwieldy. This is described in more detail in the two boxes on Information Recording Home Truths. These boxes indicate that the solution is a proper database system to record the risk information.

There are several such systems commercially available. The best ones are web-enabled to allow the risk information to be easily shared amongst all the stakeholders who need it. They generally contain lots of attractive facilities for generating and using risk matrices. However, it is a sad fact that these tools tend not to focus on giving their users the convenience of spreadsheets or the discipline of audit trails, whilst providing them with other information such as the before and after facility criticised above. More could be done to reflect the real requirements of risk management in organisations by an enterprising software company.

Information Recording Home Truths – The Problem

Because the idea of a risk register is a simple one, the technical difficulties of implementing one are underestimated. The Australia/New Zealand standard provides an indicative register of how much data and information must be supplied. The handbook, *Risk Management Guidelines* (HB 436: 2004) contains columns (on page 99) for:

- Reference ID [number]
- The risk
- What [event] can happen?
- How can it happen?
- What [consequence] can happen?
- Existing controls
- Effectiveness and implementation of existing controls
- Likelihood
- Consequences
- Level of risk
- Risk priority
- [Whether to] treat risk (Y/N)
- Further action.

Following this (on page 101) is a risk treatment schedule plan containing:

- Possible treatment options
- Preferred options
- Result of cost–benefit analysis (accept/reject)
- Person responsible for implementation of the action
- Timetable for implementation
- How will this risk and the treatment be monitored?

Both of these are presented as tables, that is, two-dimensional matrices. The implication is that these registers will be implemented as spreadsheets. Since this is a technology which most people have available and understand, this is very much a preferred option. In practice however, this is sub-optimal because of the large number of columns and the point that, even so, much useful information is missed. For example, the crucial role of risk owner has been left out. Taking a different tack, there might be a requirement for an audit trail setting out how the risk originated, how it has changed and why.

Information Recording Home Truths – The Solution

In fact a risk register should be implemented as a relational database because what is recorded is relational data. For example, a risk may have several treatments – or none. (Note the infelicity of one column for possible options and another for preferred options in the Standard.) Indeed, a treatment may address several risks.

Other examples of relational data might be a complex categorisation scheme or the steps in an audit trail. And in any case there are far too many data items for an individual risk to allow the sort of spreadsheet report that is sometimes attempted. (The examples in the Standard would actually be plain silly in regular use.) The risk database will present the information on a specific risk as a form which may well spread over several pages.

The problems with this are two-fold:

*   relational databases are less available and familiar to people than spreadsheets;

*   people confuse themselves by not distinguishing between the data itself and the tools which might be available for importing, exporting or reporting information.

So there is no reason why a tabular format such as that used to record the ABCo sessions reported above, implemented as a spreadsheet, could not be imported to the risk register. There is no doubt that spreadsheets are a convenient way to record risk workshops; indeed some sadistic facilitators and their masochistic audiences like to record the session with a live on-screen spreadsheet. Similarly there will be a multiplicity of reports which might be needed depending on the purpose and there is no reason why they should not be produced in spreadsheet format or as PDFs, as well as being printed. You could even implement a relational database in a spreadsheet, if you are feeling particularly perverse.

In summary, you need to recognise that a risk management system of any complexity needs to be supported by a risk register implemented as a relational database. But this database must come with a suitable toolkit to enable it to be used in a way which supports people; not makes their lives difficult.

3 *Quantitative Risk Estimates*

Taking stock

The previous two chapters introduced risk, showed why its management is important and outlined the elements of a risk management system. The system was examined from a plan-do-review management perspective, using the term risk assessment for the planning stage of the cycle. Risk assessment is in turn split into risk identification, risk analysis, risk evaluation and decision making. Making decisions requires us to weigh risk (and opportunity) alongside other attributes of the decision such as costs and benefits. In fact this just means separating uncertain aspects of the future from certain ones, which is possibly a rather artificial distinction. In spite of defining risk in terms of essentially quantitative concepts – probability and consequence – the approach set out in the Standard focuses on its qualitative aspects. This leads into a set of ideas involving risk matrices and the so-called risk appetite. We commented that this kind of qualitative approach, especially when driven by a reluctance to commit to numbers, can sometimes be unhelpful.

This chapter brings us to the main topic of this book: numerical or quantitative estimates of risk where we embrace numbers rather than run away from them. Quantitative risk analysis opens up the prospect of more straightforward and more transparent means of decision making and planning compared with the matrices and prioritisation of qualitative risk management. We are not arguing that quantitative is always right and qualitative is always wrong. The aim instead is to show that there is frequently a benefit in characterising risk numerically. And on that basis, all managers – not just risk managers – need to have some basic familiarity with the relevant concepts. It is important to understand what comprises the minimum tool kit which managers need to do this.

This chapter provides such a basic quantitative risk tool kit: a set of concepts and associated jargon. It provides a simple account of probability distributions and how they can be used to build risk models. This enables us to put risk on the same basis as other important attributes: it can be measured so it can be managed. The aim is to explore what is required to counter the fear of risk numbers – not by ignoring the basic source of this fear, the profoundly subjective nature of probability estimates, but by understanding it and living with it.

To support the tool kit we build on the example of the hypothetical manufacturing company, ABCo, which was introduced in Chapter 2. We start to show how the tool kit can be applied within ABCo. In the next chapter we shall discuss how ABCo's management put it to use, and then do the same for other organisations in other environments. An overview of the chapter is provided by Figure 3.1.

In order to make the structure of the narrative clearer, each section is introduced with the challenge, or problem statement, at which it is aimed. The discussion is intended to be accessible to people with little experience of risk analysis. It is assumed, though, that readers will have some basic knowledge of what a probability of 50 per cent or 90 per cent means (covered in the early sections of Chapter 12), as well as the contents of the previous two chapters.

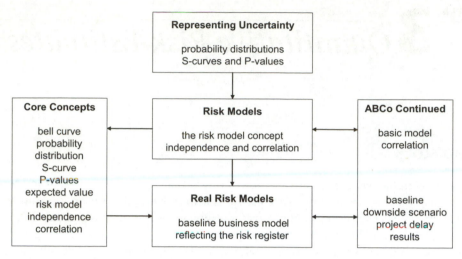

Figure 3.1   Chapter 3 overview

Representing uncertainty quantitatively

CHALLENGE 1: HOW CAN I REPRESENT RISK/UNCERTAINTY WITH NUMBERS?

The Typical Information box records a dialogue which might have taken place in ABCo to quantify the future uncertainty in the company's profit.

What the dialogue shows is that:

- ABCo's profit next year lies in a range; it is not a single number even if the business plan pretends it is;
- different people have different views on what that range might be;
- most people find it difficult to articulate this numerically, primarily because the exact nature of a specific number is at odds with their generally vague comprehension of future uncertainty.

Typical Information

Andy: *'Bill, what will ABCo's profit be next year?'*

Bill: *'Look in the business plan: £5 million.'*

Andy: *'Exactly £5 million? Couldn't it be more? Or less?'*

Bill: *'How long is a piece of string?'*

Andy: *'Well could it be £15 million?'*

Bill: *'Of course not! How could it?'*

Andy: *'£10 million, then?'*

Bill: *'Well, I suppose if that new plant came in early and the salesmen get off their you know what.'*

Andy: *'Chris, what do you think ABCo's profit will be next year?'*

Chris: '*I know the business plan says £5 million, but no one is admitting the new financial system is behind and doesn't have a proper specification – we'll be lucky to break even after fixing that.*'

You get the picture. There is plenty more where this comes from as can be seen from the risk registers in the previous chapter. It is all useful and relevant to the uncertain value of ABCo's future profit.

You can see the differing views on ABCo's prospects. The views would tend to be closer if everyone had the same information. Perhaps if Bill knew about the problems with the financial system and Chris knew about the opportunity to get the new product to market quickly, they would have a common understanding. But the range of that common understanding is likely to be much wider than either might provide individually – which management could find uncomfortable.

Based on the conversation, it sounds as if a reasonable estimate of the range of profit next year might be zero to £10 million.

Although the concept of a reasonable range within which an unknown future value can be expected to lie is what we seem to need, it is not in fact exactly what we use. Figure 3.2 shows that instead of a range, an alternative, possibly more attractive, concept is that of what we shall call a bell curve for the time being.

The curve indicates that a good central value for the profit of ABCo in the next 12 months is £5 million and that the spread of the range of plausible values is £10 million, from £0 to £10 million. It also indicates what we probably intuitively believe: that there is no such thing as definite best and worst cases. There is always some combination of events, however unlikely, which could be better or worse. These are represented by the tails at the left and right ends of the graph.

What does the bell curve represent? You can think of it as an illustration of our beliefs about the future performance of ABCo, but before we can use it effectively we need to be more specific about what it is a graph of. We also need to be clear about whose beliefs we are illustrating. There is more on this in the Subjectivity and Eliciting Data box a bit later.

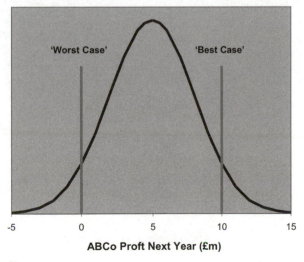

Figure 3.2   A bell curve

To give the bell curve meaning we can build on the definition of risk which involves probability, as introduced in the previous chapter. We therefore draw on the body of knowledge called probability theory to turn the bell curve into a usable concept. Specifically, we will assign a probability to each possible outcome. This is known as a probability distribution. This is a huge step. It is not the only possibility, but it is the only one this book acknowledges.

To make this concrete we draw the corresponding cumulative probability distribution, a curve which plots the probability that, given a value £x, the profit will be less than £x. This is a growing curve – increasing from left to right – because the higher x is, the more likely it is that the profit will be less than £x. It is bounded by 0 and 1 because probabilities are as well. This is known as an S-curve, for reasons which Figure 3.3 should make evident.

This book consistently uses cumulative probabilities to represent quantified risk. We reserve bell curves purely for illustrating degrees of belief, not as mathematically precise distributions. The reason for this is that few people understand what they are graphs of, and fewer still know how they would change if, for example, the units were thousands of pounds instead of millions. By contrast, the cumulative probability curve is straightforward to understand. The S-Curves and Decisions box provides a little more information about these curves and how they can be used.

CHALLENGE 2: HOW SHOULD I CHARACTERISE PROBABILITY DISTRIBUTIONS?

It is clear already that S-curves falsify the adage that a picture is worth a thousand words. They all look the same. Pretty much all that changes are the numbers along the bottom axis. An S-curve really just gives us two things: an idea of location and an idea of the spread or range. This is what we require to meet Challenge 1. The additional information contained in the bell curve and probability distribution has benefits, but unwelcome complications tag along.

The main benefits are the straightforward calculation methods of probability theory and the extra structure implied by the distributions.

The main complication is the risk of taking the additional structure too seriously and reaching unjustified, theoretical and unrealistic conclusions.

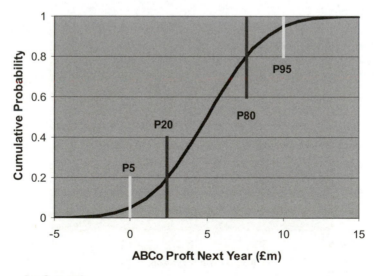

Figure 3.3   An S-curve

S-Curves and Decisions

Figure 3.4 shows a pair of S-curves alongside their corresponding bell curves. Bearing in mind the conceptual problems mentioned in the text, this is the first and last time in the book that we will show numbers on the vertical axis of a bell curve.

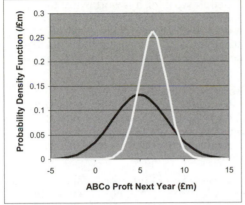 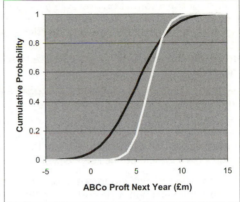

Figure 3.4   Bell curves and S-curves compared

The lighter curve has a somewhat higher central value but a smaller spread compared with the darker curve (a difference which reflects the results seen in the charts already shown in the main text).

Evidently the dark curve has the advantage that the central value of cost is lower. The light curve has the advantage that the spread – or risk – is smaller (if you think this is an advantage). Deciding which is better provides a simple first example of the balance between risk and reward which is inherent in all risk decision making.

Inspection of the probability distribution in Figure 3.3 shows that it has the property that there is a 80 per cent probability that the profit will be less than £7.6 million and a 20 per cent probability that it is less than £2.4 million (that is, an 80 per cent probability that it is greater than £2.4 million). Thus £2.4 million and £7.6 million are known as the P20 and P80 respectively. There are many other ways of characterising probability distributions, but in this book we shall feature these P-values which are easily understood and widely used. Note that this also implies that there is a 60 per cent probability that the profit will lie between £2.4 million and £7.6 million. In other words this range is a 60 per cent confidence interval for ABCo's profit next year. See the Subjectivity and Eliciting Data box for more on this.

Finally note that the chart shows that P5 and P95 (a 90 per cent confidence interval) bound a range of nothing to £10 million, our original range of outcomes. However, we have accepted that the range is not bounded by absolute best and worst cases and that there is some chance that the outcome will lie outside this range. Whether we think that chance is really 10 per cent is a topic we shall return to later this chapter and throughout the remainder of the book. Drawing conclusions and making decisions based on the tails of distributions has obvious pitfalls. Beware!

Subjectivity and Eliciting Data

The main text raises the difficult question of who could be 60 per cent confident. Does this probability distribution represent the truth? Or is it just the distribution we want to assume for planning purposes? It is the latter, of course; there is no such thing as the true or correct probability distribution. What we have is the distribution we choose to use, constructed in the light of the information available to us and the effort we think it is worthwhile to put in for its development. This means that the distribution is subjective. This can make people uncomfortable. Objective versus subjective views of probability are discussed in Chapter 12, but in business risk analysis it is best to accept this subjectivity, recognising the inevitable central role of judgement in any exercise to scope the impact of future uncertainty on an organisation.

It must be pointed out explicitly that different people and organisations are likely to have differing views of the same risk. It is especially likely that the party expecting to suffer the risk if it materialises will take a more pessimistic view than the party who does not. This has important commercial implications which, while obvious, are sometimes forgotten. In Chapter 4 we shall describe in some detail the likely perspectives of a client and a contractor working on a typical public service procurement deal.

There are ways of eliciting information from people like Bill and Chris which improve on the desultory conversation with Andy recorded in the Typical Information box. There are also processes whereby this information, when elicited, can be used to construct a probability distribution. This is discussed in more detail in Chapter 12, but what is important is to have an understanding of what the distribution means and what information it incorporates. We can then commit to using it in the risk analysis to help improve decision making.

Risk models

CHALLENGE 3: HOW CAN I GENERATE RISK ESTIMATES BASED ON MORE DETAIL?

The previous section provided us with a simple tool to think numerically about future uncertainty: the idea of a bell curve with a central value and a spread which can be quantified as a probability distribution. We treated it as if it could be put together directly from the views of Bill, Chris and others. Of course it can be, but one of the basic tenets of risk analysis is that we will get a better bell curve if we dig deeper into what makes up the result we are interested in – in this case next year's profit at ABCo. Where to stop is an important decision for the risk analyst. Note the comments in the 'Better' Risk Models box.

One starting point in adding more detail is to examine sales and cost separately. These are the two quantities which determine profit. This is what is done in the ABCo Basic Risk Model box. By applying probability distributions to sales and cost separately, it is possible to derive a

'Better' Risk Models

An obvious question raised in the main text is what does 'better' mean? This is a key theme for this book: how much analysis (if any) is worth doing? A common answer is 'in enough detail to totally bury the key assumptions in a mass of pseudo-scientific, incomprehensible, mathematical claptrap that I couldn't possibly be sacked for swallowing'. Another answer is 'in enough detail to incorporate clear assumptions about the key issues and to demonstrate the sensitivity of the decisions I make to these assumptions'. We shall return to this theme time and again.

probability distribution for profit which has the same properties as the distribution in Figure 3.3: a central value of £5 million and a spread of £10 million.

How do we do that?

The answer is, of course, probability theory. Turning the illustration of 'belief' in the bell curves into probability distributions for cost and sales and using the relationship between them and profit enables us to find the probability distribution for profit.

This, our first risk model, can be found in the ABCo Basic Risk Model box, an output probability distribution obtained from input distributions. There are methods and approximations for doing this calculation. They are described in great detail later in this book, but managers should not need to worry about what they are or how they work. It ought to be enough for now if you know that the main method is exotically named Monte Carlo and works by simulating the future many times, every time taking a random sample from each input. You can find out more in Chapter 13.

What you should really worry about is that there is one further and crucial assumption which has been made: that cost and sales are distributed independently.

ABCo Basic Risk Model

To develop the ABCo risk model in more detail we first note the simple equation:

profit = sales – cost,

and secondly make the assumption that if we have a bell curve for sales and another bell curve for cost, we can develop a bell curve for profit. Here are all three:

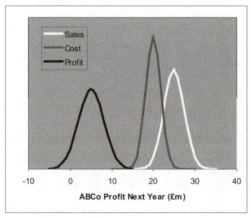 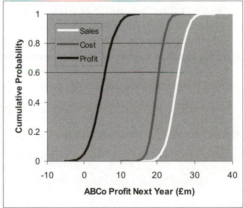

Figure 3.5   ABCo profit spread

We have assumed that sales have a bell curve with a central value £25 million and a spread of £8 million. We have assumed that cost has a bell curve centred around £20 million with a spread of £6 million. Using probability theory we find that, as before, the bell curve for profit has a central value of £5 million and a spread of £10 million, replicating the value presented earlier.

Dependence between cost and sales

CHALLENGE 4: WHAT HAPPENS WHEN THE INPUTS TO THE MODEL ARE NOT INDEPENDENT?

What this means is the distribution of cost is the same whatever the value of sales. Because it presumably costs more to make more to sell more this is probably not true. Why does it matter?

To investigate this we look at our results a bit more closely. The mathematics is shown in the Equations for Central Values and Spread box. Firstly, it is no surprise to see that £5 million central value for profit is the difference between £25 million and £20 million, the central values assumed for sales and cost.

However, the spread of £10 million that was found in the ABCo Basic Risk Model box is not the sum of the spreads in cost and sales, which would be £14 million. The lower value results from the assumption that each of the sales and cost can be considered as randomly and independently selected from its own distribution. This leads to a smaller spread.

As we have said, this is not a good assumption. Companies will have some ability to adapt their production activities, and hence their costs, to reflect demand. If they could do this perfectly, the spread would be smaller still. In fact it is reduced to £2 million, as is also shown in the Equations for Central Values and Spread box.

This is an elaborate way of illustrating quantitatively an obvious qualitative point: that a manufacturing company can manage the risk to its profit by a strategy of matching its manufacturing costs to its sales. This tends to preserve the net margin on each item sold. Note that we have implicitly assumed that a smaller spread around the same central value is lower risk – and preferable. Certainty of outcome is always desirable; later we will discuss the trade-off between certainty and the central value – risk and reward.

Equations for Central Values and Spread

The ABCo basic risk model has the property that

$$\text{central(profit)} = \text{central(sales)} - \text{central(cost)} = £5 \text{ million}$$

where central(x) is shorthand for the central value of x. This is exactly what we would expect.

Perhaps more surprising is that the corresponding equation for the spreads is, as it happens:

$$\text{spread}^2(\text{profit}) = \text{spread}^2(\text{sales}) + \text{spread}^2(\text{cost}) = (£8m)^2 + (£6m)^2 = (£10m)^2$$

where spread$^2(x)$ is shorthand for the square of the spread in x. So the spread in profit is greater than the spread in sales and cost separately, but less than their total, £14 million.

However this equation depends on an assumption of independence between cost and sales. If the assumption was that cost and sales were perfectly correlated the equation would become

$$\text{spread(profit)} = \text{spread(sales)} - \text{spread(cost)} = £2 \text{ million.}$$

You can verify this through the calculation that the worst case scenario for sales is the central value less half the spread: £21 million. In this case the costs are £17 million so the profit is £4 million. The corresponding best case numbers are £29 million less £23 million, or £6 million. This verifies that the spread is £2 million. But be careful: this only works for perfect correlation.

The theory underlying these equations is contained in Chapter 12.

Is this new assumption of perfect correlation a good one, giving credible results? Again probably not, as it is unlikely that this risk management strategy can be implemented with 100 per cent efficiency. An improved model would need to tackle this.

Modelling correlation

CHALLENGE 5: HOW DO I GO ABOUT CONSTRUCTING RISK MODELS WHEN THERE IS CORRELATION?

There are two ways to go to the next stage of modelling: either seek to model the extent to which the manufacturing costs can track sales, perhaps splitting into fixed and variable costs and modelling appropriate levels of stock, for example; or assume some gross measure of correlation halfway between sales and cost somewhere between full independence and full correlation.

We now explain both of these in more detail.

The drawback of the first method is that it will probably require brave and transparent assumptions to be made, and these could be criticised or shown later to be wrong. The drawback of the second method is that very few people know what the correlation measures mean, and fewer still know the implications of choosing halfway. (This could be viewed as an advantage by some people.)

The Modelling Correlation Explicitly box does the calculation by making assumptions about how cost and sales are interdependent. The result is that the spread is now £7 million, intermediate between the £10 million when cost and sales are independent and the £2 million when they are perfectly correlated.

The second approach to modelling dependence is to make a broad assumption about the correlation between two linked variables in terms of a suitable quantity, for example the correlation coefficient. The correlation is a mathematical measure of the extent to which two variables move in concert or not and must lie in the range of zero to one. Zero means the variables are independent and 1 means they are fully correlated. Consequently there is a tendency to select 0.5, that is, the halfway point. In this example the result with a correlation coefficient of 0.5 would have been a profit width of £7.2 million, which is not far off the previous answer using explicitly modelled dependence.

This is perhaps not surprising, given the split between the dependent and independent elements of cost was roughly 50:50. There are other measures of correlation, such as rank correlation – see Chapter 13, which would give slightly different results.

It is worth emphasising that there is a flavour of black box about using these quantities. How is the user supposed to know what a correlation coefficient of 0.5 means, and whether it is appropriate? I strongly recommend that where there is dependence between quantities, this dependence is explicitly modelled. This will require assumptions to be made, but at least these assumptions are not hidden in the esoteric mathematics of rank correlation coefficients.

Summarising the results we have found, it is the spread not the central value which is changed by the correlation. The spreads found were:

perfect correlation between cost and sales:	£2 million
modelled correlation between cost and sales:	£7 million
cost and sales independent of each other:	£10 million
combining ranges of cost and sales:	£14 million

Modelling Correlation Explicitly

Previously we assigned a probability distribution to sales and another independent one to costs. What we want now is causal relationships between these quantities, with these relationships reflected in the model. To do this we assume that production is driven by sales and that cost is driven by production. Hence sales is an important determinant of cost, but there remains an uncertainty in cost even when sales are known. An alternative approach might be to drive sales and cost from production, using an economic supply and demand approach, but this would make the example rather complicated.

Suppose, then, it turns out that 50 per cent of the projected ABCo costs are directly related to sales and can be controlled accordingly, at a value of 40 per cent of sales. Thus these 'variable' costs have a bell curve with a central value of £10 million and a spread of 40 per cent of £8 million , that is £3.2 million . The other 50 per cent of costs, reflecting overheads, depreciation, interest charges and so on, vary independently of sales achieved and can be modelled as a bell curve with a central value of £10 million and a spread of £5.1 million . These figures have been chosen so the central cost remains £20 million and the spread remains £6 million using the equations in the box above. To show this we rewrite profit as the sum of two independent variables:

profit   = sales – cost

           = sales – direct cost – overhead

           = gross profit – overhead

where

        gross profit = sales – direct cost.

Because sales and direct cost are perfectly correlated, gross profit has a central value of £15 million and a spread of £4.8. Because gross profit and overheads are independent the previous equations can be used to show that profit has a central value of £5 million and a spread of £7 million. (Note that $7^2 = 4.8^2 + 5.1^2$)

The resulting bell curve and probability distribution are shown in Figure 3.6.

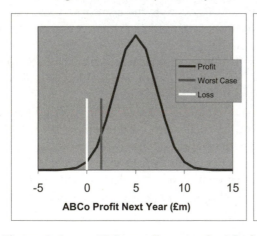
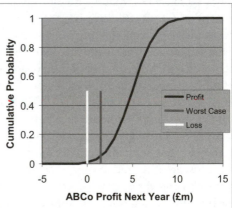

Figure 3.6   ABCo profit spread with dependence

The worst case and loss points are discussed in the Downside P-Values box.

The Combining Ranges box shows how to find the last result. It is not derived from probabilistic risk modelling. You can envisage that instead of doing all these complicated probability calculations you could much more easily just combine ranges, calculating your model twice: once with all inputs set to the worst case, then again with them set to the best case. The disadvantage of this is that it would give a very broad spread, as is the case with ABCo's profit.

The reason for this, taking ABCo as an example and simplifying slightly, is that the worst case cost is low probability and the worst case sales are low probability. The combination is therefore very low probability and is not evaluated consistently with the worst case cost and sales – assuming you buy into the probability idea. Examples of this for ABCo are provided in the Downside P-Values box.

In summary, combining the ranges with consistent best and worst cases gives a broad spread which would not be useful to managers. By contrast, the rules of probability enable us to develop a coherent view of future uncertainty which should not, for example, depend on the level of detail at which the analysis is stopped.

Combining Ranges

If we had stuck with simple ranges we would have noted the sales could have been as high as £25 million plus £4 million and the costs could have been as low as £20 million less £3 million. This means the profit could have been as high as £12 million. Looking at the downside gives a worst case of a loss of £2 million. The implied range is £14 million, higher than all the values from the probability analysis.

Downside P-Values

It is worth having a closer look at the downside estimates. From the Modelling Correlation Explicitly box we have:

worst case gross profit = £15 million – £2.4 million = £12.6 million

worst case overheads = £10 million + £2.5 million = £12.5 million

worst case profit = £5 million – £3.5 million = £1.5 million

This is higher than the profit which would have resulted from combining the two worst case figures – which, as it happens, is about zero. These values are marked on Figure 3.6. So what is the probability of making a loss?

Obviously it is lower than 5 per cent since the worst case profit is P5. Furthermore it is higher than 5% × 5% = 0.25%, since this is the probability that cost is more than worst case *and* sales are greater than worst case, which is a subset of all the possibilities leading to negative profit. In fact, Figure 3.6 shows (if you could look at it really closely) that the probability is about 1 per cent. In this case combining two P5s gives a P1, but unfortunately there are no rules of thumb which say this will be the case all of the time.

The precise numbers should not be taken too literally: they are an artefact of the shape of the distributions used in this example. However they do show that low probability tails of the output distributions are not as dependent on the tails of the input distributions as might be thought. Having said this, you could only accept 1 per cent as the probability of making a loss from this model if you were sure about the values of the distributions of the inputs at around the 5 per cent level. In practice, you would not be, and you could not take this result seriously.

We finish the initial discussion of risk modelling by looking more closely at the extreme values where the risk modelling is giving us low probabilities. The Downside P-Values box provides more detail for the case of ABCo.

While the precise results are dependent on the details of the model being examined, there are two clear, slightly counteracting, lessons which are important to bear in mind:

- treat the extreme P-values which come from risk models with suspicion;
- but remember they are not necessarily determined by the extreme P-values of the inputs.

This is important. When we discuss the calculation techniques we shall see they work regardless of the quality of the input and regardless of the quantity which is being calculated. Garbage in, garbage out is too simplistic a maxim to use for quantitative risk analysis. But the analyst does have to know what is reliable and what is not, and this is not always obvious. And the manager has to appoint an analyst who knows.

We shall return to these questions later, but now it is time to consolidate some of the probabilistic points and collate our core concepts.

The core concepts

CHALLENGE 6: WHAT DO MANAGERS NEED TO KNOW ABOUT RISK MODELLING?

We have adopted bell curves as a way of illustrating our beliefs or opinions about an uncertain quantity whilst using S-curves, or cumulative probability distributions, as a more concrete concept for calculations and modelling. Bell curves are characterised by central values and spreads whilst the S-curves can be constructed from the P-values: P5, P20, P50, P80, P95 and so on. This distinction might be thought rather artificial. Readers familiar with probability theory will probably have found the previous account rather contrived, over-lengthy and possibly even patronising. However, there is a reason.

The reason is that management-level discussion on these issues can get side-tracked because of a lack of agreed management terminology for quantitative risk (look at the case studies in the next chapter for example). Managers have varying levels of knowledge of probability, often dimly remembered from decades-old courses. This is not helped by risk advisors whose expertise is sometimes less than what might reasonably be expected at a professional level. It is taken for granted in this book that effective risk management will require quantitative risk analysis. It follows that managers will need a basic level of knowledge about probability concepts for this. This corresponds to the basic knowledge of profit and loss and balance sheet concepts, performance measurement, budgeting, business planning and so on which would also be expected of any manager. This is expanded upon in the Fitting into the Business box. One of the aims of this book is to propose a basic set of concepts which managers should acquire familiarity with: necessary but minimal.

We have already hinted that in some ways probability distributions are far too sophisticated a tool for the purpose at hand. All we really need is some form of central measure and a spread measure, together with a simple way of getting them from the data available. Now that we are committed to using probability distributions what we need is a way to extract the central measure and spread, which can be easily understood by all concerned and can be used in standard business presentations.

Fitting into the Business

The choice of the financial analogies is not coincidental. We have already identified that risk management provides an essential perspective on business planning and the delivery of the business plan. Financial measures and financial performance lie at the heart of this activity, together with other types of key performance measures for issues which are not primarily financial. Quantitative risk analysis must align with this and this is why the ABCo example will be developed around the most basic financial presentations – the profit and loss statement and the balance sheet. More generally, risk must be capable of being presented in a way which mirrors whatever numerical performance measures the organisation uses. To make this a reality will, in turn, necessitate a small broadening in the ideas and language used. Hence the core concepts.

Managers are generally fairly comfortable with the P-value concept and it would be sensible to build on this. We can use the P50 as the central value and adopt a standard range, such as P95–P5 used above, as a spread measure.

However, perhaps the most significant terminological proposal of this book is that managers should become familiar with the concept of the *mean* of a probability distribution and use that as the central value instead of alternatives such as the P50. The mean is also known as the *expected value* and represents the probability weighted average of the consequences. For the symmetrical distributions seen so far, the central value is of course the same as the mean.

You need to be aware that the expected value is a technical concept and does not necessarily agree with the colloquial idea of 'what we expect to happen'. For example if we bet on a specific horse race we probably expect to lose because experience tells us that is what happens most of the time. But technically, that is the *most likely* outcome. The *expected value* is the probability of winning (in our own opinion, not the odds!) multiplied by the win value less the probability of losing times the loss. This should be positive.

This gives an indication of the primary reason for recommending the use of the mean: the mean of a sum of quantities is the sum of the means. This is not true of P50s, for example. Thus means provide a consistent approach which can be used alongside standard financial models and forecasts without destroying the fundamental property of these models that the columns add up. This is very useful in many business risk analyses and their presentation. Indeed, one approach to selecting the single value to be used in a forecast might be to define it as the mean outcome. There is more on this in the Mean Properties box.

On the other hand, there is no fundamental problem with using the P-values as measures of spread, and this is what is recommended. Typical examples might be P80–mean or P95–P5, as before. The obvious alternative is to use the so-called standard deviation (or sigma – σ) which is described in the Standard Deviation and Variance box. This is also useful, but the manager can live without it.

Thus, a business presentation might consistently present the P80 downside results alongside the means. Just remember they won't add up: the P80 of a sum is not the sum of the P80s.

This completes the required set of core concepts which is summarised in Table 3.1.

Mean Properties

It is noted in the main text that the mean of a sum of uncertain values is the sum of their means. So in the ABCo example:

mean profit = mean sales − mean cost

This is the case whether or not cost and sales are independent of each other. We saw before that the central value of profit was £5 million whatever the nature of the correlation between sales and cost. This enables the mean concept to be applied in a simple way to quite elaborate financial models which have the property that total cost is equal to the sum of the constituent costs. The same applies to any other performance measure which is a sum. Thus means can sit alongside or be the core numbers in most financial models and forecasts.

However the mean property does not apply to all relationships or models. Just because

profit = sales × margin − fixed cost

it is not necessarily true that

mean profit = mean sales × mean margin − mean fixed cost

although, this is indeed the case if sales and margin are independent; for example, where risk management measures fix the margin, as we assumed for ABCo earlier.

Another key advantage of the mean is that it is always clearly defined. So a bet based on a fair coin in which you win £1 on heads and lose it on tails has a mean outcome of zero. The P50 (or median) and most likely (or mode) are undefined. These other measures are discussed in Chapter 12.

If you spent a day at the horse races, you could work out your mean winnings by adding the mean for each race. If you added up the P50 for each race you would assume you lose every stake of the day (unless you were an incurable optimist whose subjective probability of winning was odds on for every start).

Standard Deviation and Variance

Standard deviation is a very common measure of spread. The P95–P5 measure of spread corresponds to just over three standard deviations for an underlying normal distribution; the P80–P20 corresponds to less than 2, at about 1.7. These ratios will change somewhat for different distributions.

Mathematically it starts with the *variance* which is defined as the mean of the square of the distance from the mean. This means firstly that it does not depend on the location of the distribution. It can move left or right along the horizontal axis without affecting the variation. Secondly, because it is the mean square, it is positive: the bit just below the mean makes the same contribution as the bit just above – this is why it is a measure of spread. Because it is positive the standard deviation can be defined as the square root of the variance. It is therefore measured in the same units as the consequence concerned.

Corresponding to the useful point that the mean of a sum is the sum of the means, there are also formulas for the standard deviations of sums of quantities. However their validity is limited to situations where the quantities are independent and are probably not part of what every manager needs to know. More details are provided in Chapter 6.

We noted that the standard deviation is called sigma or σ. You may have heard of the 6-sigma management fad. The derivation of this phrase is that whilst for a normal distribution P80−mean is 0.84 sigma, P99.99966−mean is 4.5 sigma. With an assumed deterioration of 1.5 sigma you get to 6-sigma as a design criterion for systems where you are seeking to reduce failure rates to below 3.4 per million.

Table 3.1   **Core concept summary**

Bell curve	A sketch representing an individual or organisational opinion about the value of a uncertain quantity.
Cumulative probability distribution or S-curve	A graph, possibly derived from the bell curve, which plots at each point x the probability that the uncertain quantity is less than x (probability distribution for short).
P-values	P5, P20, P80, P95 and so on: the values of x where the cumulative probability is 5%, 20%, 80%, 95% and so on; can be read off the S-curve.
Mean or expected value	Of a probability distribution: the probability weighted average.
Risk model	A set of equations relating outputs (for example, profit) to inputs (for example, cost and sales) where the intention is to use the probability distributions of the inputs to calculate that of the outputs.
Independent (pair) of inputs	The probability distribution one input is not affected by the value of the other input.
Correlated (pair) of inputs	Where they are not independent.

Two further concepts can be added to the list of concepts which are non-essential, but desirable:

Standard deviation   A mathematical measure of spread generally comparable to P80 less expected value

Monte Carlo   A popular and powerful means of calculating risk models which works by simulating the possible futures many times.

That's it.

Real risk models

CHALLENGE 7: HOW CAN I MAKE MY RISK MODEL REFLECT THE RISK REGISTER?

Although we have taken the ABCo risk model through three variations, the analysis has remained quite superficial. Thinking back to the risk registers we recorded in Chapter 2, remember that ABCo is changing. It has introduced corporate initiatives to cut costs along with a new financial system. It is also bringing a new product into the market. Sales of this are planned to start halfway through the year, but are dependent on the completion of a production plant. A project risk register has been prepared specifically for this construction project. In this section we begin to look at how we use the qualitative risk registers to inform the quantitative risk analysis.

The starting point is to consider a baseline forecast which represents a particular view of the future. It can be any view – not necessarily the best estimate or an imposed budget – but it is important to understand what assumptions underline this baseline. The role of the baseline is to act as a model of the business or project or deal to which the risks can be applied. It is important that there is clarity as to what is in the baseline and what is contained in the risk modelling. The baseline for ABCo is described in the ABCo Baseline Forecast box.

ABCo Baseline Forecast

The ABCo baseline forecast indicates that the £25 million sales expected by ABCo in the next year come from two products: Product A is its long-standing cash generator produced in an existing plant and generating £15 million of sales, whilst Product B is a new product which will be manufactured in a new plant. Its sales are expected to be £20 million per year, so there will be £10 million generated in the course of next year (if we make simplified assumptions).

Further items of information are that ABCo has borrowed £25 million to finance the new plant, which is estimated to cost this amount. It will have to pay £1 million interest and repay £1 million during the year. It will also take a depreciation charge of £4 million split equally between the plants. This is all reflected in the simplified profit and loss statement and balance sheet below (see Table 3.2).

Table 3.2   ABCo Target Financial Performance (in £m)

Profit and Loss		Balance Sheet		
	Year End		Opening	Closing
Product A	15	Fixed Assets	20	41
Product B	10	Cash	25	8
Sales	**25**	**Assets**	**45**	**49**
Direct Costs	10	Loans	25	24
Depreciation	4	P&L	20	25
Interest	1	**Liabilities**	**45**	**49**
Overheads	5			
Total Cost	**20**			
Profit	**5**			

The principal simplification is to ignore all working capital effects – stock, debtors, creditors and so on. As a result the profit and loss liability is the same as the Capital and Reserves or Shareholder Funds items you would find on most balance sheets.

The consequences of the most important risks on the baseline are then considered. In the case of ABCo, the Finance Director becomes very concerned about the possible impact of a project to build a new manufacturing facility. They therefore ask for a revised forecast in which this project is delayed and then goes over cost as a result (see the ABCo Downside Scenario box). The practice of identifying specific scenarios to model is briefly described in the Scenarios box.

The downside scenario indicates a new concern, so the focus shifts to cash flow rather than profit.

At this point, recognising the possible additional impact of risks other than project delay, the FD calls for a full risk model to be developed, incorporating estimated probabilities for all the risks discussed so far to assess how bad the problem is and what can be done about it.

Effectively there are only three risks: sales of Product A, control of overheads (combining cost control and the new IT system) and cost/delivery of the new plant. Figure 3.7 shows how they feed into the profit and loss statement and balance sheet in various ways.

The sales and overheads risks are modelled in a way which is consistent with the models generated previously. However, the project risk is modelled in a different way from the symmetrical bell curves we have used so far, as shown in the ABCo Probability Distribution of

ABCo Downside Scenario

The FD is very concerned about the delivery of the new manufacturing plant. Based on painful experience of projects going wrong and a review of the risk registers, she knows that if this happens it is likely that not only will the cost increase, but also the delivery will be delayed and sales of the new Product B will be lost. She asks for a forecast for the case where the costs of the project increase by 20 per cent to £30 million and the plant opening is delayed by three months. The new projection is shown in Table 3.3.

Table 3.3   **ABCo downside scenario financial performance (in £m)**

Profit and Loss		Balance Sheet		
	Year End		Opening	Closing
Product A	15	Fixed Assets	20	47
Product B	5	Cash	25	0
Sales	**20**	**Assets**	**45**	**47**
Direct Costs	8	Loans	25	24
Depreciation	3	P&L	20	23
Interest	1	**Liabilities**	**45**	**47**
Overheads	5			
Total Cost	**17**			
Profit	**3**			

Profit remains relatively unaffected in the downside scenario, due to the ability to adjust costs in line with sales (including depreciation). The real impact of the project problems is seen on the balance sheet, where ABCo is out of cash at the end of the year. In fact it is worse than this. The company will run out of cash at the end of the eighth month, and has a cash requirement of over £3 million by the end of the ninth month, when the project is eventually completed. Cash is then generated as Product B comes on stream for the final three months of the year. Perhaps the problem is even more understated given the likely delay in getting cash in for the new product, but we keep the modelling fairly simple for the time being, recognising that some allowance for this would have to have been made in the baseline projections.

Project Delay box. Although project plans have some upside they generally have a lot more downside. The project is estimated as if everything will go swimmingly. With this as a baseline, things can only get worse. The reason for this is obvious. There is no point in making plans which contain things going wrong. Instead, project plans can contain contingency. Their financial provision or budget may contain some unassigned amount which can be released in the event of risks materialising. And from the time perspective, the project programme may contain some float; that is, it may provide scope for individual tasks or perhaps the whole job, to take longer than the minimum. These terms – *contingency* and *float* – need to be added to the core concepts. They are discussed in Chapter 7.

Notice that although the 'bell curve' is no longer very bell-like, the S-curve is fairly indistinguishable from the ones seen previously. This reinforces the point made earlier that all S-curves look the same; all that changes are the numbers along the bottom axis.

With all the inputs in place we can now calculate the ABCo risk model. The output for ABCo is shown in the ABCo Model Results and What They Mean box. This also briefly describes the implications for ABCo: different financing and procurement arrangements for the new plant will have to be sought as part of the risk management strategy.

The quantitative analysis done by ABCo yielded several benefits:

- Management – and other stakeholders – now have a view of the range in which ABCo's financial performance will lie next year; even better, they have a probability distribution.
- In particular, the stakeholders have been able to confirm the certainty in profit they will gain from matching their variable production costs to sales.
- The stakeholders have been able to understand the criticality to this performance of the delivery of the production plant project.
- The stakeholders know they must seek new financing or procurement options for this project.
- The analysis will later serve as a tool to help choose between the options and confirm their efficacy (see Chapter 4).

Scenarios

The practice of identifying different versions of the future is called scenario modelling. Companies employ it to broaden their appreciation of what might happen so that they can be ready, plan for it and have contingency plans in place.

Scenario modelling is really half of risk analysis: the consequences without the probability. This leaves the obvious question of how seriously to take specific scenarios, which is exactly the question which risk analysis tries to address. In practice, judgement is generally applied to set a boundary between plausible and implausible scenarios and this allows progress to be made. However, making the bold step of assigning (subjective) probabilities gives managers an improved handle on the future.

Profit and Loss
   Sales
      Product A
         Sales of Product A have a spread of £4.8 million
      Product B
         Sales of Product B affected by project delay
   Costs
      Direct
         Direct cost to be managed at 40% of sales
      Depreciation
         Depreciation on plant B starts with project completion
      Interest
         Interest fixed
      Overheads
         Overheads have a spread of £5.1 million
         Overhead reduction initiative has a spread of £4 million
         New IT system has a spread of £3 million
         Other operational risks have a (negligible) spread of £1 million
Balance Sheet
   Assets
      Fixed Assets
         Delivery of project may be delayed up to 4 months
      Cash
         Sales risk
         Overhead risk
         Cost of project increases with delay
   Liabilities
      Loans
         Repayment fixed
      P&L
         Derived, as above

Figure 3.7   **Consequences of ABCo risks for profit and loss account and balance sheet**

Significant shortcomings in the process should also be acknowledged:

- Most of the important sensitivities were already available from the qualitative analysis described in Chapter 2.
- The analysis does not specifically highlight the major reputational risks lurking not only in the new production facility project, with disappointed customers if the sales force has been effective, but also in the overhead costs where the IT system initiative is being undertaken: major publicised disasters in either, or worse, both, these projects could have a catastrophic effect on ABCo's share price.
- The analysis is clearly highly idealised in its cavalier treatment of working capital, for example, and also in considering only three risks.

ABCo Probability Distribution of Project Delay

Planning and managing project risks are discussed further in Chapter 7. For the ABCo model it is assumed that the cost and delivery time of the project are fully correlated. If the cost is 20 per cent over, or £5 million, the delivery is 3 months late. Moreover it is assumed that whilst the worst case is 4 months late, the best case is only 1 month early. This is modelled with a so-called triangular bell distribution with its associated cumulative probability distribution as shown in Figure 3.8. Once again we notice there is a baseline model for the project risk estimate. It comprises delivery at 6 months with a cost of £25 million. The distributions in the figure are then added on to this so that the most likely, for example, is still 6 months, while the latest time of completion is 10 months.

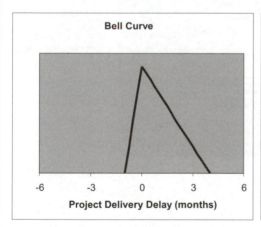

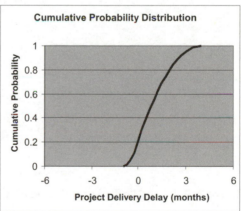

Figure 3.8   ABCo distribution of project delay

The mean delay with this distribution is 1 month (the P50 is slightly less) with a corresponding mean cost of £1.7 million. Note that because the cost and delay are assumed to be fully dependent on each other, the horizontal axis might just as well be labelled in time as cost. The translation rate is £20 million per year corresponding to the £5 million in 3 months assumed.

Note also that the probability of the delay exceeding the downside scenario value of 3 months is only 5 per cent, so the downside scenario is fairly unlikely. It could be referred to as a P95. These results were estimated prior to the full project risk estimation exercise described in Chapter 7.

However, the advantages of the quantitative work are clearly worth the extra trouble, especially as the modelling has been very simple and has not, at least until the final stage, involved very sophisticated analysis. But it would be wrong to assume this is always the case. Sometime it is very unclear if there will be any benefit from characterising risk quantitatively. If so, do not bother. A major theme of the next chapter is when to quantify risk and when to not.

ABCo Model Results and What They Mean

We can now run the analysis and the results for ABCo's profit are shown in Figure 3.9. As expected, the profit is relatively secure and indicates a very small probability of turning into a loss. Remembering that the FD's concern was cash, we can see that there is a substantial probability of running out, about 40 per cent, even though the downside scenario was P5 (equivalent to the P95 of delay; be careful about changing from numbers where good is more – such as sales – to numbers where good is less – such as cost or delay).

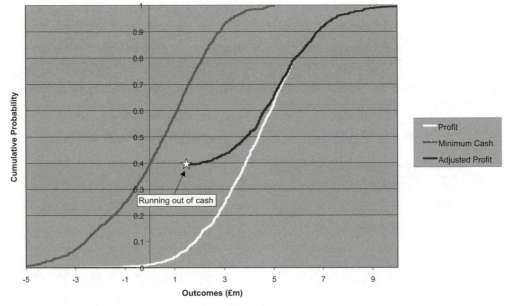

Figure 3.9   ABCo final model results

Up to this point we have assumed that ABCo finds a way to deal with this. But the fact is that if the company runs out of cash it is bankrupt and perhaps does not survive. A better representation of the profit S-curve might be to include only those situations where the company does not run out of cash. This gives the result indicated by the dark S-curve. (At last we have an S-curve which looks slightly different than usual.) Clearly a 40 per cent probability of going out of business is not acceptable to the FD and in the next chapter ABCo examines its risk management options; they need to drastically reduce the probability of bankruptcy.

Note that the adjusted profit S-curve shows that, in common with many businesses, bankruptcy arrives before loss of profitability. Even at the extreme left-hand edge, there is a £2 million profit.

Risk registers and risk models

CHALLENGE 8: HOW DO I SHOW THE RISK REGISTER IS FULLY REFLECTED IN THE RISK MODEL?

The ABCo example has illustrated the generic process for moving from qualitative risk management (Chapter 2) to quantitative risk analysis, from risk listing to risk modelling. We also noted the small number of risks in the model – many fewer than the number registered in the workshops we imagined earlier.

A common approach to risk modelling is to take every risk in the risk register, put numbers against it and then look at the distribution of the sum. This is not a good practice; for more, see the box entitled The Kitchen Sink Approach.

In broad terms the recommended approach is to register every worry and model key issues. It is important to stand back and focus on these issues and the way they interact so the analysis is more relevant, more clearly presented and less of a black box. A high-level process for doing this is described in the Outline Risk Modelling Process box.

The theme is to construct the risk model out of a relatively small number of issues. The risk register can be mapped on to the issues and a view of the probability distribution associated with each can then be taken. For the most significant issues a complete sub-model can be constructed, with the resulting output distribution used as the input distribution for the main model. As a concrete example, the probability delay risk in ABCo could be constructed from a detailed schedule risk analysis such as that used to illustrate Chapter 7.

It is important to remember during this process that we are really only trying to do something quite crude: give a broad illustration of the spread derived from future uncertainty based on gross assumptions and often little data. As we emphasised at the start of the chapter, risk modelling is profoundly subjective. At the same time, doing it wrongly – forgetting a key risk transfer or important correlation, for example – can give results which are extremely misleading. In risk modelling, the analyst must always keep an eye on the big picture and not be distracted by the minutiae of the risk register. In general the big picture gives broad – credible – spreads. Lots of little risks disappear into narrow – implausible – spreads.

The Kitchen Sink Approach

This is the name that can be given to an approach which seeks to be rigorous by quantifying every risk in the register. This approach tends to clutter the analysis; it tends to understate the key risks as the small ones make a significant, but unjustified, contribution. A noticeable tendency amongst analysts who do this is to add implausible probabilities so that the overall effect is reduced. It is much better to have a small number of important assumptions (including one which ignores swathes of trivia) than many insignificant ones which may combine to have unseen effects.

The perceived advantage of the kitchen sink is that it is considered more auditable. That is, every risk in the risk register makes a contribution to the quantitative risk estimate. This is probably the reason behind the enthusiasm for this sort of analysis. It is not directed at illustrating the spread of future uncertainty; it is just making sure that the central values account for all the issues. But a risk model is not needed for that; rather, just a spreadsheet to add up the means.

Outline Risk Modelling Process

The process for generating risk models from the risk registers should contain the following basic activities:

- generate first cut risk registers from workshops and so on;

- tidy up the wording of the registers (for example, use the phrase 'there is a risk that..');

- review the risks and actions with management to check that is what they are committed to and will really do;

- review the risks again from top down, legal, commercial, common sense and stakeholder perspectives;

- review again, ad nauseam and then some – you can expect it to be hard and painstaking work;

- start to generate the risk model in terms of key issues and the way they are mapped onto outputs;

- map the registered risks onto the key issues, if relevant;

- check that the risks which do not map onto any issues do not need to be modelled – they might be a trivial issue (or not a risk – surely not, after all that reviewing!), they may be accounted for under normal budgeting arrangements (there may be an opportunity to tease savings out) or they may be reliably transferred under the risk management strategy;

- quantify the main issues in the light of the contributing risks, probably taking a fairly broad view based on overall judgement, but if necessary focusing on the individual contributors or, indeed, building a sub-model;

- make sure correlation is accounted for.

Summary

This chapter has developed the idea of risk modelling, driven by a sequence of 'challenges', resolved largely through the ABCo case study which was introduced in Chapter 2. The key concept has been that of a probability distribution. The necessity for a core set of probabilistic concepts for managers to use has been emphasised.

Sequentially we:

- introduced the idea of bell curves to represent our beliefs about future uncertainty; in the case study, this was ABCo's annual profit;
- extended this into the concept of a probability distribution;
- noted how individual beliefs and collective appreciation of the information available can be combined into an organisational view;
- introduced the idea of a risk model which generates the probability distributions of outputs from those of the inputs;
- noted the importance of assumptions about independence and the modelling of correlations;
- noted the way in which the adoption of probabilities gives more usable results than simply combining ranges based on some estimate of best and worst cases;
- crystallised a minimal set of probabilistic jargon;

- broadened the ABCo risk model to include, among other things, cash flow concepts and the impact of an important project;
- recommended that risk models should encompass a small number of key issues analysed in depth, rather than input from each of the many items in the risk register.

This journey should have given a good appreciation of the general approach to risk modelling without covering all the aspects which might arise. These are introduced in Chapters 5 to 8.

At this point it is again worth summarising what the benefits of quantifying risk are:

- the basic definition of risk involves probability (a number) and the consequences of risk to the goals of the organisation – which on the 'if it is measured, it can be managed' principle is likely to involve a number;
- plotting risks on matrices often creates pointless or meaningless information and also tends to destroy information;
- numbers can be used much more easily in a decision-support analysis to provide more robust decisions, confidently taken, with a clear audit trail.

Against these points, it can be argued that:

- quantifying risk is likely to involve many assumptions, sometimes subjective and possibly unsupported; even more than is needed to plot matrices; it is far more difficult to get managers to agree on a probability distribution than to plot a point on a matrix, even though the implications are not much different;
- managers have to become comfortable with fundamentally different concepts and learn new jargon to do this;
- many important organisational impacts are, in fact, hard to quantify, especially reputational ones;
- producing numerical risk estimates is thought to involve much more time and money;
- producing numerical risk estimates is thought to involve esoteric black box techniques that no one understands.

These are all fair points, but they are all ones that can be addressed. Indeed many have been discussed in this chapter. No one would argue that all risk problems should be quantified. However, experience shows that there are some situations where it is certainly worth the effort and this book is aimed at explaining when this is the case, what is needed and how to avoid the pitfalls, including those listed.

The next chapter will help to illuminate the role of quantification. It provides more examples of situations where risk models can be used and the benefits which can be obtained. But before we leave this basic description of risk modelling, it is worth briefly reviewing the philosophy of the proposed approach to risk modelling; for that, see the Final Thoughts on Using Probability box overleaf.

Final Thoughts on Using Probability

In some sense this chapter has failed. We started out by recognising that we have to deal with future uncertainty and that what we wanted was some way to provide a range of plausible futures – a simple number to sit alongside the central number of the forecast. What we got was probability distributions. Probability theory is far too good for managers. Its conceptual coherence and range of application, developed over centuries, make it a sophisticated and finely tuned tool.

We use it for business risk analysis primarily because we recognise that simply defining ranges is not good enough. We have to be able to model the fact that the ends of our ranges are less likely than the central parts and that combining ranges gives output ranges which have extremes which are even more unlikely than the extremes of the input ranges. It is not probabilistically coherent.

In some ways probability is not an appropriate tool either. Probability, and our risk models, are based on the idea of randomness. In practice there is very little that is random about business risk. What we have to grapple with is poor management, dysfunctional organisations, divided attention, incomplete contracts, and so on, as well as opportunities to exploit. Ninety nine per cent of business risk analysis is analysing human frailty in the face of a broadly predictable world. Even when the occasional earthquake comes along, or a component falls off a train, it can be argued that it is not a random process but simply the outcome of a chaotic deterministic one. Life is uncertain, but not random. Using probabilistic methods is a choice, not a logical imperative.

So be it. There is no simpler or more widely understood way of achieving what we need. And probability is an excellent way of interpreting life's uncertainties in the same way that 'survival of the fittest' or 'the selfish gene' are two successful metaphors for interpreting the outcome of some complex biochemical reactions (or the strategic intent of an all-powerful deity, depending on your perspective on the universe). No one thinks genes wake up each morning contemplating what selfish acts they can engage in that day. No one thinks the failure of IT projects is a random event.

The important point is to recognise what we are taking on with probability: what it does well and what it does poorly; what can be trusted and what cannot. Above all we need to recognise the pitfalls of using a finely tuned thoroughbred theory for the crude, inexact, hand waving, illustrative calculations we want to do. This is why managers need to understand it. Otherwise they are at the mercy of the black boxes which plough through the process but do not answer these questions. More likely, managers being both practical and mistrustful, the approach will not be adopted and its benefits will not be realised. This is why this book does not focus solely on the what of quantitative risk analysis, but also on the when, the why and the why not.

4 *Using Risk Models*

Moving forward

Now that we have discussed the basic concepts of quantitative risk modelling, this chapter puts them to use. It does this mainly through two examples. The first is a continuation of the work in the previous chapter on ABCo and its plans for the future. The second looks at the risk issues associated with a hypothetical privately financed public project, especially from the viewpoint of a potential contractor. These examples can be followed using only the concepts discussed in the previous chapter: probability distributions with their associated S-curves, P-values, expected values and spreads.

Figure 4.1 provides an overview of what Chapter 4 will cover. The two examples are followed with a summary section which revisits the four key questions asked in Chapter 1.

This is the final chapter of Part I. The remaining three sections tell you how to do the calculations.

ABCo and its business plan: talking about risk

The ABCo board has now been asked to approve the 3-year business plan and next year's budget. A key element is the project to set up a facility to produce the new Product B. The board has been presented with a document which, along with lots of other material, contains a risk analysis. This risk analysis follows broadly the lines presented in the previous chapter.

What questions should the board be asking? By coincidence, very similar business plans will be being discussed by ABCo's great competitors, YZCo. Here are some questions that are asked at YZCo's board meeting:

- Will you please give us the complete risk register?
- Is this going to be based on a 'P50' or the 'most likely'?
- How much have we got in for safety management (or whatever)?
- So you're saying the chance of making a loss is 1 per cent, are you?
- Are you telling us we can't manage quality?
- So this is saying we don't know what's going to happen does it? Surely we can forecast better than this.

And so on. Of course the discussion of risk will have been left until the end of the meeting at YZCo, treated almost as an afterthought. These questions will lead to a flurry of activity in the risk team, who will be asked to report back the next morning.

Here are some questions that are asked at the ABCo meeting:

- What risk register is this analysis based on? How was it developed?
- Can you show us how the risk 'safety management' (or whatever) has been dealt with?

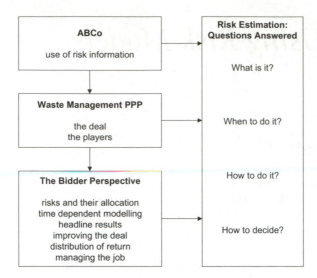

Figure 4.1   Chapter 4 overview

- Are you sure you haven't double counted contingencies in the baseline costs?
- What is the contingency plan for supplier X going bust? Is this modelled?
- What contingency do we have for things we haven't thought of?
- Have you considered the link between the market for Product A and that for Product B?
- The distribution is very broad. Is there really so much uncertainty in our business?
- What is the spread in return on investment?

And so on.

This also leads to a flurry of activity in the ABCo risk team, who will be asked to respond to all of these before the end of the meeting. The ABCo board recognises that risk is a key issue on the cusp between success and failure.

The risk team returns later with a presentation which runs along the following lines:

1. The risk register was developed in five workshops focusing on Project Beacon, the new IT system, our cost control initiative, sales and corporate issues. The dates and participants are on the handout.
2. Safety risks have been developed in a separate process over many years, most recently by looking at issues in the manufacture and use of Product B. In discussion with the HSE we have agreed that our planned control measures will reduce risk so far as reasonably practicable. Our project plans and budgets make provision for our control measures. We built a product recall into the risk model with a probability of 10 per cent in the next 5 years. This has a negligible effect on the S-curve.
3. Our guidance to the cost estimation team clearly required them not to build in any fat or contingencies. We checked this through a number of benchmarking exercises with the help of our internal audit team. However in one case we have built in an opportunity, as we, together with the internal audit team, think that there is scope to reduce costs further in production operations for Product A, compared with the figures from the plant.
4. Our risk model includes a low probability risk of our key widget supplier going bankrupt. If this does happen, it would mean a halt in production and considerable reputational

damage which we found difficult to quantify, but which could have a long term impact, even in sales of Product B, which does not use widgets.

5. We do not explicitly build in fat for things we have not thought of. However you will notice that our plans have been put together at the P80 level. The gap between P80 and the expected value is £2 million.

6. Our sales risk model includes a number of factors which introduce a dependency between sales of Product A and Product B, including a sharp downturn in our overall market and the possibility that our competitors will find a new product which leapfrogs Product B.

7. As we have just noted, there are a number of related factors which could have a significant impact on our business. These dependencies have been included in our risk model and inevitably give a broad distribution. Unfortunately competition and a demanding customer base mean that our business is increasingly risky.

8. The handout contains the S-curve for return on investment on the Product B side of the business. As you can see, we consider the chance of not meeting the rate of return set by the Chief Executive following discussions with lenders and shareholders to be only 10 per cent. Beyond this there is a 5 per cent probability that we shall run out of cash. As you can see from the chart, this is driven by the possibility that Project Beacon overruns. We have not examined the availability and cost of further funding in these circumstances, though the FD is confident that this situation can be dealt with.

In the light of this presentation, and with a certain amount of further discussion, the ABCo board decides:

1. There is a major exposure to the Project Beacon construction project. Managing construction is not ABCo's core business, so the executive team is instructed to find a company who will take on the construction risks at fixed price and put them on a contract which has liquidated damages, to ensure ABCo are compensated for the effects on their business of any late delivery. The risk analyst reruns the model in the meeting and shows that this greatly improves the downside return on investment. However, he points out that it will be difficult for ABCo to gain full compensation, for example for the impact on its reputation if customers' heightened expectations of Product B are not met.

2. Production operations for Product A will have its budget cut by 20 per cent.

3. The (new?) Production Manager will be instructed to find another source of widgets and split the orders 50:50. The board will not live with the strategic risk of production halted due to a lack of widgets.

Otherwise the risk profile is credible and acceptable and the business plan and budget are approved subject to these points. Everyone sleeps well (except the Development Director who wonders how she will find a construction contractor who meets the board's requirements).

Next morning, over at YZCo the exchange is something like the following:

-   a large document is banged on the table: 'you wanted the risk register, now read it!';
-   'the idea of Monte Carlo is to make the risks disappear';
-   'safety is paramount here: put £5 million in';
-   'we have added some opportunities to improve the forecast';
-   'that's what the last MD said when we put a risk on product quality';
-   'we have removed some of the dependencies so that the profile shows more certainty';
-   'this is too vague, give me something specific I can manage'.

When the dust has settled, the directors at YZCo decide the risk analysis did not help and take 10 per cent off the budget like they did last year (in addition to the savings on the risk team).

THE MORAL

Of course both stories are a caricature to some extent, though everything in YZCo is based on real events. The moral is that constructing risk models is a waste of time unless there is an informed audience who:

- knows what a risk model is and what its outputs mean
- knows what it can be used for
- is willing to use it where it helps.

YZCo got bogged down in the first two points; ABCo have passed them and are onto to the third. The qualification in the third point is important: the risk model does not help with many questions. For example, on what basis did the board decide to go along with the risk team against the production team and implement budget cuts?

This book takes as its premise that risk modelling sometimes helps. But it can only help where the first two questions are answered. Managers need to know what a risk model is, what its outputs mean and what it can be used for.

The waste management PPP

One of the most risk-driven areas of activity in the UK at the moment is in the placing of so-called PPP/PFI deals. PFIs are private finance initiatives in which private sector capital is sought for new or improved assets delivering public services, with the repayments on capital made from a periodic service charge for operating the assets and delivering the services. Done in the right way this keeps the asset and the liability for the loan off the public sector balance sheet, keeping the PSBR lower than it would have been. This creates the first advantage. The second is the opportunity to bring private sector management expertise to bear on the delivery of capital projects and cost-effective facilities management. The hope is that these advantages will outweigh the obvious disadvantage that private debt finance is more expensive than that available to the government – and private firms need to make a profit. PFIs are one form of PPP – public private partnership – which is a more general term. Historically the term PPP has been applied to PFIs which are particularly innovative or where the intention was to define the services supplied more flexibly, with the private sector service provider and the public sector client working together so as to achieve joint objectives.

The London Underground PPP is looked at in more detail in Chapter 9, while this chapter holds an extended discussion about an imaginary PPP. The risk picture, including the quantitative risk picture, is considered mainly from the perspective of a bidding contractor, but we also cover the perspectives on risk of the client, subcontractors and lenders.

The imaginary PPP is intended to implement a step change in a regional waste recycling strategy some years in the future. (This has been chosen to avoid coming too close to real PPPs or PFIs where commercial issues might be important.) The PPP (and we will call it that as success is going to require more flexibility than is allowed by a standard PFI term) will be let by a regional government authority.

It will involve:

- taking over the household waste collection contracts held by the various local and regional authorities and continuing to manage them until expiry;
- taking over an existing waste transporting operation with its 1000 employees and various waste consolidation sites;
- taking over some existing landfill sites which had previously been acquired by the authority in order to rationalise this aspect of disposal;
- building a new recycling plant on a brown field site (to be identified by the bidder), which will be required to carry out the separation activities necessary to produce streams of glass, plastic, paper, iron/steel, aluminium, copper, compost and so on;
- implementing new technology, not available today, but coming into use abroad at the time the PPP is let;
- the contractor being responsible for: collecting all household waste (which is expected to have been separated three ways into general domestic, paper, plastic and cans); collect all waste from civic amenities (again basic separation rules will apply, including for green waste); transporting waste as required, processing it through existing contracts, new equivalents and then the new facility; selling the product streams from the new facility; and dealing with the residual waste;
- a 25-year contract with fixed monthly service charge indexed to RPI;
- a bonus/penalty scheme relating to meeting recycling targets, reducing landfill and eliminating other environmentally damaging practices;
- demonstration of net positive energy production, expected to be achieved by the incineration of low-grade waste streams, again subject to the bonus/penalty system;
- compliance with all legislation and government and local environmental policies (including future changes).

The service charge will have to cover all the costs incurred by the contractor, who will have to borrow to finance the new capital assets and any other capital improvements, and then repay the loan, with interest, over the remainder of the 25-year period. The contractor will also have to finance any performance related service charge adjustments. In this way most of the risks associated with the project are allocated to the contractor.

The authority has pre-qualified a number of companies and consortia to bid, based on their demonstrated experience of doing this kind of thing and has drawn up tendering instructions for the bidders. The tendering instructions include a draft contract which sets the payment mechanism and the risk allocation expected, based on the standard terms, known as SoPC23 in this future time (the current version, at the time of writing this book, is SoPC3).

I have to emphasise again that everything that follows is a flight of fancy. There is no PPP/PFI planned that is of this nature, and if it were, the description of the risk and the financing is undoubtedly not realistic. This is not a book about projects and how to finance them. The purpose of this section is simply to describe the sort of risk models which prove useful in large projects, whether public sector or not.

The bidder perspective

The prospective bidder faces a number of issues, the first of which is whether to bid at all. There will be big bidding costs and no guarantee of work at the end of it. Does the business have the resources to bid, let alone the resources to deliver the project? Can the company work with the client? If it is in a consortium, can it work with the other members, especially if objectives and ways of working are not wholly aligned?

Assuming the opportunity is to be pursued, the bidder then faces a number of key strategic risk management decisions. These are to ensure a well structured chain of supply to the client. Internally, the bidder is likely to organise an SPV or special purpose vehicle. This will be the organisation borrowing the money and contracting with the client. The SPV will also have a contract with a delivery organisation, call it DelCo, which will be responsible for the bulk of the SPV's obligations to the client: ensuring the new facilities are delivered as well as the operational services, both during the capital investment and downstream, during its operation.

Both the SPV and DelCo may be owned by the bidder and its partners. The purpose of this structure is to separate the financing activities from the delivery activities. This is a basic risk management strategy. If DelCo defaults on its obligations, the SPV can in principle appoint new contractors who could continue to fulfil these obligations. This will ensure continued payment, so that the SPV can in turn meet its obligations to lenders. The lender perspective on risk is that the risk of default by the borrowers should be extremely small, especially as the project finance it is making available is likely to be at favourable rates. Lenders have a powerful position and generally have the last word on deals.

In real PFIs there are many variations on this structure which we do not need to go into. The key point is that the SPV will bear only the minimum risk consistent with its contract with the client (which might cover buying project insurance, for example), and the risks of client and delivery company default. It will aim to pass everything else down to DelCo, including, unusually in this case, the risk associated with throughput and the sales of recycled product streams.

The reason for this is that the security for lenders is the service charge and not the assets of the sponsoring companies. This is known as limited recourse funding. The price of the loan is very sensitive to the robustness of the cash flow. The sponsor companies will have to guarantee the performance of DelCo however.

I have gone into this in such detail not because we are going to model these very high level risk management arrangements. It is because these arrangements will need to be paid for. In particular, the SPV will need to keep sufficient financial reserves as a provision against the risks they hold. Keeping a cash balance to deal with problems as they materialise is the kind of language lenders understand, especially as it is they who are lending the cash balance. This means the risk management is suboptimal compared with a full portfolio approach. Keen readers might like to look at the costs of this when they have read the rest of the book.

From now on we will forget about the SPV and DelCo and consider the risk portfolio.

The next stage in developing the supply chain is to consider who will do each task. The capital investment may be subcontracted to one or more of the partner organisations or to a third party. Initial contracts may be put in place as part of the bid or the bid may be put together based on a view of the market. Whatever is decided it is very likely that the bidder will aim to allocate most of the risk associated with the development, including that associated with the performance scheme, to the subcontractor. The risk allocation picture, even for the simplest PFI, looks something like Figure 4.2.

RISK ANALYSIS

Much of this will have been done with a basic appreciation of the risks involved in the project and the client will probably have issued a risk allocation matrix of some sort. At this stage the

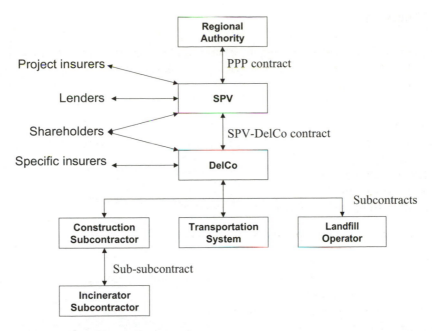

Figure 4.2   Bidder organisational structure

bidder, together with his partners, can start to build a more complete view of the risks. This would be broken down by the various activities.

Transportation

A key feature of the bid is that it will use a new type of small, unmanned, electrically powered vehicle. Guided by satellites, they collect the three full bins (each one electronically labelled) from individual households and drop off empty ones. The vehicles are then guided to the new waste processing plant: there are no economies with this system to consolidate the waste at intermediate sites (although they are locally based for recharging batteries).

The operational risks are:

- safety of the vehicles and associated third party liabilities;
- maintainability of the vehicles, including obsolescence of the electronic control system;
- availability and reliability of the vehicles;
- vandalism, both in use and at the depots;
- electricity prices;
- 25-year availability of satellite guidance, on which the system free-rides (as the economists say, meaning satellite navigation users benefit from the satellites without paying for them).

There are also risks in the procurement of the system:

- effectiveness of the new technology (although it works in Canada);
- regulatory approval including safety demonstration;
- financial stability of the supplier who owns the intellectual property of the system;
- late delivery, resulting, for example, from competition with other customers of the supplier.

Waste Processing

The new plant also has new technology to separate and process the waste streams. Specifically the incinerator is of a new type, not previously employed in the UK before. The planned processes are:

- separation
- glass production
- steel production
- aluminium production
- plastic feedstuff production
- compost production
- incineration to produce electricity.

The risks here are, for each process and product:

- volume of input
- quality of input, including effectiveness of householder separation
- process cost, including inflation
- demand for and price of output product
- plant unavailability
- maintenance and renewal costs
- environmental impact
- meeting evolving, externally imposed, environmental targets
- process safety
- change of standards and legal requirements

as well more general issues such as:

- site security
- site storage and logistics
- regulatory action and its impact across process streams.

There are further risks to developing the plant:

- construction risk – time and cost;
- technology risk – the incinerator works in France but will it here;
- regulatory risk – getting the processes approved, especially bearing in mind the potential environmental impacts;
- planning risk – finding a site where the plant can located, bearing in mind the transport and process requirements.

Residual Waste Disposal

It is envisaged that the small amounts of material which cannot be turned into a recycled stream will be landfilled in the sites retained for the purpose. The risks are:

- operating costs
- environmental impact, including leaching
- regulatory action
- landfill tax rates

- continued availability of landfill sites
- liabilities from existing sites, for which the contractor will retain responsibility even when filling has stopped
- subcontractor default.

The bidder considers that these risks will be best managed by appointing a specialist subcontractor to deal with them.

Transition Operations

The future steady state envisaged by the bidder will only be attained over a 5-year period as the new transportation system and processing facility are brought on stream. In the meanwhile, the existing waste haulage systems and recycling plants will have to be operated and then phased out. The risks are:

- defects in and safety of the ageing plant;
- performance of a shrinking, mainly ex-public sector workforce, transferred under conditions which guarantee certain rights;
- matching the phase-in of new technology with the phase-out of old;
- liabilities and inflexibility of existing contracts and equipment.

Corporate

Some risks are better considered from a whole project perspective

- inflation
- interest rates
- changes of law and tax arrangements
- residual value of the assets at expiry (or termination)
- pension liabilities
- insurance premiums and other terms
- IT system development and availability
- client approvals.

This a superficial list compiled to provide an idea of the scope of the issues which will need to be addressed.

At this stage it has become clear that the bidder would be out of his mind to take all these risks on, especially as many of them are effectively out of his control. But it is worth remembering that this bid is imagined to be taking place well into the future, say 20 years. The risks may appear differently then, compared to now. However, it is an important issue with 25-year contracts if they do not recognise how much the world changes over such a period. However well the requirement and solution are defined, it is inevitable that for all but the simplest facility or service, what is required will change and the means and costs of providing it will change. Partnerships need to recognise this.

So the bidder ploughs on, hoping to achieve eventually an equitable allocation and pricing of risk. Now the risk must be better characterised and a number of workshops are held. Each of the areas discussed is worth its own workshop and if each workshop pulls its weight, producing, say, 50 risks, the risk register quickly becomes weighed down with several hundred risks. This is the scale of the risk for this kind of activity, especially when it is remembered that construction risk ('time and cost') will perhaps contribute as many risks on its own account as many of the others put together.

The risk team sorts out the risks, makes sure each one is clearly articulated, deletes repeats, adds things which have been forgotten, collects the controls into coherent plans and then looks at the result. The risks can be allocated three ways:

1. There are issues that can be dealt with within the costings the bidder is preparing (this is likely to include those assessed as not worth worrying about).
2. There are issues for which responsibility needs to rest elsewhere than where it is currently placed – probably with the client.
3. Finally, there are issues which should be included in the bid risk model, such that we expect the bid price to be affected by them.

These decisions need to be communicated appropriately throughout the team. For example, if a business continuity issue is in the first group, it needs to be agreed and checked that the money for business continuity arrangements are included in the baseline costs. Similarly, if a risk in the second group is to be returned to the client, it must be flagged up and checked that a corresponding bid qualification (or pricing assumption or bid method statement or whatever other euphemism) is submitted as part of the initial bid. These are all part of the qualitative risk management activities which will be taken forward with the risk register.

But what is interesting for this book is what happens to the third group, those for inclusion in the risk model.

THE RISK MODEL

Each of these individual risks could be quantified on their own and added up to provide an overall model of cost, but that is generally not a very transparent approach. Nor is it likely to provide a credible estimate. It is better to prepare the risk model from the top down, aiming to minimise the number of categories and present results which are capable of being clearly understood by decision makers. For instance, the headings above could be used for the main risk inputs.

A key feature of the risk model is time dependence. The model will be used both to cost and to price the bid. To cost the bid it is essential to know when the expenditure on risk may arise so that sufficient finance to cover it is put in place (which will have its own cost). To price the bid, the spread in profit which the risk leads to will have to be considered to ensure these profits are protected with sufficient confidence, and also to ensure that the bid team is sufficiently confident that the project will not run out of cash. This is all explained in much more detail in Chapter 6 where development of the risk model is described in some detail.

Take inflation as an issue: 2 per cent per year (year on year) additional inflation over that assumed in the bid could amount to a 28 per cent increase in total costs. This is an extreme case based on uniform costs throughout the period: in reality the cost will be front loaded and the bid will in any case include in its baseline costs an estimate of the expected rate of inflation above RPI; maybe 1.5–2 per cent per year in line with increases in living standards. Inflation is quite likely to be the biggest risk in the model. Suppose the team takes the view that it could be 1 per cent per year less than what is in the baseline or it could be 1.5 per cent per year more. This is what is in the risk model. (This is actually quite modest when you think that if this is inserted with a triangle distribution the P80–P20 spread is only 0.9 per cent per year compared with the overall range of 2.5 per cent per year.)

The risk team prepares its first quantitative model. Management is provided with two charts. The first is a sensitivity chart showing how the spread in the total 25 year net cost depends on the main risk issues. In this case, net cost means total cost, capital expenditure (capex), operational expenditure (opex) less variable revenues, which in this case are performance payments and sales of recycled products. This is the amount which would have to be financed by the underlying service charge. The forecast sales are substantial and have a significant impact on the financing as we shall see.

The sensitivity chart in Figure 4.3 shows, for each risk, the minimum, P20, P80 and maximum net cost.

Not surprisingly the chart is dominated by two risks: inflation and the market price for the products produced by recycling.

The second chart, Figure 4.4, shows the proposed pricing. The small table shows the mean revenue, capex and opex risks, then an amount, which we have called the risk premium, which brings the total amount up to the P80. The evolution of the P20, mean and P80 over time are shown in the lower right chart. The top right chart shows the means in each period and, again, the risk premium amount required to bring the total up to P80.

What does pricing mean in this context? The intention is to build additional costs into the financial model to cover risk. The question is how much these costs should be and how they should be distributed in time. The bidder has taken the view that he will price at P80. That is, the cumulated amount of 'risk', as the relevant line(s) of cost are sometimes known, at every point in time is sufficient to cover the P80 level of risk up to that point. Chapter 6 discusses whether or not this is a good way of setting the price: just accept it for the time being.

With this approach the overall bid model looks as shown in Table 4.1.

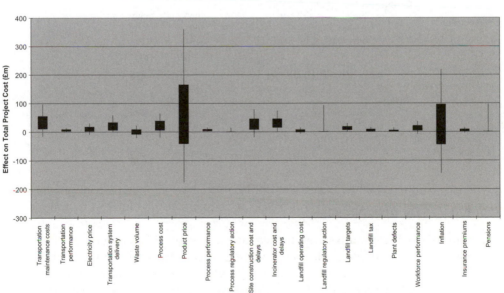

Sensitivity Chart (Min, P20, P80, Max) as at 8 Sep 2006, 17:14

Figure 4.3   Initial sensitivity chart

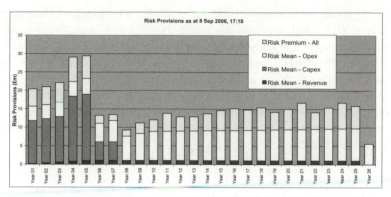

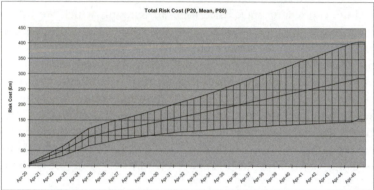

Figure 4.4   Initial risk provisions

Table 4.1   Initial bid summary (in £m)

Costs			
	capex	1000	**2000**
	opex	1091	
	performance revenue	-91	
	Sales of recycled product		**-436**
Risk			
	expected value	287	**406**
	risk premium	119	
	Total Net Cost		**1,970**

All amounts 25-year real, non-discounted

IMPROVING THE RISK PROFILE

The amount of risk is high, driven by the two main concerns of inflation over RPI and prices obtainable for recycled product. Neither of these risks is controllable by the bidder. So they decide to try an approach which leaves them with the client. Specifically, it is proposed that the client should take responsibility for selling the product and that there should be a 5 yearly cost review at which the contractor can reset prices in line with current benchmarked costs. The risk model is run again with the results shown in Figure 4.5 and 4.6.

The sensitivity chart, Figure 4.5, has changed the scale of its vertical axis and is less dominated by individual issues. The product price risk has disappeared and the inflation risk is much reduced. This is reflected in the pricing chart, Figure 4.6, where the total risk provision is now £256 million, which is £150 million lower than in the initial model.

The risk reduced model, from the bidder's perspective, can be seen in Table 4.2. The total cost has risen, but the client will benefit from the revenue from sales of the recycled products. The client will have to take additional risk, which has an expected value of £78 million – if he values it the same as the bidder – but the client will benefit overall by an amount equal to the reduction in the risk premium: £72 million. In simple terms, this demonstrates why transferring risk to a party who cannot control it is not good value for money.

THE FINANCIAL MODEL

The deal requires that the capital expenditure has to be privately funded so the real implications can only be understood when this too has been modelled.

The financial model has to determine:

- how much needs to be borrowed, at what rate of interest and when it will be repaid;
- suitable cash flows to give the bidder his required return on investment;
- the level of cash balances needed to be retained within the project;
- the underlying service charge needed be to cover all this;
- the cost to the client discounted at his 'time preference' for money, which is 3.5 per cent real per year according to Treasury guidance – see Chapter 9 for more details.

Financial models are put together by financial advisers using arcane techniques and, quite likely, at arms' length from the bid team. This does not lend itself to risk modelling but Chapter 6 describes a very simple financial model which determines all these parameters based on a requirement of 10 per cent real per year return on investment for the bidder. Because of

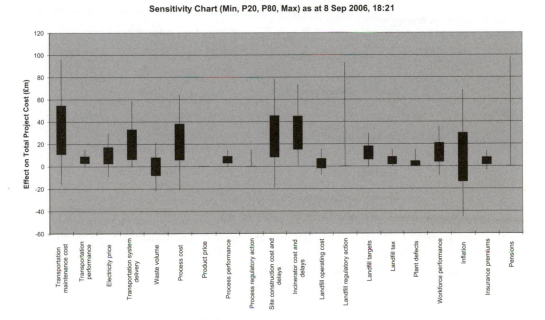

Sensitivity Chart (Min, P20, P80, Max) as at 8 Sep 2006, 18:21

Figure 4.5   Improved sensitivity chart

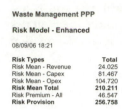

Waste Management PPP

Risk Model - Enhanced

08/09/06 18:21

Risk Types	Total
Risk Mean - Revenue	24.025
Risk Mean - Capex	81.467
Risk Mean - Opex	104.720
Risk Mean Total	**210.211**
Risk Premium - All	46.547
Risk Provision	**256.758**

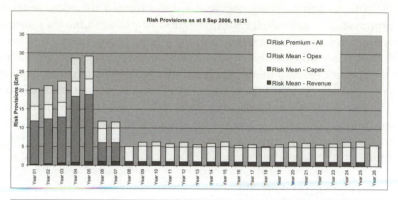

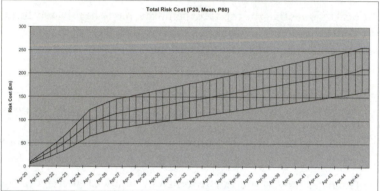

Figure 4.6   Improved risk provisions

Table 4.2   Improved bid summary (in £m)

Costs		
capex	1000	**2000**
opex	1091	
performance revenue	-91	
Sales of recycled product		**N/A**
Risk		
expected value	209	**256**
risk premium	47	
Total Net Cost		**2256**

All amounts 25-year real, non-discounted

the complexities of real financial modelling, this part of the example has a particularly strong health warning: make sure you know what you are doing before trying this in the office. The results can be seen in Table 4.3

The enhanced deal is therefore much cheaper to the client, despite the fact that he is bearing the risk of product prices and much of the inflation risk. The expected value of these was £78m, undiscounted.

What is the spread in the return on investment? The risk model is now connected up to the financial model. To do this some heroic assumptions have to be made about how shortfalls

Table 4.3 **Financial parameters**

	Initial Deal	Enhanced Deal
Borrowing	£820m	£780m
Return on investment	10% per year	10% per year
Post-capex cash	£40m	£40m
Service charge	£60.2m per year	£62.5m per year
Client income from sales	N/A	£436m
Net present cost to client	£2000m	£1865m

are funded (from the cash balance and delayed dividends) and how excesses are distributed. Note that the existence of a risk premium means that in general it is more likely that there will be excesses than shortfalls if you believe your risk model! We do not go into details of this here, except to say that these excesses are shared with the client.

More realistically there would be refinancing at the end of the investment period and this would allow the benefits of unmaterialised risk to be realised more efficiently. However, the simple financial model also provides for the distribution of this (avoiding the need for additional adviser's fees).

The risk model then provides the S-curve on the rate of return, for both the initial deal and the enhanced one (see Figure 4.7).

As you would expect, there is much more spread in the initial deal. Both models show the target rate of return, 10 per cent per year, at around P20. This is a direct result of the pricing being at P80. More precisely, it arises because the costs which are financed include the P80 risk premium, before they are paid for by the client. The P50 return is higher than target and obviously there is the possibility of much higher returns.

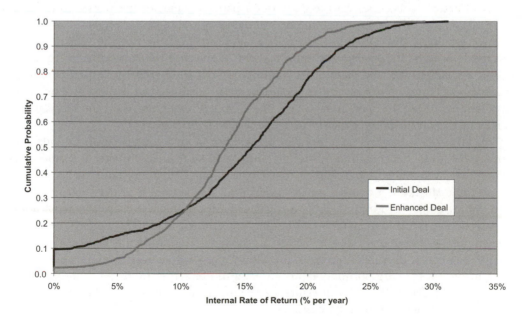

Figure 4.7 **Distribution of return**

At the left end the enhanced deal has a much higher probability of running out of cash (the return is set to 0 per cent in this case) – about 10 per cent compared with about 2.5 per cent. These numbers cannot be taken too seriously, partly because of the approximate nature of the Monte Carlo modelling, but mainly because of the shortcomings in the basic modelling of this case, such as the time dependent nature of the risk profiles and the availability of emergency funding. However the point that the bidder is much less likely under the enhanced deal to contravene his lenders' conditions will be robust.

Chapter 6 contains some illustrative models which indicate the dependence of the probability of running out of cash on the way the risks are modelled: either as long-term endemic consequences – operations simply cannot be delivered for the estimate, say – or short term immediate impacts. You need to make sure you get this right or at least understand the implications of the issue.

Of course this is all dependent on whether or not you believe the risk model. Most managers will have concerns; as we have just underlined, conclusions drawn from the extremes of S-curves are less reliable. They will ask questions such as those asked by the board of ABCo earlier on. They will comfort themselves with mysterious references to Rumsfeld and 'what we know we don't know and what we don't know we don't know'. Curves going up to 25 per cent per year will make them feel better. But it is important to get the risk model as credible as possible by covering all the issues that managers feel are important and not stinting on spreads and dependencies.

The bid team goes off to convince the client that the enhanced proposals are a good idea, making the project affordable perhaps, and that the enhancements, which are no doubt contrary to SoPC23, are worth arguing with the Treasury.

The subcontractor perspective

A subcontractor has been selected to carry out a particular part of the works: construction of the incinerator, say. At this stage the main interest of the bidder is to get an estimate of the price for doing this. Of course this price may depend on the risk the subcontractor is expected to absorb. The lenders and sponsors will be keen for the subcontractor to take all the risk associated with the plant. This would cover not only construction costs, but also revenue impacts such as lost revenue if the incinerator is delivered late or lost revenue due to unavailability during the operational phase. The sponsors might also want the subcontractor to take on risks on the price of the electricity generated (worth a try).

This gives the subcontractor a problem. He will not be in a good position to understand all the risks that he is facing. In fact, they are unlikely to be defined properly as a subcontract will not have been drafted. He is unlikely to have the resources to understand the performance scheme fully. However, a quick estimate shows that the costs of a project delay, if passed down to him, could be ruinous. It could easily absorb his profit and perhaps also bankrupt his company, which is much smaller than the bidding consortium. If, in spite of this, he reluctantly prices the risk at its extreme value, he will be accused of undermining the consortium.

The presence of the subcontractor in the supply chain will detract from the ability of the bidder to offer a true risk portfolio approach, in turn detracting from the value for money obtained by the client. Note that in Figure 4.2 the incinerator will actually be built by a sub-subcontractor, which amplifies these issues.

The immediate way out of this is likely to be uncommitted compromise between the parties, but this simply stores up problems for later. A better approach is taken in Chapter 6 where the incinerator will be built under a pain and gain sharing arrangement against a target cost supported by a full risk analysis. This gives increased confidence and risk reductions in this difficult area of the bid.

The client perspective

In putting the proposed deal together, the client will develop an idea of what it will cost him. He will be acting in close collaboration with central government and will have carried out an analysis, both of what it is likely to cost and what is affordable. This will have resulted in the award of PFI credits to allow the project to go ahead. The affordability comparison is likely to be a combination of current expenditure, together with an appraisal of the capital investment required. The key element of the cost analysis will be the Public Sector Comparator, or PSC. This is an estimate of the costs to the client of doing the same work with his own resources or using a 'traditional procurement'. It will contain its own risk assessment.

Typically bids may be a disappointment when compared against the PSC. Reasons for this include:

- the scope to which the bidders have been invited to respond contains many more items from the client wish list than had been intended or are provided for in the PSC;
- an optimistic view is taken of the productivity improvements which might be achieved;
- the PSC risk analysis omits key risks or undervalues others;
- bidders have qualified out risks which the client had assumed they would take;
- the risk analysis takes a simple portfolio approach, perhaps just adding the expected value into the overall cost estimate; the bidder, by contrast will have a much more divided risk allocation strategy, as shown in Figure 4.2, and will also have prohibitively priced those risks which he does not wish to accept because of their potentially very high consequences.

In order to compete against the PSC the bid has to find productivity or efficiency improvements which cover financing costs, a basic rate of profit and a risk premium. This assumes the bidder is willing to take a portfolio approach and to price all the risks which the client would like to see transferred. As noted, the delivery of productivity is a key risk area for bidders.

In the last few years the role of the PSC has changed. A pro-forma quantitative evaluation is carried out which includes a comparison with a traditional procurement method. Once it is established that the PFI will give best value for money, it is left to the market to finalise the price. Thus the emphasis shifts to ensuring there is a competitive enough market to deliver the deal at the best possible price. Multiple bidders need to be kept up to the latest possible stage.

The client has to decide what to do when the bidding team arrives to discuss the enhanced deal. They can see the benefits to the bidders. They can also see that the enhanced deal is potentially better value for money. But they will not be party to the full figures and they will be faced by different proposals from different bidders. They also know they need to get Treasury approval for the particular deal offered. And it has to be affordable.

Most likely they will ask for a compliant bid, knowing that the pricing of risks which the bidder is reluctant to take will be high, and a variant, incorporating the enhanced deal concepts and similar ideas from other bidders. They will start making their own appraisals of inflation risk and product pricing risk; they will also explore these ideas with the Treasury.

Negotiating

The bidder, if successful, will go through stages of getting on the shortlist, being selected as a preferred bidder, agreeing on a final price and reaching financial close before starting the job. The risk register and risk model should be kept up to date to reflect changes in the requirements, in the contract (and hence the risk allocation) and the price.

This is where the risk model can continue to add value by tracking these changes and giving a snapshot of where the complex deal is up to:

- by helping bid managers to understand which are the key issues and which are less important;
- by following the course of contract negotiations on these key issues and the many other qualifications which need to be kept in play until the negotiations close them out;
- by calculating the overall impact on cost and price;
- and doing this throughout the negotiations with both the client and subcontractors.

Managing the job

Again the risk register, in which the risk treatments have been recorded, will form the starting point. The risk management processes of the delivery team will take this on board, keep it up to date and monitor the progress of the risk treatment plans. One important question is the management of the financial side when risks materialise, whether they are those on the register or not. This tends to generate a lot of misunderstanding, so the philosophy and ground rules have to be clear.

Up to now we have tried to emphasise the need for clarity in what is included in base costs and what is included in risk. People spend a lot of time setting up rules and categories and then agonising over what is in what category: is it a risk or an uncertainty? Is it a construction risk or a contractual risk? One aim of this book is to prevent this sort of pointless activity. It starts from the view that there are two extremes: either create a baseline model in which everything turns out in the best possible way and model anything worse than this (that is, any risk which materialises); or create a baseline model in which everything turns out in the worst possible way and only model anything better than this in the risk model. Ultimately, the former contributes positively to the risk provisions, whilst the latter generates negative risk provisions.

The total cost – baseline cost plus the risk provisions – should be the same whichever approach is taken.

Most pragmatic cost and risk models will lie somewhere in between. For example, the risk model might contain a known and certain cost because the cost modellers have omitted it and the risk analyst is aware of it. It is much easier for the risk analyst to put it in the risk model than to nag the cost modellers to, and then check that they have. This is illustrated in Figure 4.8 where, independently of where the baseline sits, the risk analysis should compensate.

In Figure 4.8, Baseline 1 is very tight, and the risk provisions are large; Baseline 2 is set at P50 and the provisions are relatively small. The underlying risk curve should not change

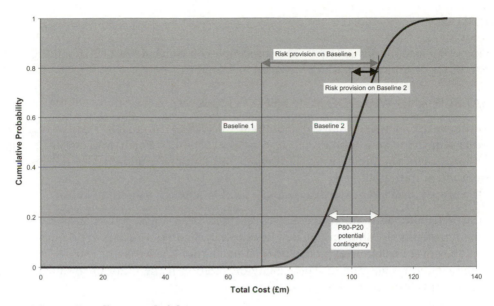

Figure 4.8   Baselines and risk

if is calculated right, and this is one of the sanity checks you can try. Looking at the overall S-curve, that is, with zero at the left end to satisfy yourself you have enough spread, is a good discipline. For example, the version of Figure 4.8 for the enhanced PPP deal would have only £94 million between P20 and P80 as compared with £2 billion of expenditure. Is this right? There are reasons why, but is there a dependency missing?

An additional process is needed when the delivery teams come to agree on budgets. Budgets need to be set with 'contingency' funds (or 'risk pots' or whatever other management euphemism) held in reserve to deal with risks that materialise. The management of the contingency funds probably needs to be at least a level higher than the corresponding budget responsibility. This is explained in Chapter 7. Rules need to be set for drawing down from the fund, which reflects as much a cultural approach to financial control as a financial one. Rules such as only allowing draw-downs for those risks that are on the register can be proposed. Other risks are supposed to be funded from savings elsewhere. This is a pragmatic approach to management, though obviously somewhat lacking in logic.

The allocation of contingency should also not depend on how the baseline is set. This is illustrated in Figure 4.8 by the light coloured arrow which represents one possible contingency amount which could be allocated at various levels.

It is not the purpose of this book to pursue these matters in great detail. However, where a deal has been priced on a portfolio approach to risk, it is important for the delivery team to appreciate what this means: that there is not enough money for each risk to be funded at its maximum worse case value. And that there is no money for risks not explicitly considered unless the delivery team get lucky on the other risks. And finally, even if you have an accurate risk analysis (which you will not) there is a 20 per cent chance that you will make a loss if you price at P80.

Summary

Having completed the discussion of our two examples we conclude Part I by revisiting the four questions about risk analysis which we posed in Chapter 1.

WHAT IS IT AND WHAT DO YOU NEED TO KNOW?

Quantitative risk analysis comprises building and calculating risk models. This involves putting together a model of your business or organisational activities which links outputs to inputs. You then specify the inputs using probability distributions and work out the probability distribution of the output.

If you are a manager acting as a customer for this activity you need to know:

- the probability distributions are subjective – there is no single, correct answer;
- the probability distributions are best described by S-curves which plot P-values – there is an 80 per cent (subjective) probability that the output is less than its P80;
- the best central measure of a probability distribution is the mean or so-called expected value – this is the probability weighted average.

As well as this bare minimum, it is useful to know two further points:

- the best approximate method for calculating risk models is Monte Carlo, which works by simulating the various possible versions of the future many times.
- another measure of the spread represented by the probability distribution is the standard deviation, which is usually of the order of the difference between the P80 and the mean.

If you are a risk adviser acting as the supplier for this activity you need to know everything in Parts II, III and IV which follow.

WHEN SHOULD YOU DO IT AND WHEN NOT?

The simple answer is, when there is a business case. It costs money to do whether you maintain a risk team with the capacity to build risk models or hire in specialists. Typically it will be thousands or tens of thousands a shot, perhaps more if you maintain a live risk model over an extended period.

So there has to be a good chance that it will be worth it; which means where there is a decision to take with a lot of money at stake. There should also be a good reason to think that going into the complexities of the decision and representing them numerically will provide some insight.

If you like you can build a model to investigate the risk that risk analysis will not tell you anything you did not already know. But be honest: a lot looks obvious in retrospect that you would not have figured out without a structured numerical approach. Making complex things obvious is a measure of the success of risk modelling.

But you should not have a risk model constructed:

- for the sake of it
- when the answer is obvious
- because you think it is good practice (or variants of this like 'I hear the FD is a Monte Carlo fiend')
- the stakes are small (or if when you run out of money you can just borrow some more)
- you think it is a fun technique.

HOW SHOULD YOU DO IT AND HOW NOT?

Here the answer is to aim for simplicity and transparency. Risk modelling is not primarily about adding up hundreds of risks in a risk register, although you can do that if you wish. It is much more about identifying the key issues, characterising them realistically and investigating the options for dealing with them. Register small worries; model big issues.

By definition there should only be a few key issues, but their modelling may require some ingenuity which goes beyond the usual practice of assigning distributions of cost and time to complete each activity. Specifically, you have to look for interrelationships between factors which might affect the results drastically: assuming independence will give unrealistically small spreads.

Ideally the model should be simple enough that, in retrospect at least, you can understand how it works and why you got the results you did. Black boxes are a breeding ground for incomprehension and errors. It is essential to carry out the sanity checks. Do I really mean this? What is it telling me? Is it right? Do not stop until you have satisfactory answers. The following sections contain some ideas for how to do this, based on some useful properties of probability distributions.

This advice applies to managers as well as the specialists.

Finally remember that the quantitative picture is not the whole story in risk management. Make sure what you are doing is safe. Remember to think about possible reputational factors which might have longer term impacts. It's a truism, but decision-support tools like risk modelling don't make decisions, just provide relevant information.

HOW DO YOU MAKE THE DECISION?

The simple answer here is to use the expected value. This is not quite right but is a good starting point which you should move away from only for clearly thought out reasons.

The reason it is wrong is that there should be a risk premium: an additional reward for taking risk. Another way of putting this is that you should take a precautionary approach where risk is involved. This is relevant especially to safety risk. What is less clear is what the premium should be. This is a recurring theme through the rest of the book and there is no single right answer.

Broadly speaking it seems that the risk premium should be high enough to reduce the probability of something really nasty happening to a reasonably low level. In business, reasonably low means somewhere in the range of one to five per cent. So in ABCo we saw the FD take action when the probability of bankruptcy was 40 per cent; in the PPP we saw risk transfer refused when the bidder would have a 10 per cent probability of breaching his banking covenants. All of this has to be viewed in the context of not taking the risk model too seriously (given its subjective nature), especially in the low probability tails of the distribution. This is the real power of measuring the likely spread in outcomes: it tells you if disaster is a possibility.

So my advice is to try to use the risk model to understand the probability that something qualitatively different happens:

* you don't recover overheads
* you make a loss on the job
* your project is so late the customer walks away
* you lose your credit rating

- your firm closes
- you are thrown in jail.

Then form a view in the light of these probabilities.

The fact that risk premiums are high is important. It means that risk transfer is expensive in a commercial environment. All else being equal, if you chop your risks up and apply a P80 to each, the total is a lot higher than the P80 of keeping them all together, which in turn is much higher than their expected value. And if the recipient is betting his farm, it may be a lot more than P80.

Finally, none of this is very difficult in concept. The idea of subjective probabilities may make you uncomfortable, especially when it comes to making career threatening decisions; but Monte Carlo, S-curves and so on ought to be a normal part of business life, moving forecasting from having no chance at all of being right to at least having some. The tricky bit is building the models and giving them credible inputs. So read on.

Risk Models

This section provides an overview of common approaches to risk modelling, mainly by using examples. The intention is firstly to provide a range of the ways in which the simple risk model concept can be applied and secondly to enable you to set about building your own risk model, appropriate to the project, system or deal you are trying to analyse.

Chapter 5 covers reliability modelling, a topic which tends not to be often used in business risk modelling. The discussion will focus especially on fault and event trees, which are useful in binary situations, when either something happens or does not.

Cost models are perhaps the most common risk application, for obvious reasons and in Chapter 6 examples are discussed in depth.

Chapter 7 introduces schedule risk modelling, which has come to be considered essential within the project risk management community. We include the way risks can be financed as they arrive through contingencies.

Finally in Chapter 8 we wrap up with a brief discussion of other types of models, focusing mainly on how to construct general risk models, rather than develop new methods for calculating them.

The summary of this section should allow you to understand the range of risk modelling approaches available to you, as a way of countering any tendency to limit yourself to only a specific sort of technique you may be familiar with.

Unlike in Part I, this section assumes a basic knowledge of probability theory and associated techniques. For reference, this material is provided in Part IV.

5 *Reliability and Other Binary Models*

Overview of reliability modelling

A longstanding area of applied risk modelling is reliability theory. Defined by a binary, on or off, character, reliability theory is concerned with whether a system or its components are working or not. This theory provides tools for estimating the probability that a system is operational at any given point in time.

These tools are very sophisticated. Their approach is to seek to build a system model in terms of individual components. As with all risk models, the idea is to use as inputs a number of probabilities which you think you know something about to find the output, a probability you know less about.

Binary risk models have traditionally been created for systems such as a radar system, an aircraft, a nuclear reactor or a process control system and reliability techniques have been developed in military and technological environments where very high reliability is required. But these models can also be created for your desktop computer or your business resumption plan following a fire. Shortly we will explore an example related to these more immediate concerns.

BASIC COMPONENT MODELS AND RELIABILITY

There are two basic concepts in component reliability modelling. The first is related to the point that we are interested in the transition from a state of 'working' to a state of 'not working'. Something happens. So the first concept is that of a transition probability, and since over some small period this probability might be expected to be proportional to the length of the period, this concept can be expressed as a failure rate. If the brake pipes on my car have a failure rate of 1 per cent per year, the probability that I will experience a failure today is $0.01/365 = 0.000027$.

Now from the system point of view cars are not very reliable. If something involved in making them go stops working, the car stops working. Manufacturers do not put a second engine drive train in the back to take over if the one in the front breaks down. But because of the importance of the brake system, it is a legal requirement that the brakes should still work with a failure in one of the pipes. Some form of valve is built into the braking system to ensure this. If this has a failure probability of 1 per cent, my probability of a brake system failure today becomes 0.00000027, or about three in 10 000 000.

This introduces the second concept in component reliability modelling, the probability of failure on demand. When the first component fails, what is the probability that the second one will fail to step in and keep the system going? This is a simple probability concept similar to the probability of a project overrunning, which we covered in Part I. It is the idea of a failure rate which we did not cover in Part I.

So returning to failure rates, we introduced this concept by saying that we expect the probability of failure during a small period to be proportional to the length of the period. The simplest model is one of a constant failure rate. It is not a very good approximation for the automotive applications just mentioned, but in general it will be a good approximation over periods where the failure characteristics do not change much. The probabilistic model which underpins this is called the Poisson process. The Poisson process is described in Chapter 12, but there are some fundamental misunderstandings around this type of model which we try to clear up in the Poisson Processes and Frequencies Box.

Poisson Processes and Frequencies

We introduced the concept of a failure rate by saying that it is a number f, which is multiplied by the time t to give the probability that an event occurs during some period of length t. So if f happens once per year, the probability of the event happening on any given day is 1/365; the probability of it happening during any given week is 7/365; and the probability of it happening during any given decade is 10. Well, obviously this cannot be the case: something has gone wrong.

The failure rate model works well for short periods where ft is much less than 1. When ft approaches 1 and then becomes much greater the interest shifts from the probability of the event happening to the number of times it happens. The Poisson process is a model of a random process in which during any small period the probability that the event happens is ft. This means the event is repeatable and in fact the expected number of times that the event happens is ft, whatever the length of the period.

Because of this, f is sometimes called the frequency, to align with the usage in statistics in which the frequency is the number of times an event occurs. More properly, it is called the Poisson parameter. For more on the Poisson process see Chapter 12.

The Poisson process can be contrasted with models involving a one-off probability. The occurrence of encountering bad ground during the construction of a bridge pier is a one-off event which would be modelled by a single probability. The occurrence of extreme weather over the course of the bridge maintenance contract could be assumed to be a Poisson process. You might be unlucky and get two storms – or even more.

Of course there is a simple relationship between the failure rate model and simple probabilities. The probability of a 50-year storm (that is, the most severe storms with a collective Poisson parameter of 0.02 per year) over a 20-year maintenance contract is about 40 per cent. (Very approximately! More accurately the probability of no storm is 67 per cent, of one storm is 27 per cent, of two storms is 5 per cent and three or more 1 per cent; the expected number of storms is 40 per cent. The Poisson process assumption is of questionable accuracy for this situation anyway as the 2005 hurricane experience in the US shows: if you get one big storm you are likely to get more.)

For some reason, the relationship between the two basic models of one-off probabilities and Poisson processes leads to considerable confusion in basic qualitative risk management. This results partly from different approaches in different disciplines. Project risk people work in one-off probabilities over the duration of the project and draw their risk matrices accordingly. By contrast, safety risk experts, for example, use the Poisson model to describe the likelihood of an accident occurring and use risk matrices where the likelihood axis is characterised by annual accident frequency. Attempts to put the two together generally lead to confusion, although there is no real need for this.

One response to the confusion is to ignore it, generally by using one formulation or the other completely inappropriately. We do not recommend this and will return to the topic in Chapter 11 where safety risk is discussed and I provide some concrete proposals for living with both.

Obviously reliability theory covers other types of process than the simple Poisson, to reflect the bedding-in or ageing characteristics or the impact of different maintenance regimes. There are many types of reliability models which can be built into the system model. Their intention is to model diverse aspects such as:

- unreliable new components;
- unreliable old, worn out components;
- differing modes of failure;
- increased reliability from more inspection and maintenance (or maybe the adverse effects of fixing things which are not broken);
- condition monitoring as a way of identifying incipient failure.

For example, Chapter 12 mentions the Weibull distribution which can be used for failure rates which either increase or decrease with time in a certain way. However, component modelling other than with a constant failure rate is beyond the scope of this book. The constant failure rate model will be used in this chapter and also in the discussion of safety risk management in Chapter 11.

Before leaving our car brakes it is worth reflecting on the unsophisticated model we developed. Will the brake valve really be as reliable as we suggested given that a component of this sort is not inspected or tested? If the brake pipes have corroded enough to reach such a condition that they leak, for example, will the valve really step in? Or indeed, is the second failure in the pipework anyway, following the correct operation of the valve?

To design reliable systems we aim to:

- first, eliminate single points of failure, where a single component transition to the 'not working' state leads to the system doing the same;
- second, ensure that we can multiply small failure probabilities to get extremely small failure probabilities;
- third, ensure that something else does not come along and dominate the small probability we have achieved.

To meet the second challenge, we need to arrange things so that the two events are independent and multiplication is permissible. In practice, achieving all of these conditions is very difficult. You should never believe in small probabilities and this advice is relevant to all risk modelling, not just system reliability.

RELIABILITY DATA

Apart from modelling binary states of 'working' and 'not working', reliability has another specific feature not commonly found elsewhere in business risk management. This is the collection and use of historical data to quantify the risk model.

Evidently there is a huge body of knowledge on how often transistors, transformers and car brake pipes go wrong. This is collected to feed into reliability models. Indeed, it is even built into design standards to ensure consistency and with the intention of providing credibility to reliability estimates. This contrasts with the approach described elsewhere in this book ,where we cheerfully accept the subjective nature of the probabilities we are using and are happy to put in guesses which have some form of consensus from the relevant decision makers.

Collecting and using information from past failures is a useful discipline, but you need to remember possibilities such as:

- your application is bigger;
- your application uses different technology;
- your application works in a different environment;
- there is no data on the interdependence effect which is killing your small probability;
- the chances are you do not even know what this interdependence effect is.

So the key lessons of this overview of reliability are:

- there is no such thing as a small probability;
- historical data is never relevant;
- but, this does not mean that history will not repeat itself: our capacity to repeat our mistakes is remarkable.

Remember these (only slightly overstated) lessons in business risk management and you will avoid many howlers.

Fault and event trees

As well as the complex component models we touched on, there are also many ways of building and calculating a system model – that is, the way the system reliability output depends on the component model inputs. These have become very sophisticated, especially when time dependence is involved. Although this generally has little application in business risk modelling, there is one set of tools which can be very useful. These are tree-like diagrams which set out to show firstly the different outcomes of a specific event and secondly the combinations of events which can lead to a specific event. They are called *event trees* and *fault trees* respectively.

The example we use to describe fault and event trees is drawn from business continuity, but on a rather personal level. A big risk in my life at the moment is losing the manuscript of this book due to some form of IT failure. To avoid this I have put in place a system which I think is very reliable. It involves synchronising my laptop computer with my desktop. I am out of the house for much of the week, so typically this happens weekly. I back up the desktop to two CDs, keeping one in the house and one in the car, in case the house burns down. I should do this every week as well, but unfortunately my experience is that this does not always happen. Losing a week's work while I am away is also serious, so I email my day's work to a dedicated mailbox managed by my ISP on the internet every evening. Finally, if all else fails, and the problem is a hard disk crash, I am told that in most cases the data on a failed hard disk can be recovered (although this was not the case the only time I experienced a hard disk crash).

My system should be reliable in that I actually have a six-fold redundancy (the laptop, the desktop, the two CDs, the internet and disk recovery). As we discussed in the context of car brakes, *redundancy* (that is, avoiding single points of failure) is the basic building block of reliable systems. Five back-up systems is impressive, even by nuclear reactor standards. But nuclear reactor experience also shows that redundancy is not enough. The systems might avoid all being destroyed in a fire, if the separation between them is good enough; but if they are all of the same design, there are likely to be other failure modes which could affect them all.

So the next tool for designing reliable systems is *diversity*. That is, the redundant systems should work on different principles. This means that common design errors or common subsystem dependencies should not cause system failure. The manuscript back-up system is also quite diverse. Hard disk crashes on the two computers should be unrelated and should be recoverable, whilst backing up to CD and emailing to my ISP are quite different technologies.

Before moving on to describe the analysis of the system it is worth concluding this general discussion of reliable system design principles by pointing out that there is one glaring dependency in all of this: people. Human error, whether of the mistake variety, the misconception variety or just plain maliciousness is just as relevant to business risk as reliability; more so in fact.

To demonstrate the technique, Figure 5.1 shows an event tree which provides an overview of the risks to the manuscript.

The diagram starts with an initiating event *Lose file from laptop*. If this happens, the most likely first thing to do is to try to retrieve the file from the internet mail box. So the initiating event is followed by a node relating to this. Doing this successfully is represented by the path which goes upward. This goes straight to the end of the tree and the outcome is loss of a day's work. On the other hand, not succeeding leads to the downward path and the next thing to try, which is to retrieve the file from the desktop. Success here is assumed to lead to loss of a week's work. Similarly, the next port of call is the back-up CDs; but because, like everyone else, I am less than scrupulous about doing this, it could be a month's work I am losing here. If all else fails I can always take the failed disk to a specialist to attempt to recover the data. It might be worth doing this even if the file is successfully retrieved from CDs, as loss of a month's work is a pretty serious issue. Because there will be a fee, marked as *Recovery charge* on the diagram, it is assumed it will not be worth doing just to recover a day's or week's work. The final outcome, at the bottom right, relates to losing the whole manuscript.

Thus an event tree starts with an initiating event and expands the possibilities for what might happen using a tree structure. As we reach the endpoints of the tree, we have explored the possible scenarios in enough detail to enable us to assign consequences. The example tree contains six different scenarios with five different outcomes. This is the qualitative side of event trees. To quantify them we need to assign a frequency (or failure rate) to the initiating event and probabilities to the nodes. This will enable us to calculate the frequency of the outcomes, and hence characterise the risk.

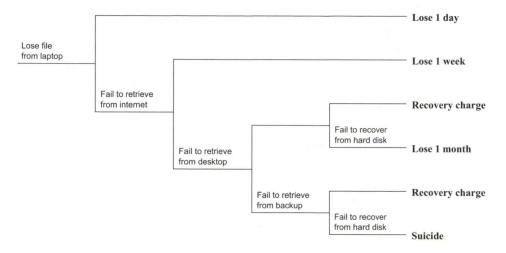

Figure 5.1   Manuscript loss event tree

We could do this directly, by assigning subjective probabilities to the initiating event and to the nodes. However, for a systems analysis problem this will not break the problem down into enough detail. Putting it another way, we think we can do a better analysis by quantifying the events which contribute to the initiating event and nodes.

This is where the fault tree comes in. It takes the opposite approach to event trees in that instead of thinking about the scenarios which might flow from a given event, it considers the ways in which the event can arise. Taking the initiating event of the event tree above as an example, we can draw the fault tree shown in Figure 5.2.

Having drawn the event tree from left to right, it would be logical to draw the fault tree from right to left. Cultural issues give us problems with this though, so we draw it from the top down instead. So the *top event* (this is a technical term, not just a casual description) is the same as the initiating event on the event tree.

It is assumed that this can arise either because there is a disk crash or because I inadvertently delete the file. Note that this is represented by a symbol called an *OR gate*. I might just delete the file by accident or I might do it while I engage in a bit of housekeeping to keep my computer clean and simple. Either way, there is a further bit of redundancy in that Windows keeps my deleted files in a trash can (sorry, Recycle Bin) from where it can be recovered if it has not been deleted from there as well. The trash can has been brought into the tree through an *AND gate*; the presence of such gates is an indication of redundancy, and hence reliability.

The bottom symbols on the tree, represented by circles, are the so-called *base events*. These are the fundamental elements of the model and are what we use to quantify it. Figure 5.2 also shows how this can be done. Each base event has been assigned a frequency or a probability as appropriate. For example, it is assumed that the probability of a disk crash in any year is 10 per cent. The frequency with which I delete the file by accident is taken as 10

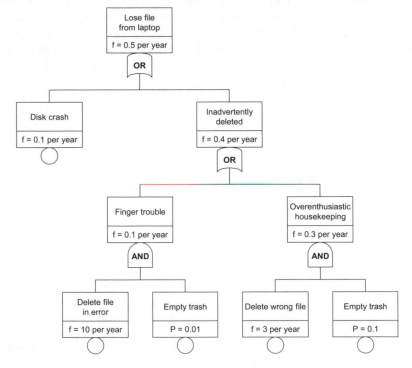

Figure 5.2   Laptop fault tree

per year, but the probability that it cannot be recovered from trash is only 1 per cent so the frequency of losing the file due to accidental deletion is 10 per cent per year (the same as disk crash). Finally, the frequency of deletion during housekeeping is smaller still. This could be expanded into a model incorporating the frequency of housekeeping and the probability of messing up.

The probability of failing to recover from trash is much higher during housekeeping than following accidental deletion since overenthusiastic housekeeping is likely to extend to emptying the trash can; an otherwise unheard-of event. Overall, the frequency of losing the file from this cause is 30 per cent per year and this is the dominating cause in the total frequency of losing the file of 50 per cent per year.

What this illustrates is that not only is human error often an important factor, but that errors made with good intentions or through incorrectly diagnosing a situation are a particular problem.

The next step is to pull together a fault tree for the first node on the event tree. This is shown in Figure 5.3. It contains similar events to the previous fault tree. Broadly speaking the recovery will fail if the back up is done wrongly, if the ISP experiences a disk crash or, again, if I delete the file in the course of housekeeping. This time the quantification is entirely in probabilities as what we are seeking is the probability of failing to recover the file, given that it has been lost.

In the specific case of housekeeping, a probability has been derived in the following way:

It has been assumed that I housekeep ten times a year and mess it up with a probability of 30 per cent. This explains the three times per year frequency on the previous tree. On any given day the probability of housekeeping the previous day is 1/30 (approximately) and the probability that it went wrong is 30 per cent. Therefore, the probability that the file is not

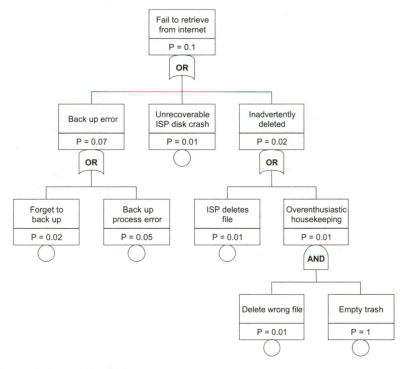

Figure 5.3   **Internet fault tree**

available due to overenthusiastic housekeeping on any day is 0.01 as shown. (Note that it has been assumed there is no trash can to pull it back out of.)

Now that we have quantified both the initiating event and the first node, we can see from the event tree that the frequency of losing one day's work is 0.45 per year, and the frequency of needing to recover from the desktop computer is 0.05 per year (see Figure 5.4).

However, there is an obvious flaw in this. If I engage in housekeeping, there is a good chance I may delete the file from both computers. To examine this I need to do two things: combine the two fault trees so that they are properly quantified and model the housekeeping in a bit more detail.

To keep it simple we consider only the parts of each tree which are concerned with housekeeping. Figure 5.5 combines the relevant sections of Figure 5.2 and 5.3.

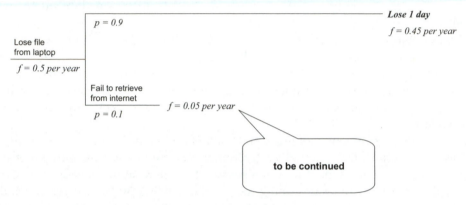

Figure 5.4   Partial quantification of the event tree

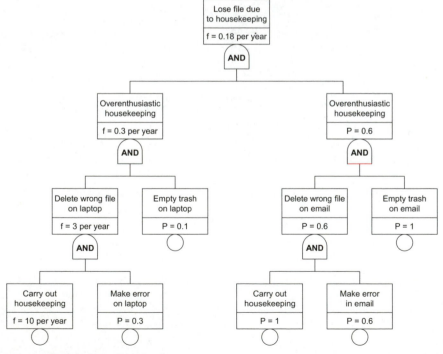

Figure 5.5   Housekeeping fault tree

On the right-hand side we have adjusted the probabilities to reflect the two points that if we are carrying out housekeeping on the laptop, then the email system will also be part of the exercise and, if we make an error on the laptop, then we are also more likely to err on the email.

As a result, the frequency of losing the file from this cause has increased from 0.03 per year to 0.18 per year, quadrupling the overall frequency of the loss from 0.05 per year to 0.2 per year. This underlines, as ever, the importance of taking dependencies into account.

At this point we will leave this example. There are still two more fault trees to develop and a number of dependencies to factor into the analysis. However you have seen enough to understand how the techniques work. And already there are a number of lessons which can be drawn.

LESSONS LEARNED

Model assumptions

It is necessary to make swingeing assumptions to develop the model, ranging from the simple – such as recovering from the internet is a day's work lost – to more complicated ones, such as the way housekeeping is carried out. These assumptions have to be made to permit the fault and event tree approach, with its binary modelling, to be used. Such assumptions are generally either 'pessimistic' or 'conservative'. That is, they are made so there is little chance of underestimating the risk. This is the case for the assumption that an entire day's work would be lost: generally it would actually be less.

Technique applicability

The techniques outlined in this section have been used extensively in reliability and safety analysis. To some extent they have been overused. The toolkit has been reached for even in circumstances where it is not obviously useful. Where a safety issue is basically a question of reliability, such as for example, the risk of nuclear reactor accidents, the approach is very suitable. When the issue has to do with the size of physical phenomena, such as the size or extent of a fire in an underground railway station, it is less suited. It is worth remembering that these techniques are addressed at binary phenomena – where it either works or it doesn't – and are not suited to continuously variable phenomena. Extending this further, although you either are or are not bankrupt, the situation will depend on the size of your cash requirement, a continuously varying quantity. So it is unlikely that fault and event trees will be helpful in determining whether you will run out of cash in the next year.

Independence

It is important to account for dependencies, either by specific modelling (for example, housekeeping) or adjusting parameters (for example, the error probabilities). I always recommend explicit modelling, but this is not always possible. Implicit in the fault tree method is the ability to model dependence by inserting the same event in different parts of the tree (but see quantification below). As well, numerous models have been developed for so-called dependent failure modelling in reliability applications. They all amount to prescriptions for increasing the failure rate compared with the independent value. Such dependent failure modelling is based on data as far as possible, but this is not necessarily very far and you make another major assumption when you decide to adopt such a model.

Dependence is a key theme of this book and I always recommend that it should be modelled explicitly (see Chapter 3). Some of the methods do this, some do not. Although both sorts suffer equally from lack of data-based verification, the methods that do explicit modelling at least have the advantage of making the presence and impact of common cause and common mode failures more visible.

Probabilities and frequencies

It is essential always to be clear on probabilities and frequencies; it is not difficult as long as you keep to the disciplines shown on the tree illustrations. The following rules may help. In fault trees each gate will be represented by a frequency or a probability. If an OR gate represents an event with a frequency, then *all* the contributing gates must also be events with frequencies. The sum of the frequencies provides the gate frequency.

If an AND gate represents a frequency event, then *exactly one* of the contributing gates must be a frequency event and the product of this frequency multiplied with the probabilities of the others provides the frequency of the gate event. Otherwise the quantification should be all probabilities: summing them at OR gates and taking the product at AND gates (but see *Quantification* below).

Although this is straightforward it is not unheard of for frequencies to be multiplied together, or for a frequency to be added to a probability. Keeping a good sense of what is going on and keeping an eye on dimensions should prevent this sort of howler.

For event trees the situation is simpler. They generally have an initiating event which is a frequency, while the subsequent nodes are all probabilities. In this case, the end points are quantified in terms of the frequency of the end point arising. However, it is possible to have event trees which use probabilities throughout.

Quantification

Several of the formulas just given for quantification of fault trees are approximate, as exemplified by the quantification of the second fault tree above. The probability of either of two independent events occurring is not $p_1 + p_2$ but $p_1 + p_2 - p_1 p_2$. Thus the accurate quantification of the tree showing failure to retrieve from the internet is not $0.02 + 0.05 + 0.01 + 0.01 + 0.01 = 0.1$ but $1 - 0.98 \times 0.95 \times 0.99 \times 0.99 \times 0.99 = 0.0967$. The approximation is not bad because the probabilities are small. More importantly, it is necessary to be able to deal with repeated events turning up in different parts of the tree when dependence is explicitly modelled. There are methods for dealing with these issues and these are described in Chapter 14.

Specialist fault and event tree software is available to implement these methods, as well as draw the trees and produce suitable reports. However, the methods in these tools are also only approximate, and are based around the situation where the probabilities are small. If this is not the case, a suitable alternative, avoiding the necessity of buying expensive software, may be simulation using the Monte Carlo technique described in Chapter 13.

You do not have to have software to use fault and event trees, as you can see from the example. Drawing trees like this helps you to structure a problem, including problems which have nothing to do with reliability. Additionally, simple quantification is very easy with a spreadsheet. There are many software packages around for doing risk calculations, but every new application increases the risk of errors and black boxes.

Uncertainty

Because reliability focuses separately on probability and consequence, it is particularly relevant to question the 'error' in the calculation. An obvious question is, 'how uncertain is my estimate of unavailability?' You could, for example, look for a technique which would provide you with a probability distribution for the unavailability. Or, given that the focus is on historical data, there are statistical techniques for putting confidence bounds on your estimates. These methods have been applied with various degrees of success – see the Aspects of Safety Risk Modelling (3): Uncertainty box in Chapter 11 for more – but are of little relevance for business risk models.

Summary

The main points from this chapter are:

- Reliability modelling is complex in general. There are lots of sophisticated techniques we have not touched on.
- High reliability comes from independence, implemented through redundancy and diversity.
- Human and management factors kill independence in business risk, even more than reliability.
- Fault trees and event trees are sometimes a good way of structuring, and then perhaps calculating, a risk model.
- But, their binary nature does have limitations.
- It is essential to understand and be able to use both one-off probabilities and frequencies.

6 Cost and Other Additive Models

Many risk analyses require an estimate of the future cost of an undertaking. This might be the cost of a small construction project, the cost of upgrading a railway or the cost of delivering a PFI contract over many years. Having estimates of the costs are a key element of deciding how to budget for a project, how to price a bid, what contractual conditions to seek, what the range of returns might be and so on.

Cost has a very obvious but important property: it is additive. The cost of a programme is the sum of the costs of the individual projects; the cost of a project is the sum of the costs of the individual tasks. This has several important and related consequences. First, the cost model is in principle very simple, although there will be lots of devil in the detail for issues such as the cost in each time period, the approach to quantification and so on.

Furthermore, there are some simple rules from probability theory which can be applied:

- the expected value of the total cost is the sum of the expected value of each individual cost;
- if the individual costs are independent of each other then the variance of the total cost will be the sum of the variance of the individual costs;
- under some conditions the output distribution will be well approximated by a normal distribution (with parameters as in the previous two bullet points).

This last result is the Central Limit Theorem, which is a very interesting and powerful result indeed – discussed in more depth in Chapter 12. It can be applied to cost risk models using the so-called direct method (see Chapter 14) as an easy way to calculate outputs.

The purpose of this chapter is to demonstrate the range of techniques which can be applied to cost modelling with risk. We begin by providing more detail of the ABCo cost model developed in Chapter 3. This focuses on the direct method. We then go on to illustrate time-dependent cost modelling in the context of the waste management PPP introduced in Chapter 4.

Finally, the additive property can apply to other models than cost. For example, if you know the critical path of a project, then the duration is the length of the individual tasks added up (assuming they run consecutively). So a simple project risk model could use the direct methods described here. This will work until the critical path changes, so this is probably only of use as a scoping or sanity-check approach: useful nonetheless. See Chapter 7 for more on schedule risk analysis.

The ABCo model

We will show how the ABCo risk model presented in Chapter 3 was actually put together and calculated.

In Chapter 3 we developed the story of the ABCo risk model by:

- starting with a simple model in which profit was the difference between sales and cost;
- noting that positive correlation between sales and cost reduced the spread in profit;
- enhancing the model to include a project to build a new production facility for Product B.

The key areas of risk in the final model were:

- overhead cost risks with a spread of £5.1 million;
- sales risks (of Product A) with a spread of £4.8 million;
- project delivery risks.

There were three major assumptions in this:

- direct costs are controllable to 40 per cent of sales;
- project costs are directly related to project delivery time (at £20 million per year);
- sales of Product B are directly related to project delivery time (also at £20 million per year).

Put another way, the first of these recognises that the spread in direct cost is 0.40 × £4.8 million = £1.9 million, but that this risk is fully correlated with sales. The other two are similar.

The overhead cost risks were in turn broken into three independent areas:

- general operating risks with a spread of less than £1 million;
- risk on an IT project with a spread of £3 million;
- uncertainty in the results of a cost reduction exercise with a spread of £4 million.

All of these are in principle the outputs of sub-models based on the detailed risk registers which ABCo has compiled.

OPERATIONAL RISK MODEL

Taking the general operating risks for example the sub-model might be as shown in Table 6.1 (with units of £k rather than the £m we have used up to now).

This shows a register of eight risks which have all been quantified using triangle distributions involving Minimum, Most Likely and Maximum values. Note that these are the yellow risks from Table 2.5. Some of the risks, such as an adverse outcome to an industrial tribunal, also have probabilities assigned (and in this case the outcome is assumed to be a point value,

Table 6.1   ABCo operational risks

ABCo Operational Risks

ID	Risk	Prob	Min (£k)	ML (£k)	Max (£k)	Mean (£k)	Var (£k)^2	SD (£k)
1	Insurance costs	1	-200	0	300	33	10 556	103
2	Office rental costs	1	-250	0	250	0	10 417	102
3	Pay claim	1	-300	0	300	0	15 000	122
4	Personal injury liability	0.2	200	250	300	50	10 083	100
5	Industrial tribunal	0.3	50	50	50	15	525	23
6	Advertising costs	1	0	200	500	233	10 556	103
7	Working time directive	0.2	0	0	500	33	7222	85
8	Waste costs	0.5	0	0	325	54	5868	77
	Total (to the nearest £k)					419	70226	265

quantified by setting the three point estimates to be the same). Others such as the uncertainty in insurance costs have a probability of one and a range which runs from negative to positive values. The negative values reflect the possibility that ABCo might improve on its budgetary estimates.

The columns on the right-hand side contain the mean, variance and standard deviation of each risk, taking account of the probability. The formulas for this are given in Chapter 12, but for convenience are repeated here for triangle distributions:

Mean = p(Min + ML + Max) / 3.

Var = SD^2

$= p((ML - Min)^2 + (Max - ML)^2 + (Max - Min)^2)/36 + p(1 - p)(Min + ML + Max)^2/9.$

The expected value of the risk is £419k, the sum of the means of the contributing risks. Because the risks are assumed to materialise independently, the variance of the total is the sum of the variance and the square root of the sum of the variance; the standard deviation is therefore £265k. (Note that the Total row of Table 6.1 has sums under the Mean and Variance columns, but not the Standard Deviation column, where it is the square root of the total variance.) In Chapter 3 we related spread to standard deviation by using normal distributions and taking spread to be the distance from the P5 to the P95. This implies the standard deviation is 0.304 × spread and applying this gives a total spread for operational risk of £872k which we previously approximated with £1 million.

If we wish to know more about the distribution of the outcome of all the operational risks we can use one of two approximate methods.

The first method is to make the assumption that with the mean and standard deviation just calculated, the distribution is normal. This utilises the Central Limit Theorem, described in Chapter 12, which states this should be a good approximation in these circumstances.

The second method is to carry out a large number of simulations of the risk model, selecting a value for each of the risks from its distribution and looking at the distribution of total costs which arises.

The latter approach is known – notoriously – as the Monte Carlo method, which is described in some detail in Chapter 13. Monte Carlo is the mainstay approximate method for calculating probabilistic risk models and it has the very valuable properties that it is both relatively simple to understand and apply, and the more simulations you do, the more accurate the approximation is.

In spite of this it is important to realise that Monte Carlo is just an approximate way to do a calculation; it is not the calculation itself. 'Doing a Monte Carlo' is not an appropriate description for developing and using quantitative risk models. The comparison is shown in Figure 6.1.

The chart indicates that using the direct method is pretty accurate. Indeed, it is hard to tell if the deviations from this are systematic or just due to the random nature of the Monte Carlo approach. Even at the extremes where the normal approximation can be expected to be unrealistic there is little systematic error.

OVERHEAD COST–RISK MODEL

Turning to the overheads as a whole, we combine the operational risks with the IT risk and the overhead reduction risk. The new, higher level model is shown in Table 6.2.

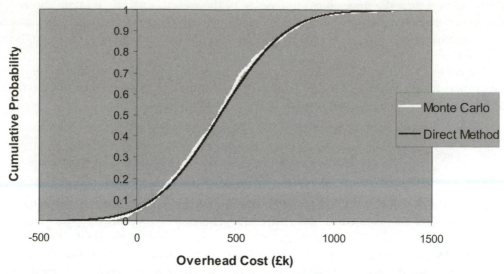

Figure 6.1   Comparison of the direct method and Monte Carlo for operations

Table 6.2   ABCo cost risks

ID	Risk	Prob	Min (£m)	ML (£m)	Max (£m)	Mean (£m)	Var (£m)²	SD (£m)
1	Operational costs	1.00		5.96		5.96	0.07	0.27
2	Overhead reduction	1.00	-5.96	-2.98	0.00	-2.98	1.48	1.22
3	IT project	1.00	0.73	0.73	4.60	2.02	0.83	0.91
	Total (to nearest £k)					**5.00**	**2.38**	**1.54**

The operational risks are now modelled as a normal distribution, with a mean of £5.96 million and with standard deviation of the operational risks just discussed. Effectively the risks from the previous model have been added to a budget estimate of £5.54 million.

The overhead reduction project is expected to halve these costs with a total range from zero to completely eliminating the costs. You are asked to ignore the point that these figures are contrived to be consistent with the round numbers in Chapter 3! They are not as contrived as you might think, though; the P20 cost reduction is £1.9 million and the P80 is £4.1 million which are quite reasonable. The maxima and minima of triangle distributions are a long way out from their non-extreme percentiles.

The IT project has a planned cost of £0.73 million, but it is thought that it could be as high as six times this (£4.6 million). Again note that the P80 is a more modest £2.9 million. Is this a reasonable range for an IT project?

You can check that these standard deviations are consistent with spreads of £4 million and £3 million (exactly) for the cost reduction and IT respectively as stated in Chapter 3.

The total overhead mean and standard deviation are given in Table 6.2 and again you can use either the direct method, with the normal approximation, or Monte Carlo to derive the complete distribution. Both results are shown in Figure 6.2, which indicates that even for the small number of quite crudely defined distributions used here, the normal approximation, underpinned by the central limit theorem, is a good one.

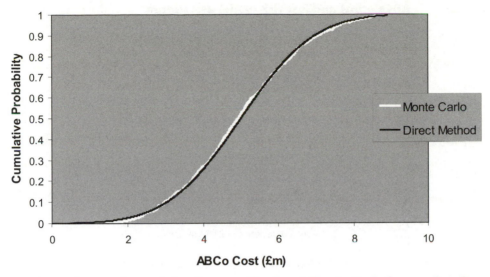

Figure 6.2   Comparison of the direct method and Monte Carlo for overheads

ABCO COMPLETE MODEL

It is now a simple task to develop the complete ABCo model, using the profit and loss statement and balance sheet formats of Chapter 3.

Taking the profit and loss for example, we have Table 6.3.

Note that this has been constructed once again so as to be a sum of independent random variables. Thus profit has a mean of £4.33 million and a standard deviation of £1.92 million. Using the normal approximation, this has been plotted on Figure 3.9 to give the result shown in Figure 6.3.

The right hand S-curves plot profit and again the approximation is good.

We can take the same approach to minimum cash. In this case the cash remaining at project completion when it is minimum since sales of Product B turn cash generation positive is:

$$\text{Minimum cash} = £11 \text{ million} + (0.6 \times S - O - £23 \text{ million})T.$$

This is the product, not the sum, of independent random variables. This means we can still work out the mean and standard deviation, using the formulas for the product of random variables in Chapter 12. The result is a mean of –£0.8 million and standard deviation of £2 million. If a normal approximation were valid the other dark line shown in Figure 6.3 would apply. This is clearly not quite right when compared with the actual minimum cash distribution.

However, since you can see from the figure that the two distributions do not have the same mean, this is not just a failure of the normal approximation. In fact, this relates to the point that the minimum cash in the 'exact' calculations is worked out only at month ends. By this time some cash may have been recovered and so the 'exact' calculations are in fact a bit optimistic, as shown on Figure 6.3. The probability of running out of cash is only 40 per cent compared with the 50 per cent found by applying a normal approximation. As an exercise, you might like to try to check to what extent this explains the discrepancy; for example by constructing a model which finds the minimum cash on a day by day basis.

Table 6.3   **ABCo profit and loss risk model description**

Sales of A	S (normal with mean of £15 million and standard deviation of £1.46 million)
Sales of B	£20 million(1 - T) where T is the time of project completion in years
Direct costs	40% of sales (of A and B)
Depreciation	£2m + £4 million(1-T)
Interest	£1 million
Overheads	O (normal with mean of £5 million and standard deviation of £1.54 million)
Profit	£5 million + 0.6 x S - O - £8 million x T

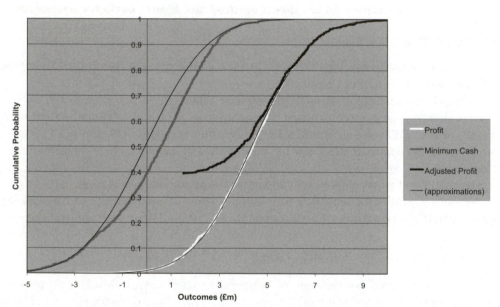

Figure 6.3   **ABCo complete model results**

The final curve, which shows the distribution of profit subject to the constraint of not running out of cash, is left to the Monte Carlo technique. The simple thing to do would be to cut off the profit S-curve at the point where it reaches the probability of running out of cash. But this is a bit crude, which is why Monte Carlo is recommended.

SUMMARY

The approximate techniques described in this section are a powerful alternative to using a Monte Carlo approach. They provide a method which does not require the purchase, learning and use of new software. More importantly, they allow a simple spreadsheet to be used in such a way that the development of the results is much more visible, and therefore open to question and challenge by the user (or anyone else). Because of this, they are recommended not so much as the main method to use, but as an adjunct which allows an early insight into the results and their main drivers.

Notwithstanding this, it will almost always be the case that the error in the results using these methods is much less than that arising from the uncertainty in the input data. Of course, the main drawback occurs when you cannot build the model with independent distributions.

The waste management PPP model

We now shift from the relatively simple approach we applied to ABCo to much heavier-duty risk modelling. The context is the preparation of the risk model which will be used alongside a cost model to support a bid for the waste management PPP introduced in Chapter 4. Many of the results could in fact be obtained by using means and standard deviations and applying the normal approximation. However, it is standard practice to develop a comprehensive Monte Carlo model for the costs which will be incurred during the many years of a PPP/PFI deal and that is what we shall do here.

CONTEXT AND REQUIREMENTS

Chapter 4 set out the overall philosophy of the PPP deal, how it is expected that risk will be allocated and the risk concerns that bidders may have. It is assumed that these concerns have been explored in risk workshops and that they have been articulated in the form of hundreds of risks relating to the various activity that the successful bidder will undertake and the specific contractual terms that have been proposed.

A risk model is needed which will provide a set of figures to feed into the financial model. This set of figures is termed the *risk provision*. The figures will be treated as just another cost in the financial model which will assume the risk provision is spent, and thus needs to be financed while at the same time giving a suitable return to the sponsors. In this sense the risk numbers play a key role in pricing the bid and striking a balance between making a profit and maintaining competitiveness against the other bidders.

Evidently the risk provision must be disaggregated in terms of time and possibly also in terms of type of expenditure. This is because the accounting treatment of different types of expenditure may vary depending on whether it is capital expenditure (capex), operational expenditure (opex) or revenue (assuming that some of the risks affect payments by the client, as would normally be the case in a PPP/PFI). Thus, it is assumed that risk numbers are required for every 6 month period in the 25-year deal and for another year beyond to cover close out. These numbers have to be broken down between revenue, capex and opex.

A large number of risks have to be entered into the model and it is required that any one risk could impact revenue, capex and opex in a correlated way. For example, there might be a risk that something will happen to impact performance and hence revenue and that money will have to be spent to correct this. The time profile of the impacts must be definable. For example, the impact of inflation will grow with time, whilst that of the discovery of a latent defect might decrease.

For the avoidance of doubt, it is worth saying that the risk model has to deal with every matter not covered within the cost model. This includes risks which may or may not occur; and also uncertainties or even known issues which have been forgotten about by the cost modellers. People can get hot under the collar about whether something is or is not a risk. The key step is for something to be covered once and once only. Only worry about whether it is risk or not once you have fixed this basic issue.

The required outputs depend on how risk is to be priced. At this is stage it is assumed that the risk provision is to be the P80. More precisely, this means that the cumulative value of the risk provision at any point in time is the P80 of the total risk cost to date.

FINANCIAL OVERVIEW

It is useful to get an idea of the overall financial sensitivities of the deal before plunging into the details. For some reason this is rarely done. Suppose it is a £2 billion deal; that is, £1bn of capital is to be spent during the 5 year investment period at £200 million per year and £1 billion is to be spent on maintenance over the 25 years at £40 million per year. These are simplified to demonstrate the points more easily. The actual expenditure in the model presented in Chapter 3 are more complex.

In order to cover this, £2 billion is required from the client at £80 million per year. For the first five years the funding gap is £160 million per year which amounts to £800 million at the end of Year 5. This is what has to be borrowed. Assuming the mean borrowing term is 15 years and interest rates are set at 5 per cent per year, means that a further £600 million of interest has to be paid, increasing the price from £80 million per year to £104 million per year.

This will increase further since:

- some of the funding will be sponsor's equity on which a higher return is expected;
- the project may have to retain some level of cash to meet unforeseen funding needs;
- the contractor may seek to recoup bid costs;
- the client may wish to pay less during the investment period since he does not yet have the new plant and services in place (though this represents very poor value for money, since it increases the borrowing requirement);
- if not already included in the costs, the risk provision has to be added.

However the price will also be reduced due to:

- the increase in revenue will reduce the funding gap (by approximately £120 million).
- interest on cash in the bank (or alternatively a reduced repayment period if the borrowing is drawn down when it is required instead of on Day 1).

Table 6.4 shows a simple financial model incorporating these principles based on 6 month periods. The loan is assumed to be drawn down on Day 1, which is rather unlikely. The sponsors provide £40 million of equity at £8 million per year during the investment period, on which they expect a return of 10 per cent per year; loan interest payments and repayments are constant over the 20 years following investment, as are dividends. Interest on cash balances is 2 per cent per year. Note that all these figures are in real terms, with inflation removed.

It should be noted that the rate of 5 per cent real per year is very high for a PFI project. Usually project finance is relatively cheap, as the income stream forms good security. However, if the borrower is taking risk on product sales revenue, the cost of the loan will certainly go up. The enhanced deal discussed in Chapter 4 where this risk is transferred would certainly attract cheaper finance. This was not allowed for and would make the enhanced deal even more advantageous. However here we are probably taking this illustrative example too seriously. See the Percentages box in Chapter 10 for some typical rates.

Table 6.4   **Simplified funding table**

Period	Costs	Revenue	Loan	Equity	Cash
1	120.00	-53.48	-634.77	-4.00	572.25
2	120.00	-53.48	0.00	-4.00	515.43
3	120.00	-53.48	0.00	-4.00	458.04
4	120.00	-53.48	0.00	-4.00	400.08
5	120.00	-53.48	0.00	-4.00	341.54
6	120.00	-53.48	0.00	-4.00	282.42
7	120.00	-53.48	0.00	-4.00	222.71
8	120.00	-53.48	0.00	-4.00	162.41
9	120.00	-53.48	0.00	-4.00	101.51
10	120.00	-53.48	0.00	-4.00	40.00
11	20.00	-53.48	31.33	2.55	40.00
12	20.00	-53.48	31.33	2.55	40.00
13	20.00	-53.48	31.33	2.55	40.00
14	20.00	-53.48	31.33	2.55	40.00
15	20.00	-53.48	31.33	2.55	40.00
16	20.00	-53.48	31.33	2.55	40.00
17	20.00	-53.48	31.33	2.55	40.00
18	20.00	-53.48	31.33	2.55	40.00
19	20.00	-53.48	31.33	2.55	40.00
20	20.00	-53.48	31.33	2.55	40.00
21	20.00	-53.48	31.33	2.55	40.00
22	20.00	-53.48	31.33	2.55	40.00
23	20.00	-53.48	31.33	2.55	40.00
24	20.00	-53.48	31.33	2.55	40.00
25	20.00	-53.48	31.33	2.55	40.00
26	20.00	-53.48	31.33	2.55	40.00
27	20.00	-53.48	31.33	2.55	40.00
28	20.00	-53.48	31.33	2.55	40.00
29	20.00	-53.48	31.33	2.55	40.00
30	20.00	-53.48	31.33	2.55	40.00
31	20.00	-53.48	31.33	2.55	40.00
32	20.00	-53.48	31.33	2.55	40.00
33	20.00	-53.48	31.33	2.55	40.00
34	20.00	-53.48	31.33	2.55	40.00
35	20.00	-53.48	31.33	2.55	40.00
36	20.00	-53.48	31.33	2.55	40.00
37	20.00	-53.48	31.33	2.55	40.00
38	20.00	-53.48	31.33	2.55	40.00
39	20.00	-53.48	31.33	2.55	40.00
40	20.00	-53.48	31.33	2.55	40.00
41	20.00	-53.48	31.33	2.55	40.00
42	20.00	-53.48	31.33	2.55	40.00
43	20.00	-53.48	31.33	2.55	40.00
44	20.00	-53.48	31.33	2.55	40.00
45	20.00	-53.48	31.33	2.55	40.00
46	20.00	-53.48	31.33	2.55	40.00
47	20.00	-53.48	31.33	2.55	40.00
48	20.00	-53.48	31.33	2.55	40.00
49	20.00	-53.48	31.33	2.55	40.00
50	20.00	-53.48	31.33	2.55	40.00
51				20.20	20.20
52				20.40	0.00

Table 6.4 shows that a model can be constructed which maintains a £40 million cash balance (paid to the sponsors at the end of the project) with a revenue of £107 million per year and a Day 1 loan of £635 million; roughly as expected when the new funding gap and the sponsors' equity are taken into account. The cash balance, about a year's expenditure during the service delivery phase, is available to meet any excess spending needs.

A good question is whether this duplicates the risk provisions in the cost model. We shall return to this when we discuss pricing. Obviously it increases the price to the customer. A different model with no cash balance after the investment period charges £1.5 million less to the customer per year and borrows £30 million less. The sponsor is compensated for the loss of the £40 million at the end of the project with £650k per year extra to provide the same rate of return.

We have gone into this in some detail because it is necessary to understand how the bidder will get his returns. You can see that the project is very highly geared: the ratio of debt to equity is nearly 16. This means that it is potentially quite risky for the lenders and also, of course, for the sponsors. Chapter 4 presents results based on this type of modelling which shows how sensitive the sponsors returns are to risks materialising. The way to do this is described later in this chapter. Doing it is good practice.

THE RISK MODEL

The intention now is to build a Monte Carlo model, based on a spreadsheet, to meet the requirements we discussed earlier. A general purpose model is sketched out in Figure 6.4 below. This shows the different worksheets which are incorporated in the model workbook.

There are many ways of creating such models. This is typical of the approach I take – more information is available from my website www.riskagenda.com if you are interested.

The starting worksheet is called Risks. This contains a list of the risks in the model and – unless something specific is built in, which it easily can – these are independent. Table 6.5 shows the structure of the worksheet.

Down the left side of Table 6.5 are the risks. The next two blocks deal with the input distributions. You can see that the same four-point approach is used as for the ABCo example earlier: probability, minimum, most likely and maximum, where probability is the chance that anything happens, and if it does the output is distributed according to a triangle distribution. However, the output here is taken to be Intensity, an intermediate quantity which is useful

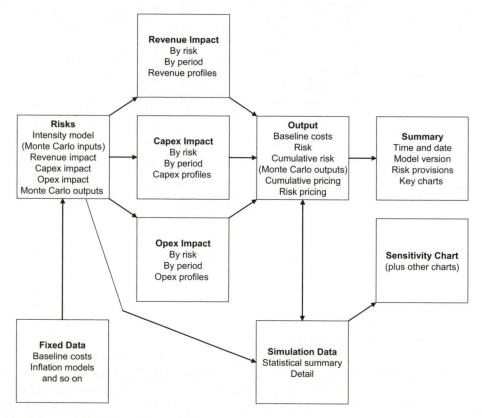

Figure 6.4   The PPP risk model

ID	Risk	Prob	Distribution Min	Distribution ML	Distribution Max	Intensity	Revenue Factor	Revenue Profile	Revenue Name	Capex Factor	Capex Profile	Capex Name	Opex Factor	Opex Profile	Opex Name	EV 287.688	Sim
1	**Transportation Operations**																
2	Transportation maintenance costs	1	-0.05	0.05	0.3	0.1							326	5	Transport	32.600	32.600
3	Transportation performance	1	0	0.1	0.5	0.2	30	6	Performance							6.006	6.006
4	Electricity prices	1	-0.1	0.1	0.3	0.1							100	3	Growing	10.000	10.000
5	**Transportation Capex**																
6	Transportation system delivery	1	0	0	0.2	0.066667				300	5	Delays				20.000	20.000
7	**Waste Processing Operations**																
8	Waste volumes	1	-0.05	0	0.05	0							439	1	Uniform	0.000	0.000
9	Process costs	1	-0.05	0.05	0.15	0.05							439	1	Uniform	21.938	21.937
10	Product price	1	-0.5	0	1	0.166667							365	10	Sales	60.833	60.833
11	Process performance	1	0	0.1	0.5	0.2	30	6	Performance							6.006	6.006
12	Process regulatory action	0.1	0	1	3	0							5	1	Uniform	0.667	0.000
13	**Waste Processing Capex**																
14	Site construction cost and delays	1	-0.05	0.05	0.2	0.066667				400	2	Investment				26.667	26.667
15	Incinerator cost and delays	1	0	0.05	0.25	0.1				300	2	Investment				30.000	30.000
16	**Residual Waste Operations**																
17	Landfill operating cost	1	-0.05	0	0.1	0.016667							153	7	Landfill	2.542	2.542
18	Landfill regulatory action	0.1	0	3	10	0							10	1	Uniform	4.333	0.000
19	Landfill targets	1	0	0.2	1	0.4	30	6	Performance							12.012	12.012
20	Landfill tax	1	0	0	1	0.333333							15	1	Uniform	5.083	5.083
21	**Transition**																
22	Plant defects	0.3	0	1	3	0							5	1	Uniform	2.000	0.000
23	Workforce performance	1	-0.05	0.05	0.2	0.066667							183	1	Uniform	12.230	12.230
24	**Corporate**																
25	Inflation	1	-1	0	1.5	0.166667				23	3	Growing	128	3	Growing	25.146	25.146
26	Insurance premiums	1	-0.3	0.3	1	0.333333				3	2	Investment	11	9	Corporate	4.625	4.625
27	Pensions	0.1	0	1	2	0							50	4	At end	5.000	0.000

Table 6.5   Risk model inputs

to inject dependence into a risk. Impact is modelled by making it proportional to Intensity with the constant of proportionality denoted by the column Factor in each of the next three sections. Thus, Intensity is generally dimensionless whilst Factor includes the financial units being used; in this case, millions of pounds.

There is a section for each of the impacts: revenue, capex and opex. Each of these has three columns. the first is Factor, as already discussed; the second is an index to indicate the time profile to be used for the impact; and the third picks up the name of the profile from the next three sheets. This is a check to make sure what is being done is sensible. This column is shaded as a means of showing it is calculated and should not be overwritten by the user.

The next column calculates the expected value of the risk using the formula:

$$EV = p(\text{Min} + \text{ML} + \text{Max})(F_{revenue} + F_{capex} + F_{opex})/3$$

where the Fs are the three Factors and the remainder of the formula is the expected value of Intensity. This assumes the profiles are all normalised to one, which should be the case. This column is for user input, as different models than the four point formulation can be employed. The total expected value is recorded at the top for checking purposes.

The final column, marked Sim, is to set up the Monte Carlo outputs relating to the individual risks. It contains the formula:

$$I(F_{revenue} + F_{capex} + F_{opex}) + \text{simulation output function}$$

to enable the risks to be picked up for investigation. Here 'simulation output function' stands for the method which is used to identify an output by the Monte Carlo tool kit. Note that the Monte Carlo inputs as identified by the software are the intensities. This is where the probability distributions are input, but they are of little interest to the analyst. This column is written by a short routine which ensures empty risk slots are ignored. This makes it easier to delete risks which are no longer needed while not affecting the presentations.

The time-dependent risk data is collected in the three sheets: Revenue, Capex and Opex. A segment of Revenue is shown in Table 6.6.

At the top are the profiles, the only user input area on this sheet. Below this are the revenue impacts of each risk. The line is empty unless the risk has a revenue impact. If there is a revenue impact, the column marked Total contains the total impact, that is, the intensity times the revenue factor from the Risks sheet. This is then distributed according to the relevant profile from the upper part of the sheet. The empty parts actually contain formulas which show a blank when the risk does not have a revenue profile. If execution time is important you can clean it up, for example, by writing a simple routine which only writes to the non-empty cells, leaving the rest genuinely empty. However, this is not an issue for the model described here, which runs in a minute or so even on my ancient laptop.

The outputs in the top row of the bottom section are added together and carried forward to the Output sheet. This develops the required risk outputs, shown in Table 6.7.

In this case, the following sequence is followed:

- the baseline costs are recorded for convenience;
- the three risks rows relating to revenue, capex and opex are copied through and a fourth is generated for the total in each period;
- for each of the four rows a cumulative value is calculated and added to the simulation outputs, $4 \times 52 = 208$ in all;
- the simulation is then run;

Revenue Risk Profiles

#	Name	TOTAL	Apr-20 (1)	Oct-20 (2)	Apr-21 (3)	Oct-21 (4)	Apr-22 (5)	Oct-22 (6)	Apr-23 (7)	Oct-23 (8)	Apr-24 (9)	Oct-24 (10)	Apr-25 (11)
1	Uniform	1.0000	0.0200	0.0200	0.0200	0.0200	0.0200	0.0200	0.0200	0.0200	0.0200	0.0200	0.0200
2	Investment	1.0000	0.1000	0.1000	0.1000	0.1000	0.1000	0.1000	0.1000	0.1000	0.1000	0.1000	
3	Growing	1.0000	0.0004	0.0012	0.0020	0.0028	0.0036	0.0044	0.0052	0.0060	0.0068	0.0076	0.0084
4	At end	1.0000											
5	Sales	1.0000	0.0000	0.0000	0.0000	0.0000	0.0000	0.0000	0.0000	0.0000	0.0000	0.0027	0.0055
6	Performance	1.0000	0.0022	0.0044	0.0066	0.0088	0.0110	0.0132	0.0154	0.0176	0.0198	0.0220	0.0220
7		0.0000											
8		0.0000											
9		0.0000											
10		0.0000											

Risk

#	Name	Profile	TOTAL	1	2	3	4	5	6	7	8	9	10	11
			24.024	0.053	0.106	0.158	0.211	0.264	0.317	0.370	0.422	0.475	0.528	0.528
1	Transportation operations	0												
2	Transportation maintenance costs	0												
3	Transportation performance	6	6.006	0.013	0.026	0.040	0.053	0.066	0.079	0.092	0.106	0.119	0.132	0.132
4	Electricity prices	0												
5	Transportation Capex	0												
6	Transportation system delivery	0												
7	Waste processing operations	0												
8	Waste volumes	0												
9	Process costs	0												
10	Product price	0												
11	Process performance	6	6.006	0.013	0.026	0.040	0.053	0.066	0.079	0.092	0.106	0.119	0.132	0.132
12	Process regulatory action	0												
13	Waste processing Capex	0												
14	Site construction cost and delays	0												
15	Incinerator cost and delays	0												
16	Residual waste operations	0												
17	Landfill operating cost	0												
18	Landfill regulatory action	0												
19	Landfill targets	6	12.012	0.026	0.053	0.079	0.106	0.132	0.158	0.185	0.211	0.238	0.264	0.264
20	Landfill tax	0												
21	Transition	0												
22	Plant defects	0												
23	Workforce performance	0												
24	Corporate	0												
25	Inflation	0												
26	Insurance premiums	0												
27	Pensions	0												

Table 6.6   Risk risk profiles

Output

Baseline

		TOTAL	Apr-20	Oct-20	Apr-21	Oct-21	Apr-22	Oct-22	Apr-23	Oct-23	Apr-24	Oct-24	Apr-25
			1	2	3	4	5	6	7	8	9	10	11
Sales	Revenue	-365.000	-0.200	-0.400	-0.600	-0.800	-1.000	-1.200	-1.400	-1.600	0.000	-1.000	-2.000
Performance	Revenue	-91.000	-0.200	-0.400	-0.600	-0.800	-1.000	-1.200	-1.400	-1.600	-1.800	-2.000	-2.000
Total Baseline	**Revenue**	**-456.000**	**-0.200**	**-0.400**	**-0.600**	**-0.800**	**-1.000**	**-1.200**	**-1.400**	**-1.600**	**-1.800**	**-3.000**	**-4.000**
Transportation	Capex	300.000	30.000	30.000	30.000	30.000	30.000	30.000	30.000	30.000	30.000	30.000	30.000
Process	Capex	400.000	40.000	40.000	40.000	40.000	40.000	40.000	40.000	40.000	40.000	40.000	40.000
Incinerator	Capex	300.000	30.000	30.000	30.000	30.000	30.000	30.000	30.000	30.000	30.000	30.000	
Capex 4	Capex	0.000											
Capex 5	Capex	0.000											
Total Baseline	**Capex**	**1,000.000**	**100.000**	**100.000**	**100.000**	**100.000**	**100.000**	**100.000**	**100.000**	**100.000**	**100.000**	**100.000**	**0.000**
Transportation	Opex	326.000	7.500	7.460	7.420	7.380	7.340	7.300	7.260	7.220	7.180	7.140	7.100
Process	Opex	438.750	10.000	9.950	9.900	9.850	9.800	9.750	9.700	9.650	9.600	9.550	9.500
Landfill	Opex	152.500	5.000	5.000	5.000	5.000	5.000	5.000	5.000	5.000	5.000	5.000	4.000
Transition	Opex	65.000	5.500	5.250	4.600	4.400	4.200	4.000	3.800	3.600	3.400	3.200	3.000
Corporate	Opex	108.750	5.000	4.800	2.000	2.000	2.000	2.000	2.000	2.000	2.000	2.000	2.000
Total Baseline	**Opex**	**1,091.000**	**33.000**	**32.460**	**28.920**	**28.630**	**28.340**	**28.050**	**27.760**	**27.470**	**27.180**	**26.890**	**25.600**
Total Baseline	**All**	**1,635.000**	**132.800**	**132.060**	**128.320**	**127.830**	**127.340**	**126.850**	**126.360**	**125.870**	**125.380**	**123.890**	**21.600**

Risk

		TOTAL	Apr-20	Oct-20	Apr-21	Oct-21	Apr-22	Oct-22	Apr-23	Oct-23	Apr-24	Oct-24	Apr-25
			1	2	3	4	5	6	7	8	9	10	11
Risk	Revenue	24.024	0.053	0.106	0.158	0.211	0.264	0.317	0.370	0.422	0.475	0.528	0.528
Risk	Capex	81.467	5.767	5.850	5.934	6.018	6.103	6.188	8.773	8.859	8.945	9.032	2.500
Risk	Opex	170.197	1.802	1.829	1.748	1.779	1.809	1.838	1.867	1.896	1.924	2.118	2.282
Risk	All	275.688	7.621	7.785	7.840	8.008	8.175	8.343	11.010	11.177	11.344	11.678	5.310

Cumulative Risk

		TOTAL	Apr-20	Oct-20	Apr-21	Oct-21	Apr-22	Oct-22	Apr-23	Oct-23	Apr-24	Oct-24	Apr-25
			1	2	3	4	5	6	7	8	9	10	11
CumRisk	Revenue	0.000	0.053	0.158	0.317	0.528	0.792	1.109	1.478	1.901	2.376	2.904	3.432
CumRisk	Capex	0.000	5.767	11.617	17.550	23.568	29.671	35.858	44.631	53.490	62.435	71.467	73.967
CumRisk	Opex	0.000	1.802	3.631	5.379	7.157	8.966	10.805	12.672	14.568	16.492	18.609	20.892
CumRisk	All	0.000	7.621	15.406	23.246	31.254	39.429	47.772	58.782	69.959	81.303	92.981	98.291

Cumulative Risk Pricing

		TOTAL	Apr-20	Oct-20	Apr-21	Oct-21	Apr-22	Oct-22	Apr-23	Oct-23	Apr-24	Oct-24	Apr-25
			1	2	3	4	5	6	7	8	9	10	11
CumRisk Mean	Revenue	0.000	0.053	0.158	0.317	0.528	0.792	1.109	1.478	1.901	2.376	2.904	3.432
CumRisk Mean	Capex	0.000	5.767	11.617	17.550	23.568	29.671	35.858	44.631	53.490	62.435	71.467	73.967
CumRisk Mean	Opex	0.000	1.947	3.922	5.815	7.739	9.693	11.677	13.690	15.732	17.801	19.897	21.773
CumRisk P80	All	0.000	9.993	20.340	30.893	41.578	52.508	64.056	78.286	92.750	107.482	122.019	128.002

Risk Pricing

		TOTAL	Apr-20	Oct-20	Apr-21	Oct-21	Apr-22	Oct-22	Apr-23	Oct-23	Apr-24	Oct-24	Apr-25
			1	2	3	4	5	6	7	8	9	10	11
Risk Mean	Revenue	24.025	0.053	0.106	0.158	0.211	0.264	0.317	0.370	0.422	0.475	0.528	0.528
Risk Mean	Capex	81.467	5.767	5.850	5.934	6.018	6.103	6.188	8.773	8.859	8.945	9.032	2.500
Risk Mean	Opex	104.720	1.947	1.975	1.893	1.924	1.954	1.984	2.013	2.041	2.069	2.097	1.876
Risk P80	All	256.758	9.993	10.347	10.553	10.686	10.930	11.548	14.231	14.463	14.732	14.537	5.983
Risk Premium	All	46.547	2.226	2.417	2.567	2.533	2.609	3.059	3.075	3.141	3.242	2.881	1.079

Risk Pricing (Annual)

		TOTAL	Year 01	Year 02	Year 03	Year 04	Year 05	Year 06	Year 07	Year 08	Year 09	Year 10	Year 11
Risk Mean	Revenue	24.025	0.158	0.370	0.581	0.792	1.003	1.056	1.056	1.056	1.056	1.056	1.056
Risk Mean	Capex	81.467	11.617	11.952	12.290	17.632	17.977	5.000	5.000	0.000	0.000	0.000	0.000
Risk Mean	Opex	104.720	3.922	3.818	3.938	4.054	4.166	3.778	3.881	3.980	4.074	4.131	3.810
Risk P80	All	256.758	20.340	21.239	22.478	28.694	29.269	11.804	11.555	5.006	6.165	6.263	5.772
Risk Premium	All	46.547	4.643	5.100	5.669	6.216	6.123	1.969	1.617	-0.030	1.035	1.076	0.905

Values for Financial Model

	TOTAL	Apr-20	Oct-20	Apr-21	Oct-21	Apr-22	Oct-22	Apr-23	Oct-23	Apr-24	Oct-24	Apr-25
Total cost net of performance and sales	2256.758	153.140	153.299	150.798	156.524	156.609	138.654	137.915	130.876	131.545	131.153	29.372
Cost net of performance and sales	1891.758	153.140	153.299	150.798	156.524	156.609	138.654	137.915	130.876	131.545	130.153	27.372
Costed risk less materialised (cum)	0	2.372	4.934	7.647	10.325	13.079	16.284	19.505	22.791	26.179	29.038	29.711
Costed risk less materialised (period)	-18.930	2.372	2.562	2.713	2.678	2.755	3.205	3.221	3.286	3.388	2.859	0.673

Table 6.7   Risk model output sheet

- the mean values for the three contributing consequence types are recorded, plus the P80 of the total, remembering that these reflect the cumulative numbers; this is done by importing simulation data in the way described below;
- these are then turned into period numbers by reversing the cumulative process (that is, taking differences);
- they are summed in pairs to give the values in each year rather than for the 6-month period used in the simulation;
- finally a further set of numbers is generated to feed forward into the financial modelling as we will describe shortly.

The reason for taking the means of the consequence types, but the P80 of the total, is that whilst we want to price at P80, we want to disaggregate the provisions into the different types of impact. The only meaningful way to do this (that I can think of) is to take the means of the contributions and call the difference the risk premium. This slightly elaborate process allows this to be done.

Of course the stage where we move from defining the simulation outputs to importing the simulation results is complicated. We have to run the Monte Carlo software and collect the data in a sheet called Simulation Data (see Figure 6.4). Although the software may have spreadsheet functions built in to do this, it can be prohibitively expensive in computer resources. All the results presented here are obtained by importing as a single page of output that records the mean variance and percentiles of the outputs. Unlike many charts in this book the main presentations do not require data from individual simulations.

Now we can present the results through graphs and tables. This is done in Chapter 4 where the first chart is the sensitivity diagram (see Figures 4.3 and 4.5). This shows the key risks in terms of their effect on total cost. Note that this is a very simple concept because of the additive nature of costs. It is very easy to understand what such charts mean.

The Summary sheet contains the main outputs as shown in Figure 4.4 and 4.6. This shows:

- information about the run;
- the total risk provisions broken down by type (including the risk premium);
- a chart showing how these are further broken down by year;
- a chart showing the growth with time of the P20, mean and P80.

In general, the Risks sheet will have changes made to adapt to specific circumstances: correlation between risks, other distributions than the three point ones, multiple profiles and so on. The template is just a starting point; obviously, it is necessary practice to keep good records of the changes made and to engage in thorough testing. Remember, no spreadsheet is without error, and you have to go to a lot of careful effort to make sure that yours contains only immaterial ones. This is where the importance of sanity checking comes in, rather than treating the model as a black box. If the result is not obvious by the time you have finished, then you need to find out why. Sometimes it will be an error; sometimes it will be something more interesting – perhaps an unanticipated feature of the model you have composed. Either way the sanity check is always worth doing.

MODELLING RISK TRANSFER AND RISK SHARING

At the centre of the PPP/PFI concept is appropriate risk allocation. In general the customer wants to transfer as much risk as possible to the contractor. The contractor in turn would like to pass risk down to his subcontractors. There are three important points here:

- risk transfer has a price: as a generalisation, the risk premium means the organisation receives poor value for money for getting rid of the risk;
- some risks may be so big they cannot be accepted, especially when transferred from a bigger to a smaller organisation;
- risks are fundamentally best-owned by the organisation best-placed to manage them; the less this is the case, the higher the risk premium.

Typically in a PPP/PFI the client will attempt to use a standard form of contract in which the contractor takes all risks for all eternity. The contractor then aims to negotiate something more reasonable. Similarly the contractor will try to place subcontracts back to back with all the vaguely relevant terms of the main contract, including performance–payment regimes and so on. He then gets upset when the subcontractor refuses to take the big risks and puts in a high price. Obviously this is a common approach to negotiating deals, but the whole process is not very sensible and serves only to line the pockets of lawyers and other expensive consultants. This increases further the costs of PFI projects. Much of this could be avoided with a more realistic approach to the three points above.

The negotiation will generally result in various types of risk sharing, for example:

- the client may share the benefits of refinancing; that is, setting up a cheaper loan structure once the main risks of the project have passed;
- the client may share in excess profits;
- a periodic contract review process may allow pricing to be reassessed as well as customer requirements to be restated;
- certain risks may be shared explicitly, for example insurance premiums which are not controllable by either party (or, more correctly, to the extent that they are not affected by the parties);
- subcontractors may be subject to a liquidated damages regime which passes on some, but not all of the financial losses suffered by the contractor;
- capital projects may be procured on a target cost basis with a gainshare regime to share gains when the actual cost is less than target and pain when it is more (perhaps creating an environment where the attribution of blame is pointless, avoiding contractual squabbles, aligning objectives, and creating a cheaper and more effective project);
- contract or subcontract liabilities may be capped.

Depending on your perspective, you might see the first two points as either the client cashing in on good risk management by the contractor or as the client reclaiming some of the risk premium.

In principle, all of these should be incorporated into the risk model. Some are easier than others. Refinancing and profit sharing are matters for the financial model to be discussed shortly. A contract review process, however, is fundamental to the risk balance in the project and ought to be included. An example of how this helps to achieve the right distribution of risk was discussed for the waste management PPP in Chapter 4.

Caps in contracts are very difficult to quantify. They are generally set at levels which are considered unlikely to be reached and, if they are reached, it is difficult to anticipate the size of the loss. Generally I would leave them out, but there is an argument for putting them in just to demonstrate that the issue of exceeding caps has been considered.

A more obvious area of modelling is gainshare contracts. These are relatively straightforward to include since a risk analysis will generally have been carried out to generate the price (from the subcontractor to the contractor). The risk analysis can be used to create a suitable risk in the main model. For example, suppose the target cost for the new incinerator facility is £300 million, and this is included in the baseline costs. Suppose this is based on the P80 of a risk analysis which shows the central cost to be £270 million and the standard deviation to be £36 million. Assume the gainshare is 50:50 between the parties. One way to model this is to note that the cost to the bidder over the baseline is given by

$$C = 0.5 \times (A - T)$$
$$= TI$$

where

$$I = 0.5(A / T - 1)$$

where A is actual cost, T is target cost and I, the intensity, is dimensionless and has a mean of –0.05 and standard deviation of 0.0594. We will further assume this is normal as it represents the aggregation of many risks in building the incinerator.

However, suppose the subcontractor has negotiated a cap on his liability where the actual cost exceeds £330 million. The cost to the contractor (the client in this case) over baseline is shown on Figure 6.5 and is given by

$$C = \max(0.5(A - T), A - T - 15)$$

$$= TJ$$

where the new intensity, J, is given by

$$J = \max(I, 2I - 0.05).$$

You will need to be careful that you generate I only once when simulating, although it occurs twice in the formula.

Figure 6.5 is a Monte Carlo simulation scatterplot which shows the relationship between actual costs and main contractor (that is, the bidder's) costs both with and without the cap. 1000 points are shown and there would be fewer outliers if this were reduced to 100.

The main impact for the overall modelling is the reduction in the width of the distribution in the main model. You may wish to insert the actual distribution in some way as shown in Figure 6.5, or you may wish to use a triangular distribution. The existence of the cap, even at this rather low level, makes very little difference to the properties of the distribution. However, you may need to be prepared to say what difference the cap makes to the distributions, something that may be challenging to do accurately with Monte Carlo. In practice the cap changes the expected value by £340k, 0.1 per cent of the project cost or 1 per cent of the standard deviation; negligible, but note that this is dependent on the wings of the specific normal distribution that was chosen.

In general, these sorts of adjustments are best analysed outside the main risk model of the project. It would be a typical reaction if, when the manager looked at the analysis, he demanded

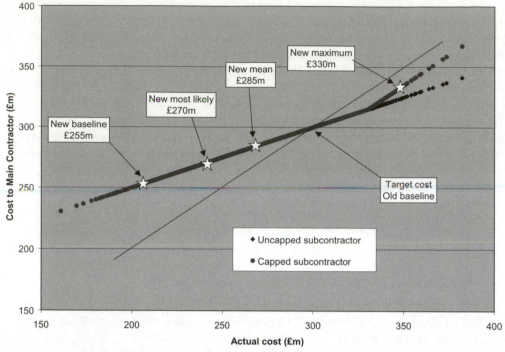

Figure 6.5   Relationship between actual costs and main contractor costs

that the baseline be reduced to £255 million so that it could be understood alongside other risks. The distribution shown on Table 6.5 with darker shading is indicated with stars on Figure 6.5. Note that the mean corresponds to the actual mean, but the most likely value is higher in order to compensate for the higher maximum value. The manager did not attach much credibility to the simulated costs below £255 million, but wished in some way to reflect the additional risk arising for the cap.

FINANCIAL RISK MODELLING

The discussion so far has been concerned with cost modelling. The basic philosophy is that we take risk into account in the costs and provide a set of risk provisions for incorporation into the financial model. The fundamental approach to risk in financial models is that different scenarios are devised and input into the model to understand what has to go wrong before the lenders start to feel some pain. The basic principle is that this should never happen. This means that bankers are not very interested in risk modelling; they feel much more comfortable with their sensitivities (if you see what I mean).

However, there is no reason in principle why the risk modelling methods should not be applied to the financial model. This is likely to be of particular interest to the sponsors who, unlike the bankers, will be the first to feel the pain of risk materialising (after the management, of course). The shareholders in the project could reasonably ask how their returns will be affected by the risk profile.

To work this out it is necessary to make suitable assumptions about how overspends will be financed. These assumptions might be:

*   use the risk premium;

- sack some people (not generally included in the risk model and possibly having the opposite effect to that intended);
- use cash balances;
- stop payments to sponsors;
- defer payments to lenders;
- inject more equity;
- borrow some more.

With enough notice of risks materialising, these tactics can generally cope with the adverse effects.

Of course the application of a risk premium means that it is more likely than not that surpluses will arise. Lenders have no long term interest in this as they do not benefit. However, in the shorter term they prefer surpluses not to be distributed so as to improve the security of the loan. Surpluses are certainly of greater interest to the sponsors, who would like to have them on the shortest possible timescale. In practice there may well be an arrangement whereby these benefits are shared with the customer and this will certainly be the case where there is a formal refinancing.

Figure 4.7 in Chapter 4 shows the output of a calculation where the distribution of the rate of return to the sponsors has been calculated. To do this it is necessary to set up a sheet with a financial model similar to Table 6.4. This can be an extra sheet with the workbook. You apply the variations in the cashflow from the assumed spend – which will include full expenditure of the risk provisions – then put in a set of assumptions about how and when these cashflows are funded or distributed, and rerun the financial model.

The assumptions will potentially be quite difficult to put together and the programming can be quite complicated, although fairly simple in concept. (I always find it takes a bit of time to sort out.) You also need to be careful about Excel's internal rate of return function, IRR, which does not always converge properly. You need to use a good starting value and make sure you investigate the reason for any errors.

This approach is not strictly correct. You would be better working out NPVs based on the required rate of return; the IRR is a somewhat unreliable concept and not always defined for the most peculiar cash flows, although such cash flows would be very unlikely to arise here. But it is more fun to look at IRR and it takes you beyond the strictly additive regime we have discussed up to now; most importantly, clients *are* interested.

Financial people tend not to be comfortable with results of this type, especially as it apparently involves risk people getting involved with the arcana of financial modelling. In fact, it is a good, simple approach to looking at variations in cash flows. However, it does not look at many other features of the financial model – for example, the maintenance of interest cover-ratios and the like – and these could be important.

Accountants need not fear. I do not think it would be worthwhile looking at the risk to the accounting treatment of these cash flows. The annual recognition of costs and revenues is an exercise which is probably not amenable to the type of simple assumptions used to produce Figure 4.7.

PRICING THE PPP

Up to now we have accepted that the deal will be priced at the P80 level. More specifically at each point in time we have inserted risk provisions which are sufficient to meet the P80 at that point. There is no particular reason to think that there is anything special about this. Furthermore it is not the case that this implies the provisions will be exceeded with a probability of 20 per cent. This is because if this is the case at any given point in time, there is some chance that it will not prove to be the case at some other point. Thus the probability of exceeding the provisions at *any* point is higher.

A key concern is clearly going to be the possibility of bankruptcy, or at least running out of cash. The financial model we described earlier showed a cash balance of £40 million, and the financial risk modelling showed this could be exhausted.

One factor which will affect this is the coherence of the risks. The modelling is generally done in such a way that the risks, if they happen, will have impact profiles which cover several or many years of the project. If the cost of transporting waste is higher than expected in one year, it will be for the succeeding years as well. In other words, it is not a one-off incident, either an accident or an episode of bad management, but a fundamental issue that was mis-estimated originally. However, it could be imagined that if the risk profile is dominated by one-off events, the probability of going bankrupt is different than if the risks are coherent.

To do a high-level investigation of this we look at two hypothetical models. They each contain ten risks which have a mean of zero and maximum and minimum values of +/–£100 million. However in the first case the risks have consequences right across the project; in the second case they occur in individual periods, each separated by 2.5 years. Either way the mean of the risks is zero and the P80 of the total over 25 years is £109 million.

Figure 6.6 shows that in the first case of risks affecting the whole project the provisions are evenly spread – as you would expect.

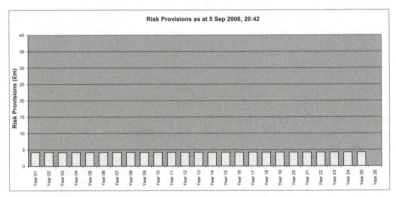

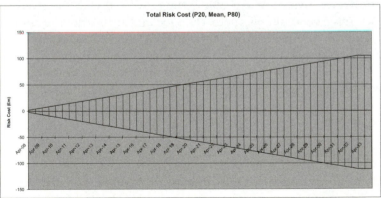

Figure 6.6   **Risk provisions for risks spread over time**

The risk provisions grow at around £4 million per year to the required total of just over £100 million. Similarly, the chance of overspending in any year is the same as the chance of overspending overall: 20 per cent and the maximum overspend is distributed in the same way as the total, so that it is distributed as the tail of a normal distribution above P80. This is shown on Figure 6.7 by the dark line.

By contrast, the second simulation shown in Figure 6.8, which has the risk consequences located at single points in time, indicates that the £100 million of provisions are much more front loaded, again as expected.

£36 million is required in Year 1; the remainder is needed in the following years. The figure shows the errors in the Monte Carlo technique, in spite of this chart having been developed from 10 000 simulations. The provisions should show a reducing pattern, but are instead quite variable. Figure 6.9 shows the exact values by comparison with those in Figure 6.8. (Although, actually they are not quite exact; the normal approximation has been used for all except the first.)

This now shows a significant difference in terms of the effect on the probability of overspending. Referring back to Figure 6.7, the S-curves are plotted for both set of provisions. The probability of overspending is higher than for the spread risks in both cases. But where the revealed provisions are used, that is, in the slightly erratic bars of Figure 6.8, this probability is much higher. To take a concrete example, the £40 million cash balance in the waste management PPP example prior to risk management was in the context of a £119 million risk premium, roughly the same as here. The probability of exceeding this with spread risks can be seen from Figure 6.7 to be about 13 per cent, with the exact provisions it is 26 per cent and with the erratic provisions, 44 per cent. Similarly, post-management the £40 million was in a context of a total risk premium of £47 million corresponding to an overspend of £92

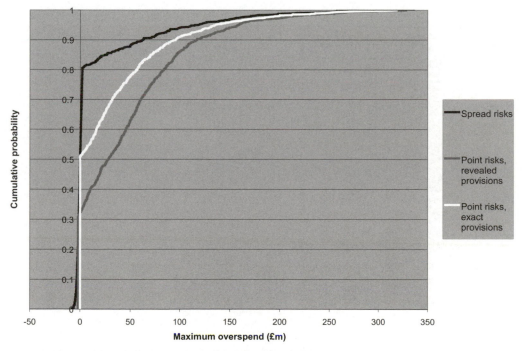

Figure 6.7   Distribution of maximum overspend

Waste Management PPP

Risk Model - Point

05/09/06 22:18

Risk Types	Total
Risk Mean - Revenue	0.000
Risk Mean - Capex	0.000
Risk Mean - Opex	0.000
Risk Mean Total	**0.000**
Risk Premium - All	108.316
Risk Provision	**108.316**

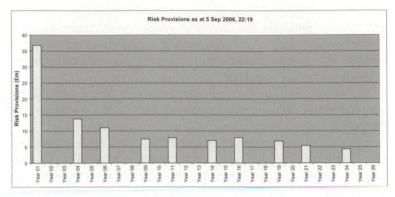

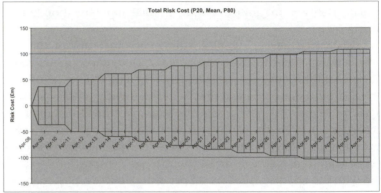

Figure 6.8   Risk provisions for point risks

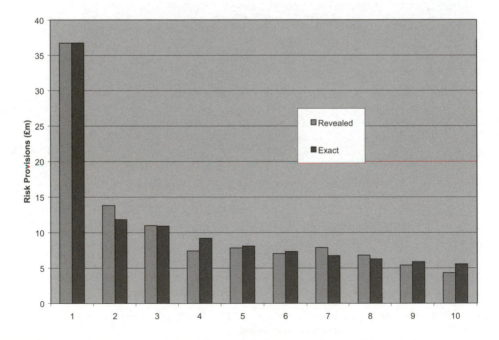

Figure 6.9   Comparison of revealed and exact provisions for point risks

million. The probabilities here range from 6 to 10 to 17 per cent. These are higher than the probabilities found in Chapter 4 because the risk is not evenly spread over time.

We have gone through this to make a number of points:

* The nature of the risks has a big impact on the probability of running out of cash. This affects pricing, but is a relatively under-explored area of risk analysis.
* This probability is also affected by the distribution of the provisions: not surprisingly, given that this event is at the fringes of the risk model.
* Monte Carlo, even after 10 000 iterations, can give some surprisingly volatile results.

Two features mitigate the situation. Firstly, many of the overspends will be in the investment phase where higher cash balances are available. Secondly, the obvious remedy for running out of cash in a fundamentally profitable business is to borrow more. But standby facilities are expensive and funders are generally inimical to project sponsors going back for more.

There is a lot more work to do to understand all the interrelationships properly.

Summary

This extended discussion of the risk modelling involved in a major deal shows that although the principles are very straightforward, the practice can be quite complicated.

First, of course, this is due to the many risks involved over the decades of the deal. They have to be identified, rationalised, mitigated and quantified. The quantification is done preferably by combining them into a much smaller number of key issues. However, to the extent that these issues are independent, they all contribute to the total project cost in an additive way. This means their means and variances can be summed to find their overall impact in the project. And the normal approximation is almost always relevant. This approach can be used for the project as a whole or for individual points in time. You will need a Monte Carlo model for any parts of the model which diverge from this, but these principles are always useful for exploring and sanity checking.

More interesting from the risk modelling viewpoint are the non-additive aspects: estimating the distribution of internal rate of return or the probability of running out of cash. PFI projects generally have robust returns, because of the need to maintain various contingencies, including the risk premium, and the existence of a healthy revenue stream.

Another under-investigated issue is how to price a PFI bid bearing risk in mind. The constraining factor appears to be to reduce the probability of needing to find extra funding. Further work is needed to determine the most efficient way to do this.

7 *Time and Programme*

One way to differentiate the activities of organisations is to separate projects from business-as-usual. The activity of business-as-usual carries on forever, with minor refinements to processes and improvements in product and service quality, controlled through an annual budget-setting exercise. By contrast, projects are coordinated activities with beginnings and ends, along with one-off objectives. Projects are sometimes grouped together into programmes with strategic objectives and common management techniques.

Some organisations are project-orientated (for example, construction contractors or consultants); others are focused on business-as-usual (for example, retailers, banks or, perhaps the best example, government). Organisations tend to develop management techniques which are aligned with their particular activity style. (See for example Tim Carroll's *Project Delivery in Business-As-Usual Organizations*, Gower: 2006.) This applies to risk management as well and the development of quantitative methods has been more advanced in the project and programme environment than in business-as-usual.

Why is this?

Arguably, project-orientated businesses are riskier, although business-as-usual organisations seem just as susceptible to big strategic risks as their project counterparts. Indeed, perhaps the biggest strategic risk for a business-as-usual organisation is failure to adapt to a new business environment, when the current business-as-usual processes and systems become inappropriate. At that point a change project is needed to effect a transition to a different model of business-as-usual. Personally I think the idea of business-as-usual is fundamentally flawed and life (including the universe and everything) is a series of projects, including those which involve processing millions of similar transactions. Thinking this way helps avoid annual performance becoming the *de facto* project.

Another reason for the greater prevalence of quantitative techniques in projects is that each project is different. Every project has different costs and different risks. Each one needs its own plan. Inevitably its managers have to take the risks on board during planning and the risks lead to bigger uncertainty in the cost, duration and performance of the project than is the case for business-as-usual operations. For them, financial and quality control through budgets and other embedded processes means that a good starting point for planning next year is this year. So although both styles are susceptible to big strategic risks, the projects have to pay much more attention to little tactical risks. That is what project risk management is about.

As a result the financial control of projects is effected not only through budgets, but also though the allocation of funds, let us call them *contingencies*, specifically to deal with risks. We shall be describing how and why this can work and how it contrasts with budget controls in a risk management context later in the chapter.

But first we turn to a more fundamental defining feature of risk management in projects: time. As well as the cost risk analysis described in the previous chapter, it is a universally held view that good practice in project risk analysis is to conduct a schedule risk assessment.

Schedule risk analysis

The idea of schedule risk analysis is straightforward. Instead of developing a model in which input distributions are applied to system components (reliability) or a set of costs, they are applied to a project plan. That is, the underlying business model is a bar chart, not a process flow diagram or a set of accounts. Whilst they can be applied to the costs of each task or to the distribution of resources, the focus is the duration of the tasks. The main output then is the probability distribution of the time to complete the project. Hence the term *schedule* risk analysis.

A project plan is basically a three-dimensional matrix of tasks, resources and time. Committing them to paper or screen means sacrificing a dimension and the normal presentation is a Gantt chart where each task is shown as a horizontal bar against a time axis. Key to the development of a plan are the interrelationships between the tasks, typically of the form 'Task B cannot start until Task A is complete'. By setting out the list of tasks, the duration of each one and by defining the interrelationships, or logic, the planner can determine how long the project will take.

This logic is fundamental to the creation of the schedule risk model. Taking as a simple example a project in which there are three tasks, A, B, and C with A needing to be complete before B and C can begin we have:

$$dur(project) = dur(A) + max(dur(B), dur(C))$$

where dur(X) stands for the duration of task X. Thus the model, instead of being additive, generally has a richer structure, as determined by the logic.

Central to this is the concept of a *critical path*. This is the set of tasks which determine the duration of the project. In the example these would be A, then whichever is the longer task of B and C. Changes in the duration of the critical path tasks directly affect the length of the project. By contrast, changes in the length of tasks not on the critical path do not affect the duration of the project, at least until they have used up their *float*. The shorter of B and C is not on the critical path and its float is the difference between the durations of B and C.

This concept allows a very crude approximate risk model to be built in which the duration of the project is taken to be the sum of the length of each critical path task. This enables the approximate methods associated with summed risk models to be used. But you need to look out for the non-critical paths losing their float and affecting the risk. Again, techniques such as this are useful to sanity check the results of your model.

There are lots of other intricacies: applying cost, working and non-working days, more complex interdependence between tasks, rolled up tasks and so on. But the basic concept is simple.

There are numerous specific tools which deal with the complicated side of project risk modelling. They generally take a plan from a planning system and use it in their own environment to generate results. For example, you can buy extensions to the @RISK Monte Carlo application to allow it to accept plans from Microsoft Project, Primavera or so on. Equally, you can buy software like PERTMASTER, which was developed as an extension of Primavera. The programs often contain default risk templates so that you avoid the trouble of thinking about the risks and can get results straightaway. The pictures for the following example were taken from a program called RiskyProject from Intaver. It is a standalone application in which you can both build your plan and do the risk analysis.

THE ABCo PRODUCTION FACILITY

For our example, we return to one of the key risks for ABCo: the construction of the production facility for the new Product B. Figure 7.1 is a bar chart for a project to put this in place.

This chart shows three strands to the project: the civil engineering project to construct the building, the specification and purchase of the production equipment and the development of the software to run the production equipment. These three strands have to be completed so that integrated system testing and commissioning can begin. The critical path is:

- concept development
- building design
- building construction
- services installation and testing
- install and test plant
- software installation and testing
- integrated testing and commissioning.

To simplify matters we apply only two risks: a global risk affecting all the task durations in the same way and a specific, higher risk for the construction task, which is seen as particularly likely to suffer delays. It is a matter of minutes to put these risks into the software and find the S-curve results shown in Figure 7.2.

Figure 7.2 shows a small probability that the project will be completed in shorter than the planned 140 days, but also indicates a possibility that it could extend up to around 180 days. (These are working days, with five per week.) This lies well within the distribution used for the initial analyses described in Chapter 3. There we saw roughly a triangle, with a minimum duration of 110 days, most likely 130 days and a maximum 215 days. These projections were put together before detailed planning had begun.

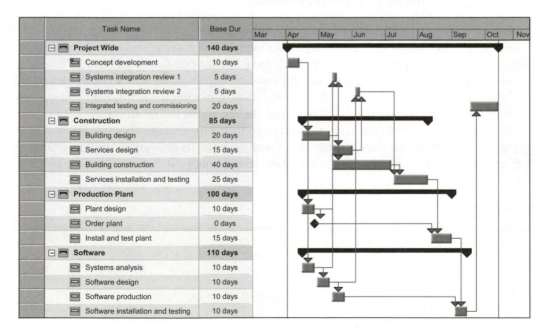

Figure 7.1   ABCo production facility schedule

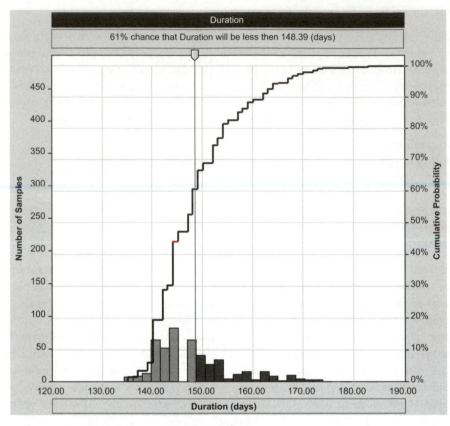

Figure 7.2   Distribution of project duration

However, there is a mistake in the plan. Although the project-wide tasks include two system-wide design reviews, they do not go anywhere; that is, there are no tasks dependent on them. A more realistic project plan would look more like the one shown in Figure 7.3.

In the updated schedule, service design, building construction and software design all need satisfactory completion of the first review. Similarly, placing the plant order and starting software production both require a second review before giving the go ahead.

The baseline project duration has now increased to 160 days, mainly because the lead time on the plant (there is a 60 day delay between ordering it and its delivery to the site, although this cannot be seen in the diagram) puts plant procurement on the critical path which is now:

- concept development
- building design
- systems integration review 1
- services design
- systems integration review 2
- order plant
- install and test plant
- software installation and testing
- integrated testing and commissioning.

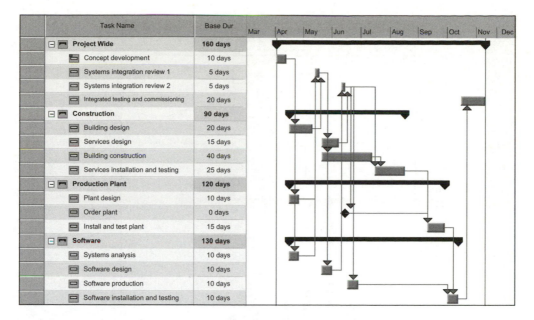

Task Name	Base Dur	Mar	Apr	May	Jun	Jul	Aug	Sep	Oct	Nov	Dec
Project Wide	160 days										
Concept development	10 days										
Systems integration review 1	5 days										
Systems integration review 2	5 days										
Integrated testing and commissioning	20 days										
Construction	90 days										
Building design	20 days										
Services design	15 days										
Building construction	40 days										
Services installation and testing	25 days										
Production Plant	120 days										
Plant design	10 days										
Order plant	0 days										
Install and test plant	15 days										
Software	130 days										
Systems analysis	10 days										
Software design	10 days										
Software production	10 days										
Software installation and testing	10 days										

Figure 7.3   Updated ABCo production facility schedule

With the same risks, the distribution of duration is now as shown in Figure 7.4.

Because the high-risk construction project has been removed from the critical path, the project has been de-risked, albeit delivered later.

This demonstrates how, firstly, it is important to get the logic right. I know this is obvious, but planners are focused on getting the right duration for their plans, not in putting in place every piece of logic which might be key to project risk. It is surprisingly difficult to get a schedule from a planning system that contains the correct logic to support a risk model. Secondly, it is hard to overstate the importance of review and approval processes in projects. Reviews often depend on external influences which are hard to manage: by definition a good review process should be independent. They can add large amounts into project duration. For example, if we add a further risk with a probability of 25 per cent that each of the review processes takes a month rather than a week, the results show the much greater spread shown in Figure 7.5.

This example is sufficient to give the general idea of schedule risk analysis. The same tools can be used to cover project cost in a similar way.

CHALLENGES

However, using these tools can be deceptive. They may be user friendly, but there are number of possible weaknesses. It does not take a very complicated project to become a difficult-to-follow black box. The effect of logic on the risk is hard to predict. This is exacerbated by the standard risk templates in the tools which may well not be appropriate to your project.

As we have already said, you generally have to work hard to get a logic which you understand and know will work when stressed with all the risks. The plan you get from the planners may well not have the right characteristics at first, especially if you are dealing with a large programme. A good example of this are approval processes, which are not seen as key to delivering the project, but are high risk. Furthermore, planners sometimes develop plans on

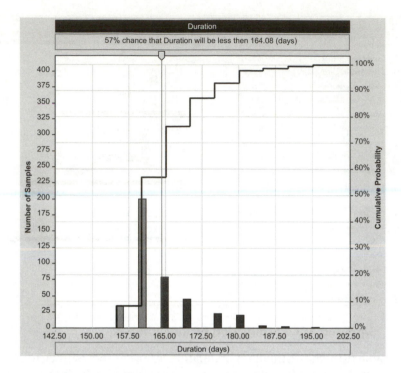

Figure 7.4   Updated distribution of project delay

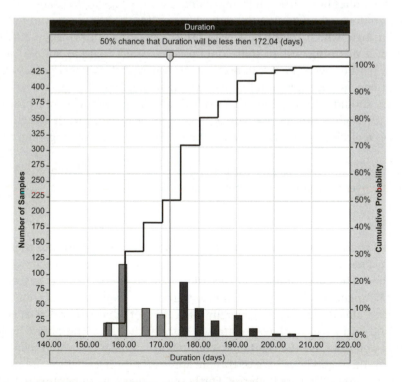

Figure 7.5   The effect of realistic review processes

their own without enough reference to project management, so the plans may not meet all the business and logistical constraints.

A specific example of inadequate logic is where tasks have been omitted because they are only needed if a risk materialises. Plans are compiled with the assumption that everything will go well, which means there is only downside risk. Take the example of the design review processes for ABCo. What if the software design is found to be incompatible with the proprietary manufacturing equipment configuration? Then a solution to the problem has to be found and we may have to go back to scratch on one task or the other. This could add months to the programme, and these are tasks in their own right. But this scenario is represented by the risk on the review task alone. You had better be sure that this represents what will really happen. When ABCo updated the project risk analysis, as in Figure 7.5, they found their hitherto assumed maximum duration was now around P50. With a further change to reflect the realistic chance of some major redesign issue, they decided to change their plans for the Product B launch. This meant borrowing more money and a significant increase in the risk of being upstaged by a competitor. There can be big stakes in review and approval processes.

I mentioned that plans are fundamentally three-dimensional but tend to neglect the resource constraint. Planning tools can be poor at assigning resources without a lot of handcrafted input, and this will be especially a weakness where they are required to do this in response to risk materialising. An example of this is described in Chapter 13.

For me there are two big messages from all of this:

1. Although schedule risk analysis is seen as basic good practice in some organisations, I think this overdone. You need to be sure why you are doing it and what you really need to know.
2. You should seriously consider whether using the standard tools, fed mechanically from a huge computerised plan, will accurately tell you what you want to know or whether you would be better off developing a simple model from scratch, using a spreadsheet and accurately modelling resource allocation, or liability pass-down or whatever else is the key feature. Using simple tools developed specifically for you, it may well be easier to understand the results and have some confidence in them.

Contingencies

Turning to how projects are financed, we assume that funds are allocated free of the annualised budget constraints that afflict projects in some business-as-usual orientated organisations. This is not necessarily a realistic assumption, but we shall not go into the details of how to resolve this technical problem. So, we are assuming that the organisation has a process to allocate funds to enable projects to be delivered, appropriate to the timescale of the project. The next question is how the funds should be allocated taking account of risk.

An example might be the kick-off of the waste management PPP. The funders have deposited the cash, a business plan has been drawn up based on the bid and the Chief Executive knows that some of the money has been labelled 'risk', and perhaps some of it even 'capex risk'. How do the Chief Executive and the Development Director decide what budgets to give to the project and programme managers?

This problem is an interesting blend of cultural and theoretical issues. Starting from the theoretical, we assume that the basic process is the allocation of a sum to each project manager to deliver their project. Recognising that risks may materialise which mean that the allocated sum is not enough, there has to be a process for applying for more funding if risks materialise (or it becomes clear that additional risk reduction measures – which cost money – are actually the most cost effective approach). Recognising that risks may not materialise, there should also be a risk release process which enables project managers to flag up when they do not expect to spend some part of the funding made available (a mini-refinancing, if you like).

A simple approach would be to fund each project at the P50 level. Half the project managers would release money, which could then be made available for the other half, who would apply for extra funding. The whole programme delivers at P50.

Simple, but, of course, it will not work. There is still some spread in the total programme cost so the balancing will not be exact; the difference needs to be funded or released as appropriate. And, there is also the exasperating problem that you will have a hard time finding the 50 per cent of project managers who are prepared to release funding – this is the cultural issue. The pressure to operate efficiently and save money is reduced in a project which is performing well compared to one where things are going wrong; surpluses tend to find their way into gold plating and other nice things to have.

This lack of symmetry creates a serious financial problem for the project organisation. Suppose you have five projects at £20 million each, and each with a standard deviation on outcome of £3 million. Figure 7.6 shows how the total cost with ineffective risk release differs from what it should be.

The ineffective risk release increases the expected cost of the programme by £6 million. You can see this approximately from the difference in the two P50s in Figure 7.6. The spread, of course, is much less, though; so if you want certainty, this is an improvement.

The only solution in the organisation where the discipline of cost control and risk release is not totally ingrained appears to be to release funds only to a much lower level and accept that the process for obtaining additional funding will almost always be attempted. This means that programme managers need an effective way to release such funds. One way is to ensure that such funding is only granted against previous identification in the risk register. This leaves the question of what to do if risks materialise which were not previously foreseen in the risk register. The brutal answer is 'tough, let the project manager find it somewhere else'. This may

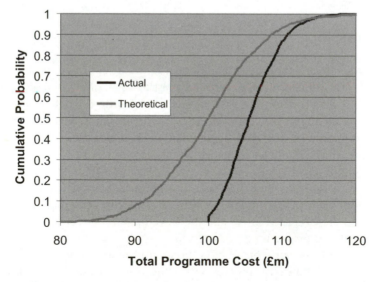

Figure 7.6   The effect of ineffective risk release

work, but is hardly conducive to encouraging managers to release money they do not need. So, the answer has to be that we keep the pressure on to release risk (have we looked hard for previously unidentified opportunities?) and bring costs to the minimum.

There is no right answer, but the strategy above has the best chance of working. As organisations become better at risk release, they can increase the discretionary funding to project managers (and economise on programme managers).

But what has this got to do with contingencies?

There is an alternative viewpoint that argues you could fund projects at the P80 level, say. The difference between P80 and P0 could then be regarded as contingent funding: for use if risks materialise; kept in the bank if they do not. We have already discussed the shortcomings of this:

- project managers will tend to spend contingencies when they do not need to;
- the sum of the contingencies over all projects is unaffordable – in the five project example above, the sum of the P80s is £112.6 million, the theoretical P97 – the budgeting process would have a nervous breakdown;
- and 20 per cent of the project managers will still come back for more.

An improved answer is to keep contingencies at a relatively high level in the organisation. Consider the organisation shown in Figure 7.7, for instance. The project managers could be allocated the P20 amounts (that is, £17.5 million each) and the £12.6 million to take the programme to the expected level could be kept as a contingency for the relevant programme manager to allocate according to an agreed set of principles. This would only take the programme managers to the P50 level, so they would need to find more funding half of the time. To do this they would have to apply to the next level up, the Development Director. It

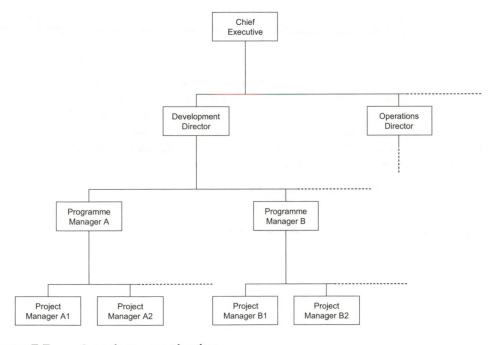

Figure 7.7   A project organisation

is more reasonable to expect programme managers to release funds that are not required than project managers – it would be part of their core function. As a result risk release becomes more effective.

A coherent picture of this system is shown in Table 7.1.

This table illustrates how the Development Director can retain the difference between the P80 and the P50 as a contingency. This is exactly what was termed the risk premium in the risk modelling of the waste management PPP in the previous chapter. But, you can see that the Development Director will still have more than his fair share. There will be virtually nothing left for operations; they will have to survive within budgets in a business-as-usual culture.

Summary

You will have noticed that I have dropped my insistence on using the expected value rather then P50 in this discussion. For these programme issues, the difference will almost always be immaterial.

The discussion in this chapter has been quite theoretical, in particular by not addressing the dependence that will exist between projects. In practice, the management of contingencies should be adjusted for this, but this does not affect the main points made.

Note that the practices discussed are not necessarily the same as distributing the money labelled 'risk' in the bid. Recall that the function of the bid risk analysis is to bridge the gap between what is in the cost model and reality. The risk element of the bid may contain expenses which are known to be required. If there is considered to be too much fat in the estimates, the expected level of cost may even be less than the baseline. It is not the central value that is important for this discussion; it is the spread. Figure 4.8 illustrated this.

It is worth underlining that the proposal in the table is not the one true 'right' answer. It is something to think about in the context of the various issues we have discussed. Each organisation will find its own way of dealing with the conflicting priorities in the cultural context.

We are now able to answer the question we started with of why business-as-usual organisations have strict budgets and no contingencies. Firstly, project managers do not have them either; secondly, the P80–P50–P20 spread is probably lower; and thirdly, the business-as-usual organisation is much better adapted to surviving within budgets, whether tight or generous, than implementing potentially expensive risk release and risk funding processes.

But this raises another interesting question: how do we incorporate the undoubted power of budgetary disciplines within our risk modelling? Surely this reduces uncertainty compared

Table 7.1   A possible contingency management system

Manager	Available Spending	Contingency
Development Director	P80 for all capex	P80 - P50 for the capital works
Programme Manager	P50 across their programme	P50 for their programme less the sum of the P20s
Project Manager	P20 for their project	None

with what we might expect? Unfortunately, I do not know. We have to be realistic about our ability to model accurately the behaviour of people in organisations.

It seems that there is an endemic inability of organisations to align individual behaviour with the optimisation of the performance of the organisation as a whole. Following from this is a management truism that a non-performing organisation should be subjected to a reign of terror to bring it back in line with expectations. But perhaps this simply leads to the good people leaving too, exacerbating a vicious circle of increasingly poor delivery. How do you model all this?

These are factors which tend to make the spread contained in the output of risk models too narrow. But, you will build them in at your peril: putting bad management in the risk register tends to attract adverse comment. You need to make your own judgement. One approach might be a diplomatically worded risk in the register to prompt a discussion – for example, 'there is a risk that day-to-day project management will not be aligned with strategic objectives'. The discussion could bring out previous experiences in other organisations and aim to identify symptoms appearing in your own environment. Credible quantification might still be difficult, but perhaps the management of the risk will improve.

8 *General Models*

At its simplest, a risk model is comprised of a set of inputs and outputs related in some way. By specifying probability distributions on the inputs and applying the model relationship, you can find the probability distributions of the outputs. In the previous three chapters we have discussed three types of models:

- reliability models where the inputs and outputs are binary – the system and its components either work or do not;
- cost models where, at their simplest, the output is the sum of the inputs;
- project schedule models where, again at their simplest, the output is the duration of the project determined through the duration, resourcing and interrelationships of a number of tasks.

Clearly these are a subset of the risk models which are possible. A quick glance at *Risk Analysis*, the journal of the Society for Risk Analysis, gives an idea of the range of risk models which are possible. Articles in *Risk Analysis* tend to cover the following topics:

- risk communication – how people and organisations describe and communicate about risk;
- risk perception – what people and organisations understand about risk and how they feel about it in the light of communications;
- risk decisions – what decisions people and organisations make about risk in the light of their perception;
- risk policy – how this is, or should be, encapsulated in the policy of organisations and government;
- risk modelling;
- historical data.

The first four topics are treated in a highly multidisciplinary way, employing social, political and scientific perspectives to generate a rich picture of how human beings do and should deal with risk. However, this is largely focused on the management of safety and environmental matters; there is little on business-focused risk management.

Similarly, for the most part, the papers on risk modelling leave reliability to one side, whilst taking an essentially scientific approach. They are focused on one or more of:

- modelling the dispersion of materials in the environment;
- modelling environmental phenomena like hurricanes (but surprisingly little on climate change);
- modelling the dose–response relationship of toxic chemicals;
- modelling the effectiveness of pharmaceuticals;
- modelling the breakdown of physical containment.

The physical risk models are compiled in spreadsheets or more sophisticated software and the risk is explained, generally, using Monte Carlo techniques. The simplicity and power of Monte Carlo for any risk model where it can be applied (that is, where there is a way of calculating outputs as a function of inputs) mean that our ability to carry out risk modelling is reduced to the ability to generate the right outputs from the right inputs.

In many of these areas these modelling questions are framed fairly easily:

- What is the dose–response relationship?
- Where does the pollutant disperse to?
- How much pressure is required to fail this containment?

The risk derives from the uncertainty in answering these questions. If you represent the uncertainty with probability distributions, you can then easily feed them into a model: the template is there. But for business risk modelling, there are often no templates. The problem is to create a framework so that you are prompted to ask the right questions. The previous chapter gave an indication of some areas where this is a challenge. A fuller list might include:

- budgeting disciplines
- value of variations and claims in a project
- impact of review and approval processes
- performance of stretched staff
- allocation of high-calibre management resources
- competitor response
- regulator response
- changing requirements over decades.

Whilst we are clear that these issues are relevant to the risk analysis, our understanding of them may range from good to a vague appreciation. Either way it is often not clear how to incorporate the issues in a crisply defined risk model. This chapter provides some thoughts on how to tackle this problem. This includes a discussion of the tools which can be used when the input/output model is not quite right.

These are complex and interesting areas and the material here gives only a very superficial view. I would heartily recommend further exploration: performing an internet search on the keywords I provide will give you plenty of material and food for thought.

Influence diagrams

We generally build risk models to make sense out of a complex mass of data and information. In business risk management, the challenge is to synthesise something workable from the horrific lists of poorly articulated worries which find their way on to the average risk register. (This was discussed in Chapter 2.)

There are simple tools to make sense of such complexity. One is to pull related things together. You can call it making lists, affinity mapping, mind maps, work (or whatever) breakdown structures, herringbone diagrams, bullet points or some other term. (I usually call it a structured hierarchy and use an indented format like a project work breakdown structure. This saves on paper compared with horrible mind maps.) This technique of creating basic groupings is very useful. For example, the approach of collecting risk register items together to create higher level risk issues for quantification and sanity checking is recommended as standard good practice in several places in this book.

Another useful set of tools are the tree diagrams described in Chapter 5. We noted there that the technique of drawing fault and event trees, which focus respectively on cause and effect, can be useful to structure a problem.

Generalising fault and event trees brings us to influence diagrams. At their most basic, they comprise a series of blobs connected by arrows which show that one blob influences another. To begin with we are not too fussy about what the blobs are supposed to represent. For example, the waste management PPP risk model could be represented by such a diagram (see Figure 8.1).

A project bar chart can be viewed as an influence diagram (with bars instead of blobs) and other blobs could be added to represent the way resources 'influence' each task they are assigned to. In Chapter 7, I argued that this might be a better approach to the initial stages of project risk modelling than loading a schedule file into a project risk Monte Carlo tool. Taking one of the risk modelling papers from *Risk Analysis* more or less at random, the issue of waterborne cryptosporidiosis in France (see: Pouillot, R. *et al.* 'A Quantitative Risk Assessment of Waterborne Cryptosporidiosos in France Using Second-Order Monte Carlo Simulation', *Risk Analysis* 24: 1, February 2004, 1–17.) can be represented by an influence diagram, as shown in Figure 8.2.

You can see that there are benefits in giving the blobs different shapes and colours. They can indicate different types of factors and make the chart easier to decipher. The authors base their risk model around the breakdown shown in Figure 8.2 (using second order Monte Carlo simulation!).

The benefits of drawing these diagrams are that they provide a way to make complex issues amenable to analysis and promote a modular approach, so that each part of the problem can be worked on separately and then drawn together to form the whole.

I recommend them unreservedly as a way of making progress.

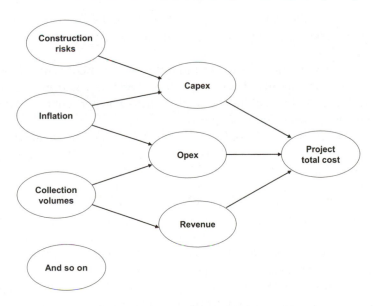

Figure 8.1   **Waste management PPP influence diagram**

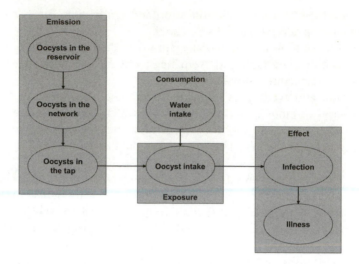

Figure 8.2   Cryptosporidiosis influence diagram

As is the case for the structured list, there are many other terms for this concept. We sad mathematicians call them directed graphs. If you put one blob inside another, you can call it soft-systems analysis. If you call the blobs objects, you are taking an object-orientated approach; if you force certain other properties on them you create an implementable object-orientated system. You can also call them Bayesian networks, and this perspective can be used to solve certain risk modelling problems which are not amenable to the Monte Carlo technique.

Bayesian networks

We will start with a simple example. Chapter 15 discusses decision trees and provides an example related to the development of a brown field site. Using this, we can draw the influence diagram of Figure 8.3.

The influence diagram represents the fact that the development gain will depend on the site condition, as will the results of a test that the developer could have carried out. The developer's view of the condition of the site is that there is a 30 per cent chance of it being bad ground and completely useless for development.

The developer also has a view about the accuracy of the tests and believes that if the site is in a good condition there is only a 8.2 per cent chance of the test giving a negative result. Conversely, if it is in bad condition there is a 23.8 per cent chance of a positive result; that is, devoid of contamination. Using probability combination rules, the chance of a positive test result is, as it happens, 71.4 per cent. But so what? What the developer is interested in is the probability that the site is contaminated, in the light of the test results. In other words, they want to know how to adjust the 70:30 probabilities in the light of new information in the form of the test outputs. This is a slightly tricky calculation using Bayes theorem (see Chapter 12 and also The Reliability of Oracles box in Chapter 15).

Figure 8.3 is a screenshot of suitable software from the Hugin Expert company, and we have input the relevant probabilities into the Condition and Test Result nodes. We have also input the net development gain in the case of good and bad conditions into the Gain node: more of this shortly. Figure 8.4 shows what happens when we tell the software to specify a positive test result.

Figure 8.4 shows that in this case the confidence that the site is good increases to 90 per cent (now a round number by design) from 70 per cent. Similarly, when the result is negative there is now only a 20 per cent chance that the site is good, rather than the previous 30 per cent.

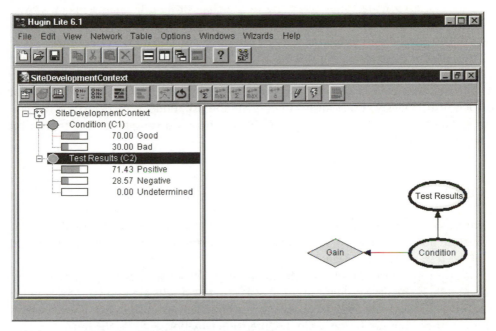

Figure 8.3   Influence diagram for site development

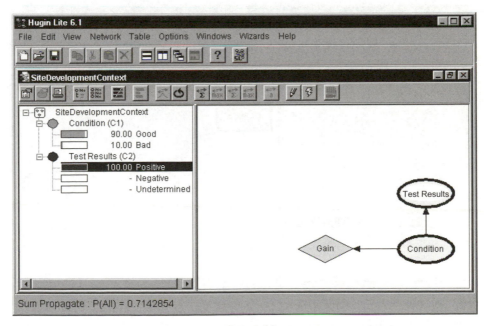

Figure 8.4   Increase in confidence with tests

This process is known as Bayesian updating. Obviously, the ability to update a risk model in the light of more information is a valuable one. Effectively it is a way to update the input distributions (in this case the site condition probability distribution) in order to reflect new information. However, the implementation of the influence diagram may already contain the whole risk model; so, instead of exporting the new model into a Monte Carlo environment, the developer can just construct it using influence diagrams where the probability distribution of the state of each node varies according to the state of its influencing nodes. Obviously, this means the model has to be rather coarsely defined. There is no room for detail about the nature of the ground contamination and the resulting clean-up costs, for example.

The key advantage of this approach is the ability to carry out Bayesian updating and it is for that reason that this type of influence diagram is called a Bayesian network. The type of software used here offers a genuine alternative to Monte Carlo in that it is not a simulation approach. It provides an exact means to evaluate the risk model not affected by the random errors of Monte Carlo. The price you pay for this is increased complexity and sophistication; and, coarseness in the distributions.

Decision trees

Returning to the developer, these probabilities can be used in order to decide whether to commission a site test. The influence diagram can expanded to include the decision and the cost of the test, as shown in Figure 8.5.

The decision is a three way one: whether to test, walk away or develop anyway. The node in the middle is the development decision after the test results are known. This is not really a decision as the developer will have already satisfied themselves that they will develop if the tests are positive, but not if they are not. Otherwise, why bother to do the test?

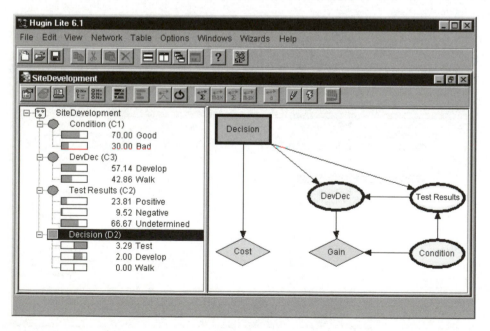

Figure 8.5   Site development decision tree

The numbers for this model have been inserted: if the ground conditions are good, the development gain is £8 million; if they are bad the loss is £12 million. With 70:30 probabilities, the option is to develop. This has an expected outcome of £2 million, compared with the zero benefit of walking away. Although the test costs £1 million, Figure 8.5 shows that the developer should commission it, as with the test result the expected outcome is increased to £3.29 million.

What you see here is an extension of Bayesian networks to cover decisions. This broadened application of influence diagrams is again an excellent way of mapping out a problem. You can see that the Bayesian network software is capable of carrying out the kind of analysis we show in more detail in Chapter 15 using decision trees. The difference is that here we look at a specific case; whereas the more general analysis in Chapter 15 enables the whole decision space to be explored.

In practice there is a whole family of analytical techniques and associated software which integrates:

- influence diagrams
- Bayesian networks
- decision trees
- object-orientated concepts (hierarchies of networks with inherited characteristics).

These techniques go beyond the bulk of what is described in this book, but it is worth being aware of their existence and having an overview of what they can do for you. I have tried to give a flavour of each.

Now is a good time for a short digression on risk software: see the Risk Software box overleaf.

Summary

The messages from this chapter are pretty simple:

- most business risk modelling is a fairly straightforward affair where we create cost models and use Monte Carlo simulations to investigate the central value and spread;
- we can apply the same philosophy to project models;
- structuring techniques such as work breakdown structures, trees and influence diagrams help us make some sense of the complexity of the environment in which we are trying to create these simple models; they can help us to frame the questions so that a model can be developed to reflect them;
- there are approaches to reliability, decision trees and Bayesian updating in the light of new information which have their own, technologically more complex, methods, including the computerised implementation of specific kinds of influence diagrams;
- whilst it is worth knowing these high tech methods exist and roughly what they do, this book is not going to describe them in detail.

Having provided this overview of the methods which are available for risk modelling, we now turn to how they have been used. In Part III we discuss how they are used to help people make decisions. Remember that a model, however sophisticated or comprehensive, does not make the decision itself. It is not even responsible for the decision.

Risk Software

You can see from the discussion up to now that the term 'risk management software' can incorporate a large range of functionality, from insurance claim management systems to Bayesian network solvers. Occasionally, buyers' guide-type reviews will appear in the risk literature, with the aim of helping you to choose from this array. They provide tables of tick lists, comparing features such as 'prints reports' or 'quantitative analysis'. They are completely useless, apart from giving you the URL of the producer.

It is hard to blame them though, when they are the victims of the grandiloquent yet vague marketing blurb which accompanies most of this software, offering spurious benefits derived from poorly described features. (My favourite was Microsoft's campaign to convince us we would be in the dinosaur age without buying the most recent version of Office, a product which I think has actually gone downhill for the last 10 years, probably because there was nowhere else to go.) It is very difficult to work out what the software actually does without the hassle of actually downloading, installing and testing. I find it frustrating that the vendors seem to be reluctant or unable to tell you anything sensible about their products.

Some risk software is very banal. Enterprise risk registers fall into this group. They are pretty simple, low-volume databases. The main feature of an enterprise risk register is that it should be quick and easy to use in a web-enabled environment. The main requirement is that the technology should be compatible with the company's IT strategy. You sometimes hear that it should be part of the integrated information system, but you need to ask exactly how and why before swallowing such a 'requirement', no matter how reasonable it sounds. Another important requirement might be a decent audit trail, but this never seems to be featured.

Monte Carlo software falls in to the same category. We have emphasised the elegance and simplicity of the Monte Carlo approach throughout this book. This means that there is not actually much to it. You just need a way to apply input distributions to a spreadsheet model and collect the output. The clever bit is the spreadsheet. Probably key is the ability to interface with your other systems, but again I think this can be overstated. I have tried to present a clear philosophy in this book that just dumping hundreds of risk register risks into a Monte Carlo calculation is not sensible (unless you just want to add up their expected value). The same applies to interfacing with a massive programme in Primavera. What I think is better is handcrafted models with a relatively small number of key issues which you understand in detail. I have used @RISK for years. It is nothing special, but does what it says on the packaging.

By contrast, some of the more specialist analysis software contains some very special intellectual property. The decision tree, Bayesian network software falls into this group, as does the fault and event tree software. Generally these are developed by small companies where there is a technology driver. Here the basic functionality is much more critical to the purchasing decision and again it is just as difficult to understand what this comprises. Obviously, there is the danger of being caught in an academic exercise or finding that the expensive software does not contain what you think is a quite basic function.

So there is a role for an informed buyers guide. It would take quite a bit of work to develop something that is genuinely useful. I am not going to do it; apart from anything else it would almost certainly be libellous. In the meantime, there is no substitute for getting on the web, searching with the right keywords, reading the hype carefully and trying out the demos.

Good luck.

Decisions and Risk

We do quantitative risk modelling primarily to support decisions. There are many types of risk decision which managers have to make:

- Should I make this investment?
- Do I need an offsite data storage facility?
- Do I need to pay a retainer to a business resumption services contractor?
- Is this plant or product safe?
- Shall I recall this product?
- What are the long-term consequences of using this chemical?
- Should I pursue this claim and risk annoying the client?
- How much of a contingency fund shall I give this project manager?
- Shall I accept this bid?
- What price will win and make an acceptable profit?
- Is it possible to win and make a profit?
- If I procure this facility with a PFI, will I be able to continue to deliver my service?
- Will I still want to deliver the same service in 20 years time?
- Shall I defraud my organisation, risking prosecution and a feature in *Private Eye*?

You can read in Chapter 15 about the theory of how to make decisions. You will see that the theory is pretty uncompromising: in non-technical terms, you should quantify the pros and cons, and their probabilities, then proceed with the approach which will, on average, be best.

In technical terms, we should maximise expected *utility*. This involves assigning a measure of desirability to each outcome as part of the risk analysis. This is its utility. We can then use the probabilities from the risk analysis to work out the expected utility. Finally, we choose the course of action with the maximum expected utility. In doing this we are demonstrating *coherence*; failure to act in this way is *incoherent* and, in principle, suboptimal. It makes us losers.

Like probability, utility is subjective: I will value differently the costs and benefits of driving a Mercedes or a Smart car to the way you will value them. There are similar discomforts in developing utilities as there are in using subjective probabilities.

This gives us a bit of a paradox. I emphasised in Chapter 3 that risk analysis was directed at providing a range of outcomes to supplement some central value. Decision theory suggests that this range is pretty much immaterial; what you need is the average or expected value. The range does enter the calculations in that expected utility is not, in general, equal to the utility of the expected value; but, as illustrated in Chapter 15, this does not generally have much of an impact.

So Part III is not so much about the application of the theoretically correct approach, as it is about the way people and organisations actually feel towards and deal with risk. This is where the ranges come in.

- Chapter 9 examines the UK public sector, which is perhaps the most theoretically correct in its approach to making decisions;
- Chapter 10 provides some points on private sector thinking, particularly where a range of stakeholder expectations has to be accommodated;
- Finally, Chapter 11 describes the approach to risk-based *safety* management which has developed in the UK; featuring significant departures from the theoretical ideal.

The examples in this section are not intended to be an exhaustive list of risk practices. The case studies provide a few insights, rather than a full review of global practice in risk decision making. Significant examples of areas omitted are:

- risk management in financial institutions
- cultural and social perspectives
- environmental risk
- war, security and terrorism
- and many more.

As well as being incomplete in its coverage of domains of application, it is also incomplete in its coverage of the theoretical foundations. This is because there are many intractable, unsolved and even insoluble challenges in the theory of personal, organisational and social decision making. This is true even when risk and uncertainty are left on one side. It is especially the case when rather than modelling the future as random, it becomes a game with your risk management competing with the rational strategies of other players.

With this health warning, what we will find is that incoherence is widespread: people and organisations demand risk premiums – that is, compensation for taking risk – which appear to greatly exceed what they would be if they were based on reasonable utility function. If this is overdone it leads to poor decisions which misallocate resources.

This is why risk modelling is important. By providing us with the ability to explore risk in as full and consistent a way as possible, albeit subjectively, risk modelling enables us to guard against the dangers of abdicating our responsibilities for risk decisions by taking the line 'it's all too hard; we'd better play safe.' Risk modelling helps to keep incoherence under control.

9 *Public Sector Decisions*

Over the last 10 years the UK government has given risk quite a high profile. One aspect of this is a number of initiatives to introduce and exploit risk management disciplines in government departments. Led by HM Treasury (HMT), the government has developed its own guide on risk management good practice, termed *The Orange Book* (2004), and has devised methods for measuring risk management performance. You can find this material on the HMT website, www.hm-treasury.gov.uk./documents/public_spending_and_services/risk/pss_risk_portal.cfm, which provides plenty of reading. However, while interesting, this material is not of direct relevance to this book.

At the same time, the government has talked of tough decisions in the allocation of resources and has issued guidance on how decisions should be made about government interventions: whether and how they should take place. Since these interventions are generally major projects, they raise significant risk issues and the guidance has to address this. So in this chapter we review the guidance for what it tells us about government decision making in the face of risk.

One area of focus is the way government seeks to transfer risk to partners where it is sensible to do so. We therefore discuss the approach used in Public Private Partnerships like the hypothetical waste management example we developed in Chapter 4. But we begin with the basic guidance.

The Green Book

If you want to understand how the UK government decides what to do, the starting point is *The Green Book* (HMT 2003, available from: www.hm-treasury.giv.uk/greenbook). This is the 'binding guidance' on, as its subtitle would suggest, 'appraisal and evaluation in central government' published by the economists at HMT. As you would expect, it is a lucid and not overlong read. All policies, programmes and projects should be subject to a cycle of action justification, objective setting, option appraisal, implementation, evaluation and feedback. You will recognise this is as a plan-do-review loop with extended planning and reviewing.

For our purposes the core of the cycle is option appraisal. Once you have identified the options, the key technique is a valuation of the costs and benefits of each option. This valuation is ideally based on market prices, although the guidance recognises that there may be wider social and environmental costs and benefits for which there is no market price, but which nonetheless have to be included. Having done this, the costs and benefits which are incurred by and derived from the policy, programme or project can be compared on a common scale by discounting and selecting the option which maximises net present value (NPV). In this way we are back to the classic approach using a utility function which is NPV, based on a value reflective of market prices as far as possible and using a discount rate which we shall discuss shortly.

TREATMENT OF RISK

How does risk fit into this? The guidance recognises that such appraisals of costs and benefits are subject to biases, risks and uncertainties. The main source of bias is thought to be the optimism of sponsors and appraisers. They are considered to underestimate costs, overestimate benefits and underestimate the time it will take to deliver them. HMT has obviously become sick of this over the years and mandates the application of large optimism bias adjustments, based on reviews of historical project overruns.

Supplementary guidance to *The Green Book* sets out maximum values for the optimism bias adjustments and provides a prescription for how they can be reduced in certain circumstances, based on a scoring scheme which takes account of specific factors within a project. The maximum values are shown in Table 9.1.

These adjustments are enormous and give a good idea of the sort of accuracy HMT anticipates seeing in appraisals. This underlines a point repeatedly made: risk assessments need generally only be coarse exercises.

Without explicitly dwelling on the point, HMT obviously recognises that optimism bias is another name for risk blindness because they accept that optimism bias adjustments are designed to complement and encourage, rather than replace, project-specific risk adjustments. In other words, the optimism biases can be reduced as the underlying costs take account of risk through steadily more detailed and realistic risk analyses.

The risk adjustments are to be the expected value of the impact of all the risks. With this we are now close to the classic decision theory approach of maximising expected utility. What else is there? Three things:

- exploring the decision space;
- the cost of variability in outcomes (or risk premium, though this is not HMT jargon);
- the relationship between discount rate and risk.

The first point makes the suggestion that you should carry out sensitivity analyses, model scenarios and enact multiple Monte Carlo simulations. All of these are aimed at providing an indication of the range of the costs and benefits and, ultimately, presumably, at providing an indication of the robustness of any decision that you might take. Particularly useful in this context are swing values: how much different things would need to be to change the decision.

Table 9.1   Recommended maximum adjustments for optimism bias

Project Type	Upper Limit of Optimism Bias: Cost	Upper Limit of Optimism Bias: Duration
Standard buildings	24%	4%
Non-standard buildings	51%	39%
Standard civil engineering	44%	20%
Non-standard civil engineering	66%	25%
Equipment/development	200%	54%
Outsourcing	41%	N/A

The remaining two points are related through a utility model based on measurements of the 'elasticity of the marginal utility of consumption'. The model simply says that an increment in consumption is worth half what it was if our consumption has doubled. Apparently this can be applied equally to individuals, to groups and to society as a whole.

This utility model has two effects. Firstly it enables a 'cost of risk' to be determined. This is what we have called the risk premium in this book. The formulas for this are in Chapter 15, but the additional 'cost of variability in outcomes' is 0.5 times the variance divided by the overall wealth of the people affected. (Note that this is dimensionally correct, unlike the formulation in *The Green Book*.) Since the denominator is large, the cost is small and, in fact, this aspect of the analysis is hardly worth mentioning: it simply underlines the point that for government, it is expected net value that is important. The uncertainty in the expected value far outweighs any correction for non-linear utility.

More importantly, the elasticity in the marginal utility of consumption is part of what determines the discount rate used for calculating NPV, or, as *The Green Book* puts it, the social time preference rate. This is split into two parts. The first is the straight discount on future consumption over present consumption, which is said to include an element to account for catastrophe risk; that is, the risk that something dramatic happens which completely changes things, with an implication that you had better consume now rather than take the risk of there being no opportunities for consumption later. Together these are said to amount to 1.5 per cent in real terms per year. This is quite small and does not appear to reflect most people's willingness to defer gratification (including catastrophe risk).

The second part of the discount rate is driven by increasing consumption and using the utility model: this adds another 2 per cent real per year. The total discount rate to be used in government appraisals is thus 3.5 per cent real per year. This is much less than the previously mandated rate of 6 per cent real per year and, indeed, lower rates are recommended for more than 30 years. The effect is to make the future relatively important in appraisals, especially when compared with the much higher discount rates used by private sector companies, as described in the next chapter.

TREATMENT OF HARD-TO-VALUE

What we have left out is any discussion of benefits or disbenefits that are hard to value. While not explicitly a risk matter, such issues are likely to contain the greatest uncertainty and are very likely to have a significant effect on decisions and their perceived riskiness. Firstly, if the preferred market pricing approach fails, the next step is to find a financial value by *willingness to pay* techniques. This reflects the amount people will pay to avoid a disbenefit – or accept to suffer it – as determined though direct elicitation or revealed by their behaviour. This is an interesting and controversial area, directly applicable to valuing risk, but we do not dwell on it here.

But what if both market prices and willingness to pay fail?

In these situations *The Green Book* recommends the use of multi-criteria weighting and scoring schemes. These schemes, if implemented fully, amount to a specific version of a utility function – see Chapter 15. However, by delaying the full integration, allowing the different criteria to be explicitly analysed and using the full integration only where there are genuine trade offs to be assessed, this issue can be side-stepped. *The Green Book* provides an example which is discussed in the *The Green Book* and Scoring Schemes box. This example demonstrates quite well some of the limitations of the approach.

The Green Book and Scoring Schemes

The Green Book (HMT 2003, available from www.hm-treasury.giv.uk/greenbook) provides an example in which a hypothetical FD must select between three IT systems, A, B and C. The analysis has been reduced to cost (fully adjusted for optimism bias and risk) and two attributes related to the performance of the system: management information and user friendliness. The performance attributes are not costed, but instead weighted and scored. The initial evaluation looks something like Table 9.2, where B is ruled out for being less preferable than C.

Table 9.2   Initial IT system evaluation

Scheme	A	B	C
Cost (£k)	-1000	-800	-600
Management information (points)	60	60	80
User friendliness (points)	160	100	80
Total points (points)	**220**	**160**	**160**
Net Value (£k)	?	C - 200	C

However, having gone through the multi-attribute approach, the FD suddenly finds that they can assign a financial value to User Friendliness, at least as regards A and C, and that the Management Information benefits are (a) worthless and (b) might be introduced later. The assessment now looks like Table 9.3.

Table 9.3   Updated IT system evaluation

Scheme	A	B	C
Cost (£k)	-1000	-800	-600
Management information (£k)	0	0	0
Future flexibility (£k)	>0	0*	0*
User friendliness (£k)	400	100*	0
Net Value (£k)	**>C**	**C-100**	**C**

* Inferred number

On this basis the FD selects A. A number of comments can be made about this:

- As it happens, A is not affordable: the budget is only £900k. This would be an offence punishable by death in the private sector, independent of value for money over the longer term; although not, perhaps, for FDs.

- The weighted and scored multi-attribute analysis was a waste of time. I think that this is nearly always the case for such schemes. A key reason is that they are implemented with little rigour: the fact that they are simple is used as an excuse to throw in any old rubbish. You must not take decisions this way. (This style of analysis is discussed further in Chapter 15.)

- A presentation like Table 9.3 is not provided in The Green Book. It is all hidden away in wordy descriptions. As a result, three items in Table 9.3 have been inferred. You can see that the relative score of B and C has changed and the starred items could change things again.

I think there are grounds for reviewing this decision, supposedly supported by 'best practice' techniques.

The moral is you will generally make the best decisions by sticking with a single measure of costs and benefits and showing clearly how they vary between options.

It seems to me that government guidance on decision making stops short of grasping fully the nettle of what to do about these shortcomings. It recognises that if the trade off is present, any decision implies constraints, at least on the relative values. As we have already mentioned, the guidance also shows that it is good practice to explore fully all the dimensions of the impacts to understand the implications of any decision rather than simply use the black box of a utility or scoring function to get the answer. But it could do more to encourage people to take valuation on a single scale as far as possible, and to guide people where this is not possible. See the example in the Health Effects box for more evidence.

MAKING THE CHOICE

Leaving all this information on the costs and benefits on one side, how is the best option to be selected? The first criterion is to select that with the highest risk adjusted net present value. Remembering that the risk adjustment is an expected value this amounts to maximising expected utility.

However, the selected option has to be affordable. Government is good at developing and evaluating options that it then finds it cannot afford – this is its own version of optimism bias, perhaps. The guidance is at pains to point out the difference between cost–benefit analysis

---

Health Effects

As an example, Annex 2 of *The Green Book* (HMT 2003) provides some detail on valuing health benefits. It is strong on the kind of measures to look at when comparing healthcare options, but generally silent on how to turn them into money. For example, it puts forward the quality-adjusted life year (QALY) as a good common measure of factors with an impact on health. The concept is one of measuring life expectancy and quality of life in a single measure. It is a cold-hearted concept and attracts extensive criticism; but it is a rational way to try to measure the potential benefit obtained from medical interventions against their cost.

In the next section, *The Green Book* goes on to note that the value of a prevented fatality might be £1 million or so. On the basis that the average life contains some 100 years, this might value a QALY at around £10k. Crude, but no cruder than most risk numbers. Cruel, but not as cruel as condemning people to negative-quality life years because resources are spent on small reductions in, for instance, railway risk. The QALY is only weakly endorsed as something you might try.

In fact HMT has more recently issued a supplement to *The Green Book* on appraisals where health effects are involved. This makes the same logical step as the previous paragraph and then suggests that QALY might be worth £20k–£30k. Obviously your quality of life goes down after 30 and is not worth living after 50. The QALY is also given a much higher profile as a useful measure. This is progress.

But the supplement also engages in an activity which has blighted risk modelling as a decision tool which is to emphasise the negative points without asking if there is anything better.

Specifically, there is a section which seeks to compare and contrast cost–benefit analysis (using willingness to pay for risk aversion) and cost–effectiveness analysis (using QALYs and its associated measures of health status). The guidance takes the line that they are two different things and although you might use one, you might not use the other: 'it all depends'. I think they are two perspectives on the same thing. There is a tendency to make risk modelling difficult when in principle it is not. That is why I recommend starting from a can-do viewpoint of quantifying and taking expected values, and only moving away from that for well understood good reasons.

– getting the best net outcome – and cost–effectiveness analysis – getting a specified outcome at the lowest cost. Affordability is in some sense the complementary idea: getting the best outcome at a specified cost.

The guidance, in an uncharacteristic departure from its logical approach, also suggests using a risk averse decision criterion it calls Maximin: select the option which gives the least bad outcome if the worst possible conditions prevail. No hints are given as to when it might be preferable to use this instead of maximising present value, and no guidance is given as to what constitutes 'the worst possible conditions'. Our probabilistic philosophy would at least try to set a P-value for what this might be. This is discussed further in the Maximin and Minimax box.

Procurement and risk transfer

A key factor for government in developing and evaluating its options is how to work with potential partners. This could be characterised as different procurement options – how to buy things. But the real issue is that by working with a range of organisations in different ways, the public sector can potentially:

- reduce costs
- increase benefits
- change the timing of costs and benefits
- and, most importantly from our point of view, reduce risk by transferring it to someone else.

Maximin and Minimax

The surprising departure from coherence recommended by HMT's economists in putting forward Maximin does have some form of justification, but this justification exists in a different field: game theory. Throughout this book we have adopted the philosophy that future uncertainty can be modelled in terms of probability: the future is the outcome of a random process. We have commented on this at various points, but have not developed alternative modelling techniques. Game theory, a much richer and more difficult field, imports the twist that future uncertainty is in part determined by the unknown decisions and actions of others. In other words, randomness is replaced by, or modified by, the rational behaviour of people. Because this behaviour is rational, driven by objectives which might be misaligned with yours, it is likely to be a poor approximation to model it as random.

Many business risk issues are game theoretic by nature. Business is competitive and there are plenty of situations where you face opposing objectives, such as when you try to negotiate the best prices or lowest wages.

Returning to HMT, a simple decision rule in game theory is minimax, as it is more usually called. The idea is that you enumerate the possible actions of your opponent, work out your expected loss for each such action and for each option. You then choose the option for which the maximum expected loss is minimised. In other words, you assume that whatever option you choose, the rational opponent does whatever will maximise your loss.

The separation of the rational from the random is important. Making this distinction means that you are being risk averse and this is not incoherent in *game theory*. But if the 'worst possible conditions' are effectively random, then the approach is indeed incoherent. The example given in *The Green Book* is the demand for services, so arguably this is the case.

In any case, this risk averse approach is especially surprising for a Government which, in its promotion of risk management for its activities (through *The Orange Book*, for example), is explicitly seeking to engender a less risk averse mindset in its policy makers and implementers.

If risk is reduced enough it may even be possible to take potential liabilities for future costs off the balance sheet so as to support the political objective of reducing public sector borrowing.

Whilst there are options for cooperation between different parts of government, and for involving the voluntary or charity sectors, the main issue is how the public sector works with the private sector. The relevant point is that for any activity that needs to be undertaken, there will be a private sector organisation for whom that activity is a core competence. That organisation will have honed its processes and costs in a hostile competitive environment in such a way that it can deliver the goods or services related to the activity more cost effectively than the public sector could.

This is a bit theoretical. As a generalisation, the public sector buys goods and delivers services. Where greater cost effectiveness is being sought is in relinquishing management and financial control of procuring significant goods (for example, buying a hospital instead of making it, in the jargon) and in outsourcing the provision of services (operating the hospital). PFI deals of the sort we have already discussed combine the two and add private finance into the mix.

Why go into this? Changing the way things are done is politically sensitive; especially when a service which has hitherto been delivered by public sector employees is outsourced to the private sector. Because of this political sensitivity, it has been normal to introduce a further option into the analysis called the Public Sector Comparator (PSC). The purpose of the PSC is to demonstrate that keeping the activity within the public sector has been explicitly considered in an evaluation of a new policy, programme or project. In this sense it is a bit like the *do nothing* option (or *do minimum* as *The Green Book* rather prissily calls it) which should always be one of the options on the table in a decision analysis. For us the PSC is important: firstly because it is a risk model and secondly because it will tend to crystallise the discussion of risk; both its transfer and its valuation.

Use of the PSC has not always been very successful. It is difficult for the public sector to generate accurate estimates of the risks which will materialise if it keeps in-house the management of a building project or the exploitation of a medical facility over 30 years. The result is fundamentally hypothetical cost estimates which have to be compared with the prices received from bidders for doing the job. The bidders' risk models may be just as flawed, but the prices are prices, so the public sector has some certainty in the options which involve procurement as opposed to the PSC.

As a result, the role of the PSC has changed over the years. Formerly, providing better value for money than the PSC was a strict hurdle for private sector bids to overcome. However now it is recognised that this is an unrealistic process, and the best way to ensure value for money is to have bidding that is as competitive as possible.

To take this forward HMT have issued guidance entitled *Value for Money Assessment* (2004, now updated from www.hm-treasury.gov.uk./documents/public_private_partnerships/ key_documents/ppp_keydocs_index.cfm), which provides a new three-stage process for PFI projects. The PSC is developed in a formulaic way during Stages 1 and 2, with the intention of showing (or not) that a PFI will offer best value for money for the specific project, that the project will be affordable, and that a market will exist to demonstrate value for money.

Progressing into Stage 3, the PSC is forgotten – the guidance explicitly says it should not be revisited. Instead, an effective competition should be set up to obtain the best terms from the market. If the market falls away for some reason (for example, if bidders withdraw), it may be necessary to stop the PFI procurement and choose some other method. One of the functions of Stages 1 and 2 is to ensure this contingency plan remains available.

The quantitative part of the assessment during Stages 1 and 2 is carried out according to *The Green Book* approach using a mandatory spreadsheet. Specifically this includes optimism bias and expected values for risk. The focus is on sensitivity analysis for the different options and showing the changes in assumptions necessary to cause a change the decision. The development of risk models is not seen as necessary, and, by implication is thought to be overcomplicating things – see The London Underground PPP box.

It is also worth noting that the analysis must be done with a risk allocation which reflects the government's standardised form of contract for PFI deals, SoPC3 (HMT 2004). You can see that the thinking on how to set up and analyse PFIs has become a standard process. This is intended to save huge transaction costs on some deals, but I think the jury is still out on how successful this is in practice.

The London Underground PPP

The biggest PPP/PFI deal to date has been the London Underground PPP. This comprises three contracts for the maintenance and renewal of the Underground infrastructure (track, stations, signalling and trains) for 30 years. It is expected to result in the expenditure £15.7 billion (NPV at 6 per cent per year) by the two private sector consortia who have taken it on.

As well as being the biggest deal financially, the three contracts are subject to a number of other superlatives. The London Underground PPP deal is:

- the riskiest, potentially, given the volume of worn-out, hard-to-inspect assets taken on and the challenging timescales for delivering new fleets of trains and signals;

- subject to the most highly developed performance specification in order to deliver the outputs a railway operator (who remains in the public sector) and its customers need;

- the most politically fraught, with a newly elected London mayor with no faith in the PPP solution and (initially at least) at loggerheads with the Government;

- and (partly because of the previous point) the most publicly discussed.

This last point makes this PPP particularly significant and a useful case study. By the time the deal had been in operation for a year, there had been no less than three National Audit Office (NAD) reports, which is probably another record. (These reports are obtainable from www.nao.org.uk.) Transport for London, the customer, also publishes its own annual reports on PPP performance, replete with performance data and commentary on the contractors. On its website (www.tfl.gov.uk), you can also find a number of older reports, produced as critiques of the deal at the time it was being set up. (You can even access the contracts themselves by searching for 'PPP', if you want some light reading.) Finally, the contractors, Metronet (www.metronetrail.com) and Tube Lines (www.tubelines.com), produce their own reports on what is going on, which you can find on their websites.

As in many PFI deals, the public sector – in this case London Underground Limited (LUL) – produced a Public Sector Comparator (PSC). It was intended to provide a benchmark for the private sector bids. The NAO have commented three times on this PSC. In their 2004 report London Underground PPP: Were They Good Deals? (HC 645 Session 2003–2004: 17 June 2004) they reiterated their previous comment that the financial analysis (that is, the PSC and its comparison with bids) provides useful but incomplete insight into the value of alternative approaches. They go on to say:

With hindsight, London Underground agrees that some of the cost, particularly the production of refined cost projections, extensive Monte Carlo simulation and the overly detailed documentation associated with the model's development was unnecessary given inherent weaknesses in the underlying data. Aspects of the model, however, did have value, for example the investment in base cost analysis, which was relatively high level and could usefully have been developed at lower levels, gave the project team a general idea about what the bidders' proposals would cost. The risk analysis work was also available and was used productively outside of the PSC, for example in informing contract negotiations. (NAO 2004, 29).

Don't even think you can win with the NAO! It is an important lesson that a risk analysis should not be developed in more detail than is supported by the data or evidence. The NAO report gives a good overview of the approach to risk analysis used by LUL (2004, 1–2).

Coming back to 'were they good deals?', which of the two possible answers did the NAO give? Here are paraphrases of the four key points from their executive summary:

- it was a complex deal;

- there is limited assurance that the prices were reasonable;

- it was an expensive deal to close;

- compared with the previous investment regime, there is an improved prospect, but not certainty, that the upgrade investment will be delivered (NAO 2004, 1–2).

'Haven't a clue,' would have saved paper.

Given the money involved, you would think that the public sector would be able to do better than that to demonstrate its stewardship of public money. Perhaps the PSC needed to be a better risk model; perhaps the NAO's criticism of LUL is misplaced. You can see from this how the stage is set for the Treasury's revised approach on PSCs, as described in the main text.

Summary

This chapter has shown that the public sector aspires to take a broadly coherent approach to deciding what to do when taking account of future uncertainties. It seeks to maximise the value for the money it has to spend on government interventions where these are considered necessary to address inefficiencies in the operation of markets or to achieve equity objectives. In doing this it can afford to use the expected value of the outcomes of the risk issues.

The approach is centred on economics and, to the extent it can be, is based on market prices and social preferences. It takes a long term view. The main challenges in this straightforward world are to value everything on a monetary scale and to develop realistic estimates of the expected values. It has found these challenges difficult to meet: guidance on hard-to-value attributes remains woolly and risk modelling takes a back seat, replaced by market competitions.

So risk modelling plays a relatively low-key role in public sector affairs. In part this is perhaps because the focus is on expected values rather than spread. You can also detect an element of suspicion, as reported on the part of the NAO in The London Underground PPP box, that risk modelling is overly sophisticated and wasteful of resources. There is little recognition that there are likely to be substantial risk premiums when government procures projects from organisations whose decision criteria are less coherent, financial rather than economic, driven by shareholder value rather than social welfare functions, and with a short term focus. We come to these organisations next.

10 *Private Sector Decisions*

All companies, or rather their managers, have to take decisions about risk. They do this in the light of the expectations of their various stakeholders: shareholder owners, funders, employees, customers, neighbours and, of course, the managers themselves. How can the risk models described in this book assist in these decisions? Our starting point is with the shareholders, the group for whom the company, in principle, is being run. We will then look at how managers react to shareholder expectations, putting them alongside those of a host of other stakeholders, including themselves. Finally, we discuss how the approach to risk this reveals might interact with the public sector in procurement situations where risk is being transferred.

What investors expect and what they get

Much of the theory around how companies should decide to invest (that is, enter into projects), is based around investor expectations. It starts with two observations:

- returns on shares are more volatile than returns on, say, Treasury bonds;
- over the long term, returns on shares are higher than those on bonds.

In other words, when investors buy shares in companies instead of buying low-risk bonds, they are foregoing more certain returns for higher, albeit riskier, returns. Historically, the stock market has outperformed low-risk investments such as Treasury bonds (or gilts, an expression which implies no risk) by perhaps seven per cent per year. This is another example of a risk premium.

This is what investors have got, and this can also be considered to be what they expect. In fact, there is some evidence that they would be happy with a lower risk premium.

Investors' expectations are, in fact, a bit more subtle than this because they recognise that some companies are higher risk (than the market average) and some are lower risk and they will demand a higher premium for higher risk.

The way this works is that investors normally hold portfolios of shares. To some extent, the returns on each share will move in concert with the market, and to some extent they will move independently. This is *systematic risk* and *unique risk*. By holding portfolios, the unique risks are thought to net off or *diversify*, leaving the investor to manage the systematic risk element of the portfolio. This is a considerable simplification. Some investors will reckon to identify those companies where unique risk is well managed and this is obviously a central concern to each company's management, so we shall return to this later.

By comparing the monthly returns, for instance, on a company share over several years, with the market average monthly returns, the investor can identify the correlation between the two. High correlation means low unique risk, but whatever the correlation, the slope of the fit between the share returns and market average returns indicates systematic risk. If the slope is small, the share has low systematic risk, or low beta, as it is called. If it is highly correlated, it has high systematic risk and high beta. The portfolio beta is the weighted average beta of each share in the portfolio.

This is known as the Capital Asset Pricing Model, or CAPM for short.

You can see where this is going: the focus of investor concern is systematic risk and it is thought that investors expect a higher return when beta is higher. To be specific: the expected return is the risk free return if beta is zero; the risk free return plus the market risk premium if beta is one; and linear in between (and beyond). In practice, there is no overwhelming evidence that investors have actually received higher returns, in line with this model, by investing in high beta shares. Note that on this model the risk premium is proportional to the standard deviation of the systematic risk, not the variance, as utility theory would imply. See the Are Investors Coherent? box for more on this.

Managers can infer their marching orders from this: they should only invest in projects which will deliver returns in line with shareholder expectations, or better. Financial managers implement this by:

- measuring the company beta;
- working out the required return to investors by adding beta times the market risk premium to a suitable risk-free return;
- working out the cost of debt, basically the interest rate the company has to pay to its lenders, adjusted for tax;
- working out a *weighted average cost of capital* (WACC) by averaging investor expectations and the cost of debt in line with the company gearing – the proportion of debt to equity;
- setting a hurdle rate for new investments or projects equal to the WACC;
- reserving for themselves the right to change this depending on whether the project is considered to be more or less risky than the company standard (as reflected by the company beta).

If adventurous financial managers select projects which will not deliver the expected return, investors will seek the same returns from lower risk investments. Equally, if cautious managers do not invest in projects which will deliver the expected return, investors will invest where they can generate these returns. One result of this is that if managers overestimate investor expectations they will not invest. It is possible that there is systematic under investment arising from inferred expectations that are too high. (CAPM is only one way to do this, but it has not been demonstrated to reflect expectations.) This is perhaps one example of the misallocation of resources which can arise from dealing too prudently with risk.

The last bullet point above indicates a role for modelling, though this role is vaguely defined. Ideally you might work out a project beta to test its returns, but this is simply not a definable concept given that beta relates to the periodic performance of shares in a market. In practice, the whole process can be done simply by forming a subjective view of the riskiness of the project.

This brief introduction shows that, in contrast to *The Green Book* rules in the previous chapter, the private sector has to make decisions in ways which are fundamentally determined by risk. The rate of return on costs *which include the expected value of the risks which could materialise* must be higher if the risk is higher. In general, though, the relevant benchmark for risk is the company's global systematic risk, perhaps modified by project-specific factors, but in a way which remains undefined. This might mean that risk modelling for investment decisions is of little value except, perhaps, to get the expected costs.

Are Investors Coherent?

In this book we have emphasised that decision makers ought to maximise their expected utility. If they do not, they are acting incoherently and there should be a way to make money out of them. It does not look as though investors are doing this. Why do they demand a premium for investing in risky or volatile equities? Surely their utility of money is not so risk averse that it would give rise to this. One way to look at this is to simulate the returns on a portfolio of equities by creating a risk model of their returns. For example, you can imagine that each month the return is one of two values – one represents a positive return and one a negative – which are randomly selected but are chosen such that on average the return grows at the market rate. You can simulate higher volatility by increasing the gap between the gain and the loss, whilst keeping the average constant.

Figure 10.1 shows the output of several such models run for 5 years with different volatilities. The risk-free part has been stripped out. The line marked with diamonds is the expected return, which is constant by design. The line marked with squares represents the expected value of a possible utility function, chosen to be logarithmic on the value of the portfolio (that is, the loss of the complete portfolio has infinite negative utility). This is the same model as that used by HM Treasury for the 'cost of variability in outcomes' reported in the previous chapter. It is normalised so that the marginal value of utility at the expected return is equal to one. At high volatility the expected utility is lower, indicating some sort of risk premium. But as you would expect, this does not increase linearly away from zero risk, but quadratically (we show why in Chapter 15). As a benchmark, market volatility on this chart is around three to six per cent per month, so there is not a huge risk premium, even with a fairly extreme utility function.

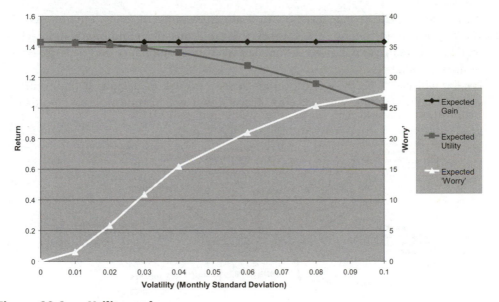

Figure 10.1   Utility and worry

However, it is sometimes said that the return demanded by investors is the reward for waiting (this is the risk-free return) and the reward for worrying (the risk premium). It is reasonable to think that worry is proportional to volatility. To find a measure for 'worry' we use the fact that the higher the volatility, the more likely the portfolio is to go though periods where the gain is negative (that is, less than a risk-free portfolio). The triangles on Figure 10.1 show the expected number of months out of 60 where this will be the case. Sure enough, this grows roughly linearly away from zero: our investor might demand a risk premium roughly equal to the market returns if their anxiety is raised in this way perhaps a third of the time.

This emphasises that risk premiums arise when downside outcomes are valued much more negatively than a utility of money approach would suggest. This is a key difference between the public and private sectors. The public sector simply maximises its linear utility (at least if it is only money – see the discussion on safety in Chapter 11). The private sector charges disproportionately for downside risk because of its nasty consequences. This starts with investor expectations, but does not stop there.

The Percentages box contains a collation of the percentage rates which we have been referring to. You may find this useful as a tangible background to the discussion.

What managers do

We have seen that if managers do not invest when there are opportunities to do so at rates above investor requirements, investors will actively seek higher return opportunities. We have also seen that if managers invest below the rates investors expect, investors will seek less risky opportunities. Either way, the share price will fall and managers will be failing in their prime duty. However, managers face other pressures which are of little concern to investors. For example, Figure 10.2 shows the expectations different stakeholder groups have about risk.

Putting more detail on some of these elements shows what a range of risk issues a manager has to deal with.

Regulators will tell the manager how to deal with a range of safety, environmental and corporate issues, amidst many others. Often these will take a precautionary approach – see Chapter 11. The manager will need risk models to ensure compliance and perhaps assess the risk of non-compliance.

Lenders will cast a beady eye, expecting to see zero risk of default. If there start to be indications that their conditions are being breached they will intrude more and more into the

Figure 10.2   Stakeholder expectations on risk

Percentages

To provide an overview of the different annual percentage rates used in the various calculations we have described, Table 10.1 shows some rates current in September 2006. The aim is to separate clearly nominal from real values. The table also indicates the difference between risk-free returns and the rates that companies set for their investments. As well, it shows the rates we have assumed in the waste management PPP example of Chapters 4 and 6. Obviously these rates are provided for illustration only.

Table 10.1   Percentage reference table

Percentage Table

	Nominal	Real	Differences	Comment	Ref
Inflation Rates					
RPI	3.30%				HMT
RPIX	3.10%			RPI excluding mortgages	HMT
CPI	2.40%			RPIX excluding housing costs	HMT
Assumed current inflator/deflator	3.00%*	0			
Interest Rates					
UK base rate	4.75%	1.75%*			FT
LIBOR					
overnight	4.89%	1.89%*			FT
1 year	5.24%	2.24%*			FT
Bank deposits	4.45%*	1.45%*	-0.30%	Compared with LIBOR	AL
Interest on PPP example cash		2.00% †			
Corporate borrowing	5.75-7.75%*	2.75-4.75%*	+(1.00-3.00)%	Compared with LIBOR	PF
PFI projects	5.25-6.75%*	2.25-3.75%*	+(0.50-2.00)%	Compared with LIBOR	PF
Interest on PPP example loans		5.00% †		High revenue risk for a PFI	
Rates of Return					
UK Government bond yields	4.16-4.94%				FT
UK indexed bond yields	5.00%	2.00%		In recent years	FCF
Bonds					
UK investment grade	5.00-5.43%				FT
Share market			+7.00%	100 year risk premium in UK	FCF
Assumed current risk free return	5.00%*	2.00%*			
Discount Rates					
UK Government projects					
current		3.50%			GB
former		6.00%			GB
Equity funded projects					
'typical' projects/companies	12.00%*	9.00%		Current risk free plus market return	
Return in PPP example		10.00% †			

Key
FT   *Financial Times* (29 August 2006)
HMT   *HMT Treasury Report* (31 August 2006)
FCF   Brealey, Marcus, Myers (2006), *Fundamentals of Corporate Finance*, 5th Edition (McGraw-Hill)
GB   HM Treasury (2003), *Green Book*. Available from www.hm-treasury.gov.uk/greenbook
AL   Alliance and Leicester website (10 September 2006), '30 day notice'. Available from www.alliance-leicester.co.uk
PF   Phone a friend: thanks to Helen Garlick and Matthew Crosse

* Inferred numbers; the rest come from the data
† from hypothetical PPP example

running of a business or project and put their prices up. Your credit rating is a precious asset; what is the risk of losing it?

Consortium partners may constantly jostle for some form of advantage. How do you know that you all have an equitable position on the risk–reward diagram? Will it matter if you don't?

Suppliers will seek the highest possible price for their goods and services. Normally, you will seek to negotiate a good price from a supplier. But what is the risk that it bankrupts him, or he simply walks off and finds other customers? Do the consequences matter?

Your workforce may be your biggest asset, but what if you win too much work and can't resource it with the heavy-hitting managers and skilled staff it needs? What would be the effect on delivery, quality and the resulting impact on your reputation with shareholders, lenders and customers?

Customers look for you to take on risk whether in the formal risk transfer of a PFI, on-time delivery to ABCo of their new factory, or a consumer money-back guarantee in case of dissatisfaction. If you cannot deliver, you will not win business. This has certain and unpleasant consequences.

Coming full circle, the *investors*, in spite of their portfolio approach, presumably expect managers to maximise the returns on the non-financial assets available to them – including equipment, buildings, systems, people and core competences, intellectual property, brands and so on. Investors will hope to steal a march on the market by picking winners: managers and firms who excel at dealing with unique risk. That is why risk management was invented.

All of these interested parties create risk for the managers themselves, who just want to continue to earn an honest crust by dealing with this environment. Messing up with any of the above bears the risk this modest objective will not be met.

So, it is not surprising if managers go beyond the wishes of investors. They may well act to diversify the risks the company faces; or protect their jobs; or optimise the fruits of their reward schemes; or simply have a quiet life.

For all of these reasons, company managers will not make decisions by folding in risk just as an expected value. That is why we need risk models: to explore upsides and, especially, downsides, so that managers can ensure that the probability of really horrible things is sufficiently remote. Examples we have listed elsewhere in this book include ensuring the risk of bankruptcy or running out of cash is sufficiently low, ensuring banking covenants are not breached and pricing at P80.

Needless to say, this is not codified. Private sector managers do not have a Green Book, at least not one that covers everything in Figure 10.2. As we would expect, the results of risk models play – at best –an informative role, rather than a determining one. But, referring back to Chapter 4, the S-curve of return on investment for the waste management PPP (see Figure 4.7) should be of interest to investors, not least to show how the company is dealing with the very unique risk profile of that particular project.

There is much that can be done to build these insights and approaches into a coherent way of dealing with risk, or even to explain why managers make the decisions they do. Going back to the theme set for Part III, incoherence is not demonstrably under control and risk modelling can perhaps help.

To finish, one specific and rather obvious point about risk modelling is that it prevents the idea that you need to make an individual provision for every single risk, perhaps at a 'reasonable worst case value'. Clearly this makes you uncompetitive. By definition risk modelling takes a portfolio approach to the risks you face. As ever, though, there is a warning about modelling dependence correctly. Provisions for individual risks reflect the gut feeling that everything may go wrong at once.

Can risk transfer be value for money?

To finish this chapter, we return to the public sector and ask what happens when it attempts to procure goods or services with better value for money than if it made the goods (or at least managed their production) or delivered the services itself. Tied in with this is the idea that some risks will be transferred from the public to the private sector. Can this be value for money given the concerns that private sector managers are trying to balance?

It is clear this issue is problematic. Tables 10.2 and 10.3 provide some of the pros and cons of the situation respectively.

These tables show that there are substantial and measurable costs to procuring from the private sector, including the increased cost of private finance and risk premiums. Against this are the less measurable benefits sometimes called private sector efficiencies, which are primarily effective project and facilities management capabilities.

A good example of an activity which has rejected outsourcing risk management is BAA's Terminal 5 project. BAA is a UK airport operator, formerly in the public sector and now expanding the capacity of Heathrow Airport with a huge new terminal costing £4.2 billion. This has been managed by BAA with in-house skills either developed or bought in. Risks have been managed centrally with the amount transferred to contractors remaining quite small, even where rework is necessary. BAA recognises that transferring risk can be ineffective and will certainly cost money.

So is risk transfer to the private sector value for money? It can be as long as:

- a portfolio approach is taken; especially, when an additional risk is transferred, as the marginal risk premium is quite small (*But*, lenders may insist that some risks, such as contractor defaults, insurance or assets renewed earlier than planned, for instance, are provided for separately; in which case they will have their own premium and the marginal transfer will not be value for money);
- the risk can be managed more effectively by the private sector because it is a fundamental part of the activities they are undertaking (*But*, not if the risk is very big and unquantifiable: for example, when the managing cost increases over inflation is a basic activity for a contractor; but it is affected by uncontrollable factors such as regional overheating in an industry, such as that caused by the 2012 Olympics, for instance);
- the risk does not have a highly unpleasant downside, such as bankruptcy; that is, the private sector has the capacity to manage the risk.

Table 10.2   Factors which improve value for money in procurement

Factor	Response
Access to specialist core capabilities – people, processes, systems – honed in a competitive environment	But service delivery skills may be in public sector already; other skills can be bought in. This will often just come down to (project) management capabilities which will also include risk management
Stronger incentives on people to deliver	Again, an aspect of (project) management
Greater cost certainty	Not such a big concern for the public sector as the need to avoid surprises for the private sector
Reduced costs if performance is reduced	Yes, but this is not what you want
Detailed specification of what is required and disincentive to change requirement	Yes, but should be standard practice. Clients changing their minds are still commonplace and a major source of cost and time overruns

Table 10.3   Factors which detract from value for money

Factor	Response
More expensive finance (both debt and equity).	As we have discussed, debt will be possibly several per cent per year higher and there is a need to make a profit in line with investors expectations. But remember there is still a profit when skills are bought in by project managers.
Risk premiums.	Will be enormous if each risk is priced separately, but still substantial if a portfolio approach is taken. Increased by risk allocation through complex structures. Will also be big for long term risks such as inflation. Over the long term the range of possible futures is large and perhaps unimaginable.
Lack of flexibility.	This is not often valued, but even after a year or two of operation it can become apparent that you do not want, or have a use for, what you thought you wanted. Again predicting the future over many years is a very risky undertaking.

All of this means that the allocation of risk in public sector deals has to be carefully thought through and tailored to the specific circumstances. Where risk modelling can help most is in providing a quantitative understanding of how risk premiums affect prices in specific circumstances.

11 *Safety Decisions*

This book is primarily about business risk modelling. But it would not give a proper perspective without some discussion of the quantitative techniques used to estimate and control safety risk, that is, the risk of people being killed or injured. We saw in the previous chapter that a prime use of risk models is to explore downside risk, and it is no surprise that this has been done in great detail where the potential downside is so serious. A key question is how to take account of the risk of death and injury in making decisions. The political, social, cultural and ethical dimensions of this, when set alongside the managerial dimension, contribute to making this an issue that many have struggled with, without reaching any real consensus.

Perhaps the single most persuasive idea to emerge is that the approach should be precautionary. Phrased simply, this just means we should be extra careful when it comes to people's safety. This is not a lot different to the emphasis on downside risk we discussed in the previous chapter except that we do not call it a risk premium. Exercising caution is obviously a good thing, but we still have to decide how much caution is enough. This is what this chapter is about. We shall also draw out three aspects of risk analysis which receive different emphasis when the subject is safety risk, rather than business risk. These things are worth bearing in mind by all risk modellers.

Although our discussion in this chapter will focus on safety risk, similar issues, or perhaps even more intractable ones, exist for environmental risk. These include the uncertainty and incompleteness arising from the complexity of the physical modelling involved, the huge number of possible consequences – pollution, loss of amenity, extinction of species, destruction of the ozone layer, climate change and so on – and the enormity of some of the issues which threaten our own way of life and the development or survival of others.

A brief history of safety risk modelling and its use

Modelling safety risk has been, perhaps alongside reliability, the most active area of risk modelling. It is not hard to see why this is the case. People are worried about safety and go to great lengths to reduce safety risk. As a result, the chances of things going wrong are low and require more sophisticated approaches to estimate.

The simplest model begins with a list of situations which have the potential for harm; such situations are known as *hazards* in the safety field. The first aspect of safety risk is that such lists should be as comprehensive as possible (see the Aspects of Safety Risk Modelling (1): Completeness box). The model can then be calculated by quantifying each hazard.

The development of more substantial models, with a more complex function relating the outputs to the inputs, began in earnest when people started to model the consequences of accidents in nuclear reactors. It was discovered that the radioactive material released could disperse over large areas, directly irradiating people, getting inhaled, settling on the ground and entering the food chain, or travelling though many other pathways to humans. This,

---

Aspects of Safety Risk Modelling (1): Completeness

A key feature of all safety risk modelling is the emphasis on completeness. This means taking the aspiration to identify all the safety risks associated with an activity seriously. Of course, any risk model should aim to do this, but we know that we have to balance this aim with the realisation that adding more risks to our register is subject to the law of diminishing returns and indeed runs the risk of cluttering up the register with unmanageable amounts of dross. Much better (though easier said than done), is to have an 80:20 first shot and then carry out regular reviews which include asking whether there is anything material missing.

When we deal with safety issues, we recognise that the diminishing returns kick in much later. This typically results in much more structured and detailed risk workshops using, for example, a technique called HAZOPS (hazard and operability studies). Again, fault trees might be developed in such a way that they contain every possible source of failure. As a result, safety risk models tend to contain large numbers of individual risks, many of which have a very low likelihood.

---

combined with a dose–response model which postulated that any small dose of radiation brings a small (and proportional) chance of fatal cancer, meant that the worst case scenarios were very bad indeed: hundred of thousands or millions of people might die. Furthermore, the economic impact would be enormous too. The Chernobyl accident demonstrated these consequences in an all too real and tragic way.

However, pre-Chernobyl, it was thought that such worst cases should be very unlikely. This was because the reliability measures would make the chance of an accident remote, the containment measures would make the chance of a release of radioactive material even more remote and finally the environmental conditions would only rarely lead to the worst cases of irradiation.

As a result, a major activity began in the nuclear industry in the 1960s to create risk models of nuclear reactors. The models used fault trees to estimate the frequency of accidents in which the energy-generating and radioactive core of the reactor is destroyed, generally because it could not be cooled. The models went to great lengths to model the actual probability with which highly redundant and diverse safety systems might nonetheless fail. They used event trees to model the likelihood of the physical failure of containment systems – typically very strong reinforced concrete domes. They used other physical models to examine the dispersion in the environment of any radioactive material which could be released and what its impact on people might be.

The results were presented in various ways, but perhaps the most useful was the fN-curve which is a variant of the S-curve we have seen so many times, but adapted for this specific purpose (see the box Aspects of Safety Risk Modelling (2): Frequencies).

Aspects of Safety Risk Modelling (2): Frequencies

In analysing project risk, we develop risk registers which are based on probabilities; each entry contains the probability that a risk emerges during the project. These probabilities will often be small and will generally be based around the idea that the risk can happen at most once during the project.

In Chapter 5 we discussed a slightly different model for basic risks based on the idea that the probability of a risk materialising during a given time interval is proportional to the length of the interval, with the constant of proportionality called the frequency. Again, this is used where the probability is small. The statistical model underlying this is the Poisson process, which allows the possibility that the risk could happen more than once and indeed, where the interval is sufficiently long, forces it to do so. The relationship between the Poisson parameter, the frequency and the classical definition of frequency as the number of observations was discussed in Chapter 5.

The frequency model is what is invariably used in safety risk modelling. As a result, instead of drawing S-curves, it is usual to characterise the output of safety risk models by fN-curves. The consequence axis is typically the number of deaths which might be caused, N, and the probability axis is replaced by a frequency axis, hence the term fN. What is drawn is the frequency of incidents which cause N fatalities or more. This can be contrasted with the S-curve – as shown in this book – where we plot the probability of consequences equal to C or less. Thus, whilst the S-curve has a positive slope, the fN slope is negative. The reason for this is the emphasis on high consequences in safety analysis and, specifically, the possibility that some accidents may have consequences an order of magnitude more than others, hopefully with probabilities that are at least an order of magnitude less. This leads to the other difference in fN-curves: they are logarithmic. You can make accountants nervous by talking about the logarithm of their money, but safety people are well used to looking at the logarithm of fatalities. Of course this opens up the criticism that this approach de-emphasises very large accidents. For an illustration of the techniques, see the Case Study: Single Lead Junctions box.

Putting frequency models alongside probability models sometimes causes great confusion. There is no reason for this. All you have to do is define a period T over which you will look at the probability of safety incidents. For a risk which has frequency f and consequence N you now have several one-off risks depending on the number of times the event happens. The probability that it happens n times is $e^{-ft}(fT)^n/n!$ You can use this to draw a S-curve as shown in Figure 11.1 for the case where f is once per year, T is a year and $N = 1$.

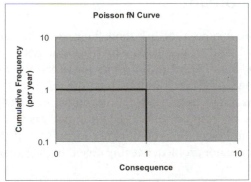
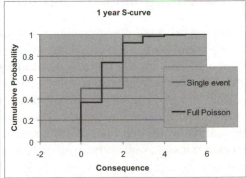

Figure 11.1   fN-curves and S-curves

It is less complex to replace the Poisson risk profile with a single one-off risk with the same expected value and variance. This has probability $fT/(1 + fT)$ and consequence $N(1 + fT)$. Such a single point risk is also marked on Figure 11.1 by the lighter, thinner line. Where fT is small, that is, the time interval is small enough that the possibility of more than one event can be discounted, the probability is fT and the consequence is N, as you would expect. In this way you can put your safety and reliability events into your probability risk register. If you do not have a fixed length project, use $T = 10$ years. It really does not matter, given the uncertainty of most risk estimates. And, if you have a frequency risk register you can do the reverse, taking T as the duration of the project or perhaps the actual frequency during the time you are exposed to the risk.

Although the fN-curve is not immediately easy to grasp for most people, it enjoys the advantages of S-curves discussed in Chapter 3, and is very good way of representing risk. As a result, it was immediately considered for use when it came to making decisions about the acceptability of the various risks which had been estimated for nuclear reactors. A number of lines were proposed, with the intention that they should represent at each point an upper limit on what could be allowed for the fN-curve of a nuclear facility.

The risk work had represented a major investment by the nuclear industry, both to make reactors safer and to convince others of their safety. Other industries soon began to build on this. First the hazardous chemical industry developed safety risk models for processing sites, including offshore installations, driven partly by the Flixborough accident and later by Piper Alpha. The Seveso accident in Italy contributed to European legislation on major hazards and prompted other countries, notably the Netherlands, to support their hazard control and safety regulation activities with quantified site risk models. The philosophy and techniques used were similar to those developed by the nuclear industry; although obviously the physical mechanisms modelled for the release and dispersion of dangerous substances were different from those of the way they can injure and kill people.

The transport of hazardous materials was also an issue which could be addressed through quantitative analysis and, naturally enough, so was the transport of people, especially by rail. A series of serious accidents on the railways, of which the most serious was the Clapham Junction accident in 1987, indicated that railway risk models could also be beneficial (see also the Case Study: Single Lead Junctions box).

Risk based regulation – a rational dream

In parallel with these developments it became obvious that risk modelling could be used as a tool to support decisions about safety risk and in particular whether an activity was safe enough. This applied not only to complex, high-hazard technologies for which the risk models were needed, but also to more mundane workplace risks for which the risk could be calculated straightforwardly from statistics. You might have needed a risk model in 1990 to see what the risk reduction to passengers might be from advanced signalling systems which could automatically stop trains passing signals at danger, but you only needed to look at the number of trackside workers being killed to find a major problem needing urgent management action.

Broadly speaking, the aspiration was to have a process in which:

- you calculate the risk;
- you calculate the cost of reducing the risk;
- you adjust for other factors which you think are important, such as the size of individual accidents (multi-fatality risks as shown on fN-curves), the controllability or familiarity of the risk and so on;
- if the cost is too high, the activity is safe enough.

This, it was thought, would enable transparent regulatory decisions to be made which would enjoy universal consensus because of their obvious rationality. It would avoid resources being dissipated in making safer those activities which were already safe enough and free them up for something more useful. This might include improving the safety of other activities which were not safe enough and, once everything was considered safe enough, enjoying an

Case Study: Single Lead Junctions

This is based on a real example of a safety risk management problem, although the model and numbers are completely fabricated and unrealistic.

In the 1970s and 1980s British Rail achieved maintenance economies by removing track. Railway junctions and their points are maintenance intensive, especially where one line crosses another. You can remove this by having single lead junctions where the branch line is reduced to a single line before it meets the main line (see Figure 11.2).

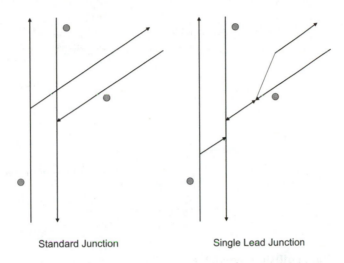

Standard Junction   Single Lead Junction

Figure 11.2   Comparison of standard and single lead junction

The single lead arrangement removed some track, along with the troublesome flat crossing. This means that in spite of doubling the number of points from two to four, it is easier to engineer the main line for increased speed, especially where the main line is curved. (Think about how it all works with the cant, or camber in road terms.)

However the single lead, marked with an arrow at each end showing that the section must carry trains in each direction, clearly increases risk. Single track lines with bidirectional working capability are inherently higher risk, necessitating the use of tokens, for example, to ensure that only one train at a time uses a stretch of line. But tokens are clearly impractical for the short stretches at single lead junctions, so safety depends on a signalling system.

All junctions carry the risk that train drivers will not stop at signals and cause collisions. For example, a train moving downwards at the standard junction on the main line will conflict with a train moving upwards on the main line onto the branch. If the signaller resolves the conflict by holding the main line train, but it does not stop, there is likely to be a collision. Note, however, that if the signaller resolves the conflict by holding the train turning onto the branch, and that does not stop, the collision is likely to be avoided because the signalling system will ensure it carries on the main line harmlessly, at least for the time being.

But the single lead arrangement adds a conflict which did not exist before. Trains moving simultaneously on and off the branch line do not conflict in the standard arrangement, but compete for the single lead in the new one. This creates the possibility of head-on collisions. The main additional risk is where the train from the branch line SPADs (commits a Signal Passed At Danger), coming into conflict with trains signalled onto the branch line, or moving downward on the main line. There are specific reasons why this error is more likely, especially where the signal is at a station and the train is starting away.

The event tree in Figure 11.3 shows what can happen. The probabilities are highly dependent on the circumstances which might promote driver error, such as the acceleration of the trains, lateness and many other factors. The split between high and low consequence is also determined by many things: train speed, loading, time of day, local topography, but is highly uncertain in any case.

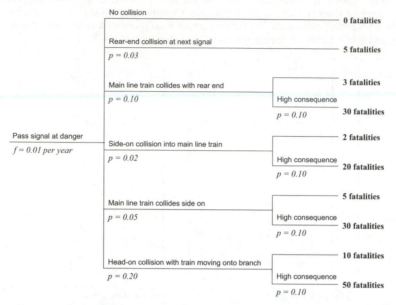

Figure 11.3   Train collision event tree

These figures are presented solely to provide an illustration of fN-curves; they are not intended to represent any real situation. Altogether there are 9 fatal accident sequences – the number of end points on Figure 11.3 ignoring the zero fatality 'safe' sequence at the top – and the fN-curve for this is shown in Figure 11.4.

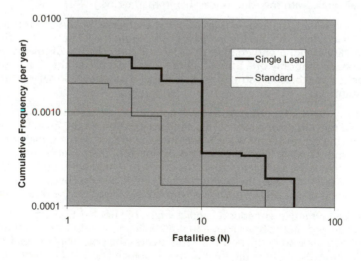

Figure 11.4   Train collision fN-curves

Removing the head-on sequence by reverting to the standard layout greatly reduces the fN-curve. If you calculate the product of frequency and consequence for each sequence, you can show that the expected number of fatalities has reduced from approximately 0.04 per year to 0.01 per year, a risk reduction of about 70 per cent.

Unfortunately British Rail did experience a number of fatal accidents at single lead arrangements in the 1980s and 1990s and, supported by risk assessments, their use was phased out. They were no longer good practice.

improved standard of living in other ways. The adjusting factors in the third bullet point on page 160 are interesting: they show the need for estimates of the spread in consequences, but also ring an alarm bell as to how rational the process could be.

In the UK, the legal environment was amenable to this approach. In a landmark judgement in 1949 (Edwards v The National Coal Board, 1 All ER 743) the Court of Appeal clarified the term 'reasonably practicable' which then, as now, is the standard for reducing risk:

'Reasonably practicable' is a narrower term than 'physically possible' ... a computation must be made by the owner in which the quantum of risk is placed on one scale and the sacrifice involved in the measures necessary for averting the risk (whether in money, time or trouble) is placed in the other, and that, if it be shown that there is a gross disproportion between them – the risk being insignificant in relation to the sacrifice – the defendants discharge the onus on them.

This is roughly in line with the approach outlined. The judgement introduces the term 'gross disproportion' to indicate there must be enough clear water between the risk and the cost (or 'sacrifice' – a rather emotive term!) to justify that the activity is safe enough. The judgement introduces an appropriate element of caution in favour of doing something unless it is demonstrably not worth it, but otherwise the risk based approach could usher in a brave new world of rational allocation of resources even for safety issues, including those major technological hazards which, it was feared, would be difficult to get a grip on.

The approach was also auspicious as there was a move toward a regulatory safety case regime. The idea of this was that operators would have to produce a document, the *safety case*, in which they told the story of why their operations were safe enough. Part of this would be a detailed explanation of the risks the operations entailed, how they were each controlled and what the level of residual risk was once the controls had been imposed. This regime started out in the nuclear industry and was imported successively into the hazardous chemical, offshore oil and gas and railway industries, chasing the development of safety risk models.

The awakening

Of course, the dream remained exactly that. Broadly speaking, there were two main reasons it did not work out:

1. Risk analysis was not up to the job.
2. Most people do not buy into rationality.

As a result, there was – understandably – another reason:

3. lack of commitment from the regulators.

RISK ANALYSIS WAS NOT UP TO THE JOB

This is no surprise to those of you who have read carefully up to now. We have cheerfully accepted the subjective nature of most business risk models. We have argued that rough sketches of outcome ranges provide useful data, but do not represent any fundamental or scientific truth. To think you can avoid this is an illusion. Safety risk models are built with much more care and can, with much better justification, be quantified using historical data. But they still struggle to deal with many areas of technological and scientific uncertainty. And, even more fundamentally, they still have find a way to deal with managerial error. You only have to look at the space shuttle or Clapham Junction to see that (see the Management as a Source of Risk box).

So, regulators had to deal with large amounts of uncertainty in risk modelling; there was little that could be done about that (see the Aspects of Safety Risk Modelling (3): Uncertainty box). This problem was supplemented by what might politely be called poor quality risk analysis and safety cases. Much of the risk modelling contained howlers of one sort or another, and did not own up to their shortcomings, whether these were totally guessed failure probabilities or inappropriate coarseness in the modelling. Many people doing risk analysis simply did not understand the regulatory guidance. Safety cases also tended to degenerate into copied and pasted variants of each other, with far more importance being attached to the contents of each chapter satisfying a pre-ordained checklist, than telling a coherent safety story.

Understandably, this riled regulators. Perhaps the approach was too sophisticated to be carried through.

MOST PEOPLE DO NOT BUY INTO RATIONALITY

A more fundamental problem is that the approach, however well explained, however scientifically based, would never gain universal acceptance.

It is not the place of this book to describe cultural theories of risk perception and risk acceptance. But only a minority buy into the hierarchical model which is implicit in the concept of a government regulator taking decisions on our behalf, telling us what to do based on sums which apparently optimise social welfare functions (as utility is known in this context), throwing in a handful of the precautionary principle here, going the extra mile for safety there, and making sure some weight is given to equity considerations.

Management as a Source of Risk

Although many of the railway accidents in the 1980s and 1990s were caused by trains passing signals at danger because of driver error, Clapham Junction was not: the signal showed green when it should not have. This is called a wrong-side failure and is considered rare because signalling systems are designed to be fail-safe. Clapham Junction was caused by a signalling maintenance error which would typically not form part of a risk model. Similarly, a wrong-side failure caused by poor signalling maintenance practices probably led to the chilling railway accident in the Severn Tunnel in 1991, which is not widely known as no one was killed.

The point I am making is that driver error was a long term problem which received close management attention over decades; maintenance error did not. This was a management failure. There are many more examples and they tend to undermine risk models.

Aspects of Safety Risk Modelling (3): Uncertainty

Whilst business risk modellers live with subjectivity, helping their clients understand and reach an agreed view of the appropriate risk model for their organisation, this is not a luxury open to safety risk modellers. Most people would take a dim view of a safety decision made on the basis that '10^{-4} seemed about right to me,' without some good supporting evidence.

This requirement for sound decision making led to work on understanding the uncertainty in risk models. The question which seemed sensible to ask was: 'what range of risk might reasonably be estimated from the information available?' I was closely involved in some of this work.

Various approaches were tried:

- ranges

- statistical confidence bounds

- probability distributions on the risk parameters

- complex degree of belief formalisms such as fuzzy set theory.

The probabilistic approach in particular was vulnerable to the criticism that it dealt in probabilities of probabilities, which some people found difficult; although not those used to Bayesian inference, an approach which utilises exactly this concept.

What was evident though, was that people did not know what to do with the results. It was more information than they needed. To the extent that, for example, knowledge of the uncertainty in a risk assessment could help people take a reasonably precautionary approach, it was apparent that people felt much more confident with a single, conservatively derived, risk number. It might therefore become a matter of negotiation about the degree of conservatism to be applied, rather than an examination of the full range of possible results. This was especially the case where this range was very wide and a precautionary approach could turn into total inaction because of the possibility (albeit with small probability, you might think) of the risk being very high.

However, it still seems to me that a formal exploration of the set of risk analyses which are consistent with a set of suitable and agreed-upon evidence is a useful idea and deserves more attention in the safety arena. It might be an improvement on the vague Treasury guidance referred to in Chapter 9, urging us to explore the decision space.

On this theory, other people are variously individualists, egalitarians and fatalists, and with this comes their own philosophy of how governments should behave and their own, dearly held rationality. You can see that the title of this section is a bit provocative. By rationality I mean using the results of risk models to allocate resources. That is what I think is rational and I believe in this enough to get angry if I see resources being allocated in some other way. But, I also recognise that telling people who think differently that they are wrong will not be effective. This causes frustration among the hierarchalists who seem committed to the belief that if they shout loud enough people will understand.

For example, the UK Health and Safety Executive (HSE), in its 2001 document *Reducing Risk, Protecting People*: *HSE's decision making process*, (available from their website at www.hse. gov.uk) says:

Other studies on perception of risk have led to a theory which considers that it may be simplistic to believe that it will be possible to derive a quantifiable physical reality that most people will agree represents the 'true' risk from a hazard. (11)

If you have understood this book at all I hope that by now you will be saying 'no kidding, Sherlock'. After some discussion they go on to conclude:

The net result is that, increasingly, people are having to rely on authoritative bodies such as HSC/E as a source of reassurance about the arrangements in place for protecting people and the impartiality of those arrangements. These bodies for their part are acutely aware that they would not be able to provide reassurance unless they are trusted and that trust will not be bestowed but will have to be earned. (HSE 2001, 19)

I think the first quotation means they are wasting their time in the second. It certainly does not win them *my* trust. This naturally leads on to the third point.

LACK OF COMMITMENT BY THE REGULATORS

Regulators like the HSE are in a difficult position. They cannot please everyone, but can easily please no one. Their built-in response to this, as members of the hierarchy, is to flood us with apparently reasonable and clearly written documents. They cannot afford to commit to new approaches and the rational allocation of resources. Needless to say, their document on decision making does not say 'less than one in a million per year is OK; more is unacceptable', nor even 'maximise expected utility where the value of averted risk is £1 million per expected fatality', although buried within it is a conclusion with similar wording.

To understand what they do say, we need to look at a bit more history. The turning point was the inquiry into the Sizewell 'B' nuclear reactor. The inquiry inspector, the admirable Sir Frank Layfield, examined the approach to risk based regulation put in front of him at the inquiry and was broadly supportive of a risk based approach, but felt there was lot missing. He therefore administered a well deserved kick up the backside to HSE and required them to issue more complete guidance. This they did in a document called *The Tolerability of Risk from Nuclear Power Stations* (1988) and 13 years later they formalised this as their approach to all decision making about risk. Naturally this took account of another 13 years of experience across the different industries where risk models and safety cases had been applied, and also of course, where they had not been.

Stripping out the verbiage, and especially the ifs and buts, the HSE approach now has three broad threads:

1. There is a level of risk which in unacceptable; below this we will tolerate risk in order to secure benefits as long as it is not reasonably practicable to reduce the risk.
2. Good current practice is (by definition) reasonably practicable.
3. Where there is uncertainty we apply the precautionary principle.

We will discuss each of these in a little more detail, but you can see already that the HSE has provided itself with a couple of ratchets in the second two points that will take us beyond the possibly rational approach of the first.

Unacceptable and tolerable risk

It is reasonable for the HSE to set unacceptable levels of risk. They make this one in one thousand per year for a worker, as part of their work, and one in ten thousand for everyone else. It is an equity based criterion, not a utility based one; that is, it considers the rights of individuals for protection, not just the good of the whole. Furthermore, with regard to the risk of a multi-fatality accident in which 50 or more people are killed, it is considered unacceptable for the frequency to be more than 2×10^{-4} per year: one in 5000 years.

Assuming the level of risk is not plainly unacceptable, it might be tolerated because there is a benefit, but only if there is no reasonably practicable way to reduce it. We have discussed the 'gross disproportion' interpretation of reasonably practicable, and this is a utility based idea where 'gross' implies a generous valuation of averted risk. The HSE propose a number in the order of £1 million per averted expected (in the statistical sense) fatality. They also introduce a level of risk which is broadly acceptable. This is simply a level (set at a risk of death of one in a million per year) below which there is a presumption that further improvements will not be reasonably practicable. You are not relieved of your reasonably practicable duties below this level, so it has little practical effect.

You should also read the HSE spin on gross disproportion and, apparently, guidance to inspectors, taken from their website (www.hse.gov.uk/risk/theory/alarpglance.htm) in August 2006:

> *In essence, making sure a risk has been reduced ALARP is about weighing the risk against the sacrifice needed to further reduce it. The decision is weighted in favour of health and safety because the presumption is that the duty-holder should implement the risk reduction measure. To avoid having to make this sacrifice, the duty-holder must be able to show that it would be grossly disproportionate to the benefits of risk reduction that would be achieved. Thus, the process is not one of balancing the costs and benefits of measures but, rather, of adopting measures except where they are ruled out because they involve grossly disproportionate sacrifices.*

If you re-read what the Appeal Court actually said, you may think this goes a step further than they intended.

Good practice is reasonably practicable

This is intended to reduce the amount of sophisticated risk analysis. It is presumed that once a practice has hit the standards or codes of practice it is good practice and, by definition, reasonably practicable. Needless to say, while you cannot avoid implementing good practice, you are not relieved of a duty to look for and implement something even better if it is reasonably practicable. It is indeed a ratchet.

The precautionary principle

As is this relatively new idea. It originated in 1993 at the Rio summit (officially called the Earth Summit: The United Nations Conference on Environment and Development [UNCED]), whose official statement said:

> *Where there are threats of serious or irreversible environmental damage, lack of full scientific certainty shall not be used as a reason for postponing cost effective measures to prevent environmental degradation.*

Whilst originally drawn up in the context of environmental risk, the HSE plausibly adopted this for regulating safety risk. You could reasonably ask what it is supposed to mean. How do you know it is 'cost effective' if there is no certainty? Does it just mean 'if people are worried, do something – anything'?

In practice, the HSE apply the precautionary principle in many layers which will make the risk assessment conservative – that is, so as to overestimate the risk. This is similar to the bounding methods we discussed in Chapter 3. It may be necessary to meet people's concerns about safety, but it takes us a long way from reaching a balanced view where we can be confident that we are not systematically and knowingly misallocating resources. Arguably we have reached the point where we have no confidence that our risk taking is balanced, and we cannot demonstrate we are allocating our resources sensibly in a world which remains full of danger, in spite of its comfortable gloss for those of us lucky enough to live in affluent western societies.

As a matter of interest you can read 'The Precautionary Principle is Incoherent', a paper by Martin Peterson (in: *Risk Analysis*, 26:3, June 2006) which proves its title mathematically. This apparently contradicts HSE's view that their framework is coherent, although it is unlikely they would recognise Peterson's premises.

DOES IT MATTER?

It is easy to poke fun at the hapless HSE. Their business is improving safety at work and they explicitly disown responsibility for the wider impacts of their action. It is not for them to worry if they make railways too expensive and force people into dangerous and polluting cars. This, they say, is a matter for government. In response, the Treasury have supplemented *The Green Book* with guidance on risk to the public. (This was touched on critically in the Health Effects box in Chapter 9.) This document too is verbose and inconclusive. None of this is surprising: if safety regulators do not retreat into a cloud of impenetrable precaution, they will be replaced by others who do exactly that.

But I think it does matter. We do not have unlimited resources. We cannot afford excessive levels of caution. Yet we live in a world where precautionary behaviour is seen as increasingly acceptable. The police are allowed to inflict high economic costs on society through increasingly long accident investigations which prevent resumption of services. One of the most unbalanced decisions ever taken must be Railtrack's 'nervous breakdown' in the wake of the Hatfield accident, closing large parts of the system for months and inflicting untold inconvenience on passengers, for reasons which any cigarette packet risk calculation would have told you was not worth it. We strangle ourselves in increasing red tape, putting trivia in risk registers, whilst we fiddle ineffectually in the face of big risks like climate change, or low profile risks like inadequate access to healthcare. We take an age to recognise that we are not receiving the benefits – reduced risk of waiting, reduced risk of discomfort and pain, reduced risk of death – of increased expenditure on the NHS. The individual risk of death to British service personnel in Afghanistan, at the time of writing in September 2006, is running at 15–25 times the maximum tolerable limit for workers set by the HSE. Risk in wars is always excluded from the normal framework. Why?

We need more confidence that we are getting the most from what we have available and that is why I would like to see renewed commitment to the idea of using risk analysis and making it work instead of worrying ourselves into inaction over its failings.

What does it mean for business risk modellers?

I included this chapter to broaden perspectives a bit, by providing risk modelling experience from another area, and by emphasising the point that not using risk analysis can be risky. You need to pay attention to downsides, but not the very low probability downsides which are the domain of safety people. No one ever got rich by worrying about one per cent chances, let alone one in a million ones.

Yet perhaps there are some lessons here for the business risk modeller:

1. your assessment is worthless if you leave something important out: it is worth being very careful not to do this by inviting a wide range of views and not rejecting ideas too early;
2. probabilities and frequencies are both legitimate models: be comfortable with both and work with both;
3. remember that you are dealing with subjective probabilities: what other assessment might you or someone else make in the light of the evidence available?
4. you will not do anyone any favours by applying excessive caution, layers of conservatism or anything else which distorts your risk model: unlike the HSE you will go out of business;
5. whilst avoiding excessive caution, we have seen that greater concern about downside risk is legitimate, in business risk as well as safety: the key issue is not to let this ratchet out of control;
6. and finally, safety management is extremely important and must be reasonably precautionary: be very careful about thinking about safety risks in the same way you think about business risks.

To build on the last point, some people like the idea of integrated risk management systems where all risks are kept on the same database and subject to common analysis. 'After all,' they argue, in a vaguely plausible way, 'many risks have both financial and safety consequences.' It works in principle, but in practice it is fraught with problems. Think safety, then think business.

IV *Techniques*

This section underpins everything that goes before. It contains:

- a description of probability theory in enough detail (but no more) to support the previous sections;
- a review of the most popular technique for calculating risk models – Monte Carlo – which should enable you to produce useful results and understand the shortcomings;
- a brief summary of some other techniques, most notably the direct method, which will enable very simple calculations to be carried out in some circumstances;
- and a summary of decision theory, again in just enough detail to enable you to compare and contrast the theory with what people actually do when making risk decisions, especially with reference to Part III.

This section is much more mathematical than the previous ones and is directed at practitioners. However, I have tried to give fairly informal explanations, so I hope that some of it will be accessible to the general reader.

12 *Probability*

This chapter provides a review of probability theory focused on those aspects of this extensive body of knowledge which are useful to develop and understand the risk models described earlier in the book.

We shall begin by describing the concepts of a random process and random variables. From this we can define probability and probability distributions. The main characteristics of probability distributions are defined and a summary of the best known distributions is provided in terms of these characteristics. This will provide a set of building blocks for risk models.

We then go on to some of the most important approximate properties of random variables. These enable us both to predict – to some degree – the results of risk modelling and to understand the results when we have them. This mitigates the black box effect.

Finally we consider the relevance of all this to risk analysis in organisations.

Random processes and random variables

Some things that happen in the world are pretty much predictable, especially if they are related to some basic physics. The sun will rise at the time printed in the paper. Your alarm will go off at the time you programmed it to. When you switch on the kettle for coffee, it will draw perhaps ten amps, depending on its rating.

But most things are less predictable. You do not know exactly what time you will arrive at work and you certainly cannot be sure what awaits you there. You do know it is much more likely to be something that ratchets up pressure and stress levels than the opposite. More mundanely, the ten amps will vary, depending on the voltage delivered by the power station that morning. It changes a bit, but hardly ever enough to make a noticeable, let alone significant, difference.

'Much more likely?' 'Hardly ever?' We certainly have a rich vocabulary to use to describe these unpredictable situations. The challenge is to see if we can do a bit better than to tell the chief executive, 'we are pretty unlikely to go bankrupt'. It is 'odds on' that this will make increased stress a self-fulfilling prediction, with a 'remote chance' of an early reunion with the coffee kettle at home.

One solution is to develop the idea of *randomness*. This means that, for at least some part of the model, you abandon the idea of a deterministic relationship between cause and effect, between input and output, and replace it with something which is explicitly unpredictable. You can then ask what characterises this unpredictable element.

To make further progress we introduce the idea of a *repeatable experiment*. We can measure the supply voltage at 7 o'clock each morning. We can measure the number of radioactive decays in an hour. We can measure the lifetime of a batch of bulbs. We can measure the number of defective items on a car assembly line. We can measure the number of days per year it rains in Manchester. We can measure the number of Virgin trains from Manchester which turn up on time in London each day. We can measure the number of Labour victories in general elections since 1900. By examining these measurements, and by imagining that we could obtain an unlimited amount of data by repeating the experiment indefinitely, we can start to understand the nature of randomness and replace deterministic predictions with something else.

It is clear this is an idealisation. For a start there is no such thing as an infinitely repeatable experiment. There is only one set of election results since 1900. There are only a finite number of days since Virgin trains have been running from Manchester. Secondly, we know intuitively that this exercise is only going to be useful if none of the underlying factors changes. Virgin bought some new trains and ran them according to a new timetable on an upgraded infrastructure. All of this is going to change the characteristics of randomness as it affects punctuality. Thirdly, the world, and particularly the world as modified by human decisions and actions, is profoundly not random; just uncertain.

We shall return to this at the end of the chapter, because the nature of this uncertainty is obviously very important for risk analysis in organisations, where it is exactly human decisions and actions which are responsible for outcomes. But for now we take a more positive approach to the idea of repeatable experiments and ask what it can do for us.

It certainly does a lot for bookmakers who deploy the randomness concept to good effect. The idea that the outcome of a horse race can be considered the result of a random process is a credible one. But you can bet on many other propositions for which this is less the case. For example, at the time of writing the English football authorities had just appointed a new manager and before the appointment you could place bets on who the successful candidate was going to be. Given that the appointment would be decided by a small number of people in suits, it is not at all clear that that this could be considered as random (although in fairness these are suits celebrated for their capriciousness and absence of logic). Predictably there were allegations of bet fixing.

The key idea for turning repeatable experiments into something usable is *statistical regularity*. This means that the fraction of experiments with a particular outcome, the *relative frequency*, tends to stabilise to a particular number. For example, the number of experiments in which there is exactly one radioactive decay in an hour might be:

- 4 in the first 10 experiments
- 33 in the first 100 experiments (4, 5, 0, 1, 2, 2, 5, 4, 5, 5 in each batch of 10)
- 355 in the first 1000 experiments (33, 39, 31, 31, 33, 36, 42, 36, 40, 34 in each batch of 100)
- 3677 in the first 10 000 experiments (355, 365, 366, 356, 365, 379, 355, 392, 370, 374 in each batch of 1000).

You can see that the fraction of experiments with one decay is stabilising around 36.8 per cent, which was the 'correct' value for the way I designed the 'experiment', which was actually a numerical simulation of the random process.

You can also see that the relative frequency of an outcome, or event, has some specific properties. It must lie between zero and one, inclusive. The relative frequency of the combination of two mutually exclusive events is the sum of their individual relative frequencies. And the relative frequency of the event which comprises all possible outcomes is one.

Obviously, it is only a short step conceptually from a stabilised relative frequency to a *probability*. That is, the probability of an outcome, or event, is the stable value of the relative frequency with which it occurs in a large number of repetitions of the experiment. Equally obvious, the three properties of relative frequencies just mentioned also apply to the probability of events. It turns out that this is enough to develop the whole theory of probability, although we do not need to explore this further here.

To summarise, if you have a repeatable experiment you can define the probability of one of the outcomes of the experiment as the stable value of the relative frequency of the outcome you would find as you repeated the experiment an ever greater number of times. The important point is that the theory you can build on this basis *can* be used even where there is no underlying repeatable experiment. Whether you *should* use it is discussed later.

It is worth giving a warning whilst the data from the simulated experiment is fresh in our minds. Perhaps you were surprised that there were four occurrences of five decays in the first ten batches of ten. Could that really have happened by chance? In fact the chance of this is pretty low: there is a probability of 17 per cent of having exactly five incidences of a single decay in ten experiments. This translates to a 6 per cent probability of having exactly four incidents of this in ten such super experiments. But it is not that low. You can naturally find apparently non-random patterns in any simulation of a random process. Be careful not to be fooled: many have been.

The final concept here is that of the *random variable*. Instead of the number of experiments with a certain outcome, consider some function of the outcome which could be scored, that is, could be represented as a number. For example, the following lists the total number of radioactive decays in the simulation described above:

- 8 in the first 10 experiments (2, 0, 1, 0, 1, 1, 2, 1, 0, 0 in each experiment)
- 111 in the first 100 experiments (8, 11, 17, 12, 8, 8, 12, 16, 10, 9 in each batch of 10)
- 1038 in the first 1000 experiments (111, 98, 95, 113, 119, 98, 95, 102, 107, 100 in each batch of 100)
- 10 086 in the first 10 000 experiments (1038, 1031, 963, 967, 946, 1023, 1076, 1024, 995, 1023 in each batch of 1000).

The number of decays is a random variable. Its behaviour is determined by the probabilities associated with each outcome (0, 1, 2, … decays in the hour of the experiment). The data show that again the random variable is stabilising in some sense to around one per hour, which is, of course, exactly how it was designed.

The random variable can take several values, each one having a probability. This is known as a probability distribution. You need to keep clear in your mind the distinction between the probability of an event and the probability distribution of a random variable. To repeat, the distinction is that the random variable is a numerical function defined for each event.

Other random variables more relevant to organisational risk analysis include the total cost of a project (or its duration), the internal rate of return of an uncertain cash flow, the number of performance points for collecting waste in a timely way and so on.

Probability distributions

Without being too mathematical, we have defined the probability of events and how this leads into the probability distribution of random variables. These probability distributions are the basic building blocks for risk models which are concerned with calculating the probability distribution of output random variables based on the probability distribution of input random variables.

We now describe some simple random processes and the probability distributions they give rise to. They can be grouped into either discrete distributions, where there are separately identifiable possible outcomes, or continuous distributions, where the random variable may take any value in a range.

DISCRETE PROBABILITY DISTRIBUTIONS

Coins, dice and uniform distribution

The best known probability distribution is that which arises from the toss of a fair coin. There are only two events, heads or tails, and the fact that the coin is fair means each is equally likely. Since the probabilities add to one, there is no choice but to make the probability of each event 0.5. Another example is the throw of a fair dice, where the same reasoning says the chance of any of the six possibilities is 1/6.

Neither of these is a probability distribution as such, as there is no random variable, but if we identify the score on the dice as the random variable, then it takes the values 1, 2, 3, 4, 5 and 6 each with a probability of 1/6.

Repeated coin tossing and binomial distribution

If you toss a coin N times an obvious random variable is the number of heads. If you toss it three times, then there are eight outcomes, each with an equal probability of 1/8. Of these, one has three heads, three have two heads, another three have one head and one has no heads. So the corresponding probability distribution of the number of heads is: pr(0 heads) = 1/8, pr(1 head) = 3/8, pr(2 heads) = 3/8, pr(3 heads) = 1/8, where we are using the convention that pr(E) represents the probability of event, E.

For a more general case, where there are two possibilities, the event either happens at each experiment (with probability p) or it does not (with probability $1 - p$) the corresponding result for the number of times the event happens in N trials is:

$$p_n = pr(n \text{ events}) = (N!/n!(N-n)!)p^n(1-p)^{N-n}$$

where $n!$ means n factorial, that is, $1 \times 2 \times 3 \ldots \times (n-1) \times n$. Broadly speaking the $p^n(1-p)^{N-n}$ term is the probability of any of the sequences in which the event happens n times (and therefore does not happen $N - n$ times), and the $N!/n!(N-n)!$ term is the number of such sequences. This discrete probability distribution, described by p_n, is known as a binomial distribution.

The Poisson process

The previous section provided data on a radioactive decay process. The underlying process was assumed to be one where the probability that a given atom decays during a short interval is proportional to the size of the interval. Suppose there are N atoms (a very large number) and that the probability of any one of these decaying during the interval is FT where F is the decay rate and T is the size of the interval. In these circumstances the number of decays during the interval is given by the binomial distribution:

$$p_n = pr(n \text{ decays}) = (N!/n!(N-n)!)(FT)^n(1-FT)^{N-n}$$

$$\approx e^{-NFT}(NFT)^n/n! = e^{-ft}(fT)^n/n! = e^{-q}q^n/n!.$$

Note that $N! / (N - n)!$ is approximately N^n and $(1 - FT)^N$ is approximately e^{-NFT}, which you can see by taking logs of both sides and noting that $\ln(1 - FT)$ is approximately $-FT$.

In the formula $f = NF$, the product of the large number of atoms and the small probability of any individual one decaying per unit time, is assumed to be roughly comparable with the inverse of the observation time T, over which a reasonable number of decays might be seen. That means the parameter $q = fT$ is of order one.

In risk analysis, the Poisson process is important because it represents events that may happen several times rather than just once. This is typically the case for safety risk analysis, where the chance of an accident occurring might be represented as once every thousand years, for example. This means that $f = 0.001$ per year in the formula. So the probability of one occurrence in 10 years is $q = 1$ per cent and the probability of two is $q^2/2 = 0.005$ per cent, which is very small.

CONTINUOUS PROBABILITY DISTRIBUTIONS

Some random variables can take a continuous range of values and their probability distribution is correspondingly defined on a range. This necessitates an additional concept, the probability density function, which locally is the probability that the variable falls within an interval divided by the size of the interval. Probability density functions can be quite difficult to understand for non-specialists. An alternative is the cumulative probability distribution, which is defined as the probability that a random variable is less than some value. We denote probability density functions by $p(x)$ such that:

$$\int_{x_1}^{x_2} p(x)dx = \mathrm{pr}\,(x_1 \leq x \leq x_2)$$

and cumulative probability functions by $P(x)$ so that:

$$P(x) = \int_{-\infty}^{x} p(x')dx'$$

from which

$$p(x) = \frac{dP(x)}{dx}.$$

The uniform distribution

The idea of a probability density function is most easily understood in the context of a uniform distribution. Say that all that is known is that the random variable lies between a and b. Then the width of the interval is $(b - a)$ and the probability density is $1 / (b - a)$, that is:

$$p(x) = 1 / (b - a) \text{ for } a \leq x \leq b$$

$$= 0 \text{ otherwise.}$$

Obviously $p(x)$ satisfies the normalisation condition that the probability of all possibilities is one:

$$\int_b^a p(x)\ dx = 1.$$

The cumulative distribution is given by:

$P(x) = 0$ for $x < a$

$\quad = (x - a)/(b - a)$ for $a \leq x < b$

$\quad = 1$ for $b \leq x$.

The exponential distribution

Going back to the Poisson process, another random variable is the length of time until a particular atom decays. If we write $P(t)$ as the probability that it has decayed at time t, we know that this must satisfy the differential equation:

$dP/dt = (1 - P(t))F$ with initial condition $P(0) = 0$.

Therefore:

$P(t) = 1 - e^{-Ft}$.

$P(t)$ is the cumulative probability distribution. The probability density function of the decay-time random variable is:

$p(t) = dP/dt = Fe^{-Ft}$.

which is called an exponential distribution. The fact that this function is decaying represents the point that as time goes on the atom is less likely to decay because the chances are that it already has. In this case we can see again that, arguably, it is easier to deal with the cumulative function, or S-curve as we have already called it, than the probability density function.

The normal distribution

This is the most important distribution of all. Unlike the others, the initial formula for the distribution is not rooted in a specific random process:

$p(x) = (2\pi\sigma^2)^{-1/2}\exp(-(x - \mu)^2/\sigma^2)$.

This represents a distribution which is symmetrical about $x = \mu$ and has a distance scale of the order of σ; that is, by the time x has reached $\mu \pm \sigma$ the density function has dropped off significantly. It is the archetypal bell curve from Chapter 3. The initial, inverse square root factor is there to ensure normalisation.

To understand its importance, consider its logarithmic derivative:

$d\ln(p)/dx = -(x - \mu)/\sigma^2$.

This is the distribution whose logarithmic differential is given by a straight line passing through zero at the maximum.

Take the Poisson distribution, for example, in the case where q is very large. The most likely value of n is of the order of q and we can in fact write:

$\ln(p(n)) = -q + n\ln(q) - \ln(n!)$.

Hence, effectively turning n into a continuous variable:

$d\ln(p)/dn = \ln(q) - \ln(n) \approx -(n - q)/q$.

This shows that the number of events in a Poisson process which is sufficiently long for many occurrences to be expected is distributed as a normal distribution with $\mu = \sigma^2 = q$.

This is intuitively reasonable. In the example we had a decay rate of 1 hour and the experiment lasted for 1 hour. So the number of decays ranged from zero to seven in the sample of 10 000 we looked at. If each experiment had lasted 100 hours, we would expect to see 100 decays with much smaller relative variation. Figure 12.1 shows the results from the sample of 10 000 considered as 100 experiments of 100 replications. It shows how the frequency of the number of decays in each experiment cluster roughly around the expected normal and that the cumulative is pretty close to its normal approximation.

You can do the same thing with the binomial distribution. If the number of experiments is large, you can show that the number of successes is normally distributed with $\mu = pN$ and $\sigma^2 = Np(1 - p)$. If you followed the argument for the Poisson process, you might like to try that here as well.

So the point about the normal distribution is not that it describes a specific individual process, but that it is the limiting distribution in some very important circumstances. The cases we have just seen are not the only ones.

The cumulative probability for the normal distribution cannot be written in closed form, but is available from tables (or more likely via the appropriate spreadsheet function, NORMDIST in Excel).

Mean, variance and percentiles

The next step is to look in more detail at how these distributions can be characterised. We have already noted that it is fundamental that the sum of probabilities is one, which is the normalisation condition:

$$\sum_n p_n = 1 \qquad\qquad \int_{-\infty}^{\infty} p(x)dx = 1.$$

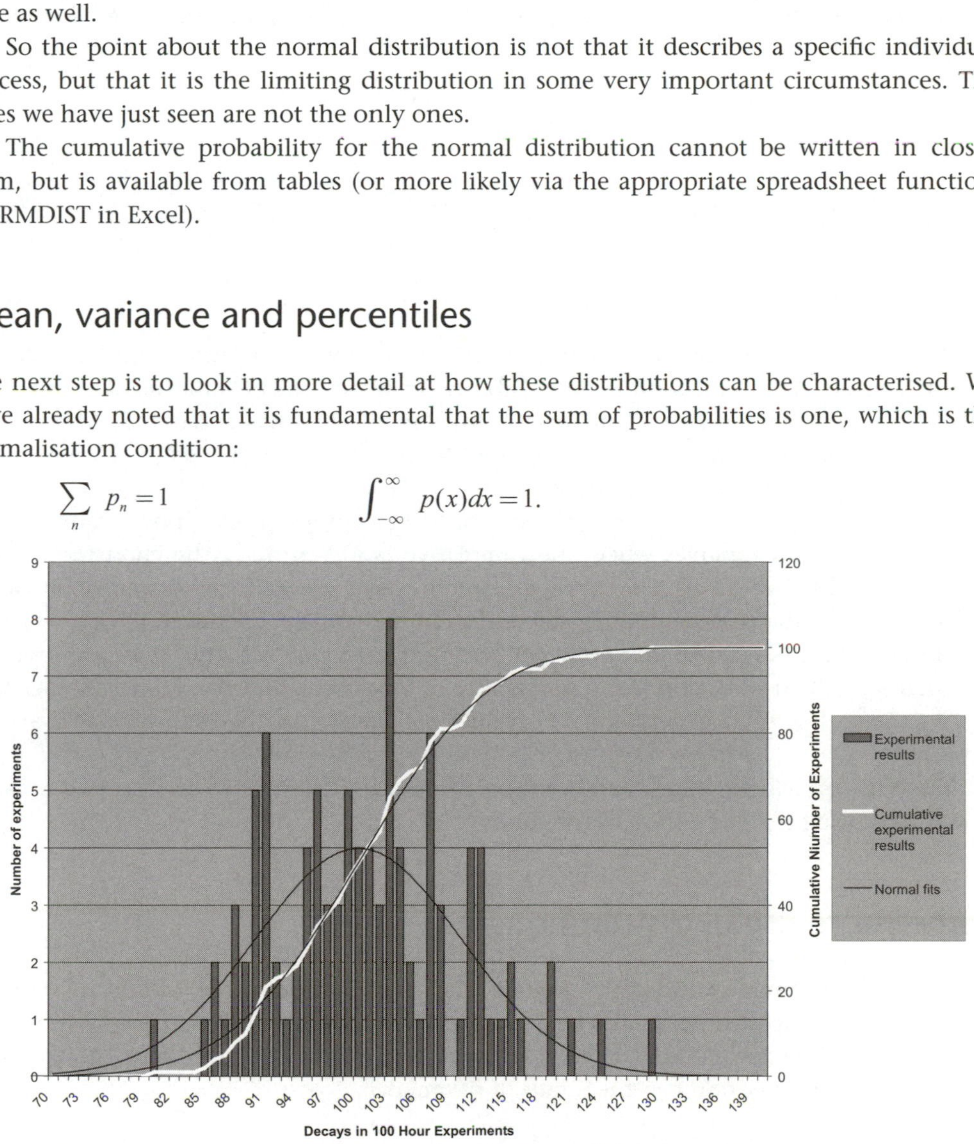

Figure 12.1   Decays in 100 experiments lasting 100 hours each

It is natural to try to determine the central location of the distribution which we could expect to be the probability weighted mean:

$$\mu = \sum_n x_n p_n \qquad\qquad \mu = \int_{-\infty}^{\infty} xp(x)dx.$$

This is also known as the expected value (in the mathematical sense).

Finally, we would like a measure of the spread of the distribution and it makes sense to look at the mean square departure from the mean. 'Square' ensures we get something that is positive; 'from the mean' ensures we eliminate the central tendency. Thus the *variance*, σ^2 is defined to be:

$$\sigma^2 = \sum_n (x_n - \mu)^2 p_n \qquad\qquad \sigma^2 = \int_{-\infty}^{\infty} (x - \mu)^2 p(x)dx$$

and the square root of this, σ, is called the *standard deviation*.

These three sets of formulae are tied in with what are known as moments. The *r*-th moment (about the origin) is defined by:

$$M_{or} = \sum_n x_n^r p_n \qquad\qquad M_{or} = \int_{-\infty}^{\infty} x^r p(x)\, dx$$

whilst the r-th moment about the mean is:

$$M_{mr} = \sum_n (x_n - \mu)^r p_n \qquad\qquad M_{mr} = \int_{-\infty}^{\infty} (x - \mu)^r p(x)\, dx$$

and for second order moments you can show that:

$$\sigma^2 = M_{m2} = M_{o2} - \mu^2.$$

The equation is sometimes useful to calculate the variance and standard deviation of distributions. Third and fourth order moments provide further information about the distribution in terms of *skewness* and *kurtosis*. Skewness is the third order moment about the mean divided by the σ^3 and kurtosis is the fourth order moment divided by σ^4. It is said to represent the peakiness of the distribution.

What is often more useful for risk analysis is percentiles. These apply particularly to continuous random variables where the cumulative is a continuous function from which specific values can be read off. The concept is simply one of selecting specific probability levels and determining the corresponding value of the random variable. For example, for a normal distribution there is a probability of 20 per cent that the value is higher than $\mu + 0.84\sigma$ (or less than $\mu - 0.84\sigma$) whilst there is a probability of 5 per cent that the value is higher than $\mu + 1.64\sigma$ (or less than $\mu - 1.64\sigma$). The values are known as the P80, P20, P95 and P5 respectively.

Table 12.1 provides the mean and variance values for the distributions discussed so far, as well as reiterating the probability distributions.

Some more useful distributions

There are plenty more distributions around. Many are mainly of application in statistics; we shall meet some of them in the next chapter. This section provides a brief list and the distribution gallery (see Table 12.1) provides more details. They are introduced because they have been shown to be of use as the inputs of risk models.

Table 12.1   **Distribution gallery**

Discrete Probability Distributions	Probability Distribution	Mean	Variance
Uniform	$p_n = 1/N, 1 \le n \le N$	$(N+1)/2$	$(N^2-1)/12$
Binomial	$p_n = (N!/(n!(N-n)!))p^n(1-p)^{N-n}, 0 \le n \le N$	Np	$Np(1-p)$
Poisson	$p_n = e^{-q} q^n / n!, n \ge 0$	q	q

Continuous Probability Distributions	Probability Density Function	Mean	Variance
Uniform	$p(x) = 1/(b-a), a \le x \le b$	$(a+b)/2$	$(a-b)^2/12$
Exponential	$p(x) = Qe^{-Qx}, x \ge 0$	$1/Q$	$1/Q^2$
Normal	$p(x) = (2\pi\sigma^2)^{-1/2}\exp(-(x-\mu)^2/2\sigma^2)$	μ	σ^2
Triangle	$p(x) = 2(x-a)/((b-a)(c-a)),\ a \le x \le b$ $= 2(c-x)/((c-b)(c-a)),\ b \le x \le c$	$(a+b+c)/3$	$((c-b)^2 + (a-c)^2 + (b-a)^2)/36$
Gamma	$p(x) = k^{s+1}x^s e^{-kx}/s!, x \ge 0$	$(s+1)/k$	$(s+1)/k^2$
Chi-Square	$p(x) = 2^{-n/2}x^{n/2-1}e^{-x/2}/(n/2-1)!, x \ge 0$	n	$2n$
Beta	$p(x) = K(x-a)^s(b-x)^t/(s!t!(b-a)^{s+t+1}), a \le x \le b$ where $K = (s+t+1)!$	$((t+1)a + (s+1)b)/(s+t+2)$	$(s+1)(t+1)(b-a)^2/((s+t+2)^2(s+t+3))$
Weibull	$p(t) = abt^{b-1}\exp(-at^b), t \ge 0$	$a^{-1/b}(1/b)!$	$a^{-2/b}((2/b)! - ((1/b)!)^2)$
Lognormal	$p(x) = (2\pi\sigma^2 x^2)^{-1/2}\exp(-(\ln(x)-\mu)^2/2\sigma^2), x \ge 0$	$\exp(\mu + \sigma^2/2)$	$\exp(2\mu + \sigma^2)(\exp(\sigma^2) - 1)$
Mixed	$pr(x=0) = 1 - p$ $pr(x\ne0) = p$ with (μ, σ) distribution	$p\mu$	$p\sigma^2 + p(1-p)\mu^2$

THE TRIANGLE DISTRIBUTION

As its name suggests, this distribution has a triangular shape and is described by its minimum, maximum and most likely values. The most likely value is the peak of the triangle. It can be symmetrical, where the most likely value is midway between maximum and minimum, or skewed.

The useful feature of this distribution is that it is easy to elicit from subject experts. Generally they feel most comfortable in providing the three parameters. And the fully skewed triangle, where the minimum is also the most likely, is a useful concept for when things can only get worse; for example where a project has been costed at the best case, or nearly so.

However, it is worth giving a word of warning: the triangle distribution is narrower than it looks. A symmetrical triangle distribution has a standard deviation which is only 41 per cent of the distance from the centre to the extremes, and the P20 and P80 are only 37 per cent of the way out. The P5 and P95 are 68 per cent of the way out.

For a fully skewed triangle, the standard deviation is 24 per cent of the width and P5, P20, P50, P80 and P95 are at 2.5 per cent, 11 per cent, 29 per cent, 55 per cent and 78 per cent of the way out respectively.

Both of these distributions and the percentiles are illustrated in Figure 12.2.

One response to this is to fiddle around with the distribution, setting the minimum and maximum at P5 and P95, for example. However, a better approach is to force the experts to expand the range of possibilities, using the percentiles as evidence of the need for them to do so (as well as people's war stories from when they have underestimated the range of possibilities).

THE GAMMA OR CHI-SQUARE DISTRIBUTION

The Gamma distribution is a generalisation of the exponential distribution described previously. The exponential decays from a fixed value at $x = 0$; the Gamma has a more general power law at $x = 0$:

$$p(x) \propto x^s e^{-kx} \text{ with } s > -1.$$

For s between -1 and 0, the probability density function tends to infinity at zero; above zero, the probability density function grows at first as x increases and then decays as the exponential term takes over. The exponential distribution corresponds to s = 0.

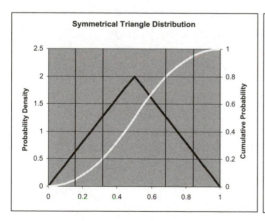
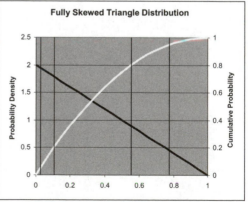

Figure 12.2 **P5, P20, P80 and P95 for symmetrical and skewed triangle distributions**

The mean and variance of the Gamma distribution are given by:

$$\mu = (s + 1)/k$$

$$\sigma^2 = (s + 1)/k^2$$

that is

$$\sigma = \mu/(s + 1)^{1/2}.$$

Thus for large values of s, the standard deviation is small compared to the mean and, in fact, the Gamma tends to a normal distribution. (You can prove this with the logarithmic derivative technique discussed above.) As s becomes negative and approaches -1, however, the standard deviation becomes much larger than the mean. This is a useful property on occasion.

The chi-square distribution is a special case of the Gamma (with $k = 1/2$ and s restricted to half integers). It is important in statistical inference because it is the distribution of the sum of squares of normally distributed random variables.

THE BETA DISTRIBUTION

The beta distribution can be a useful distribution where it is desired to fit elicited data with a maximum and minimum, and power law behaviour near the extremes. Thus:

$$p(x) \propto (x-min)^s(max-x)^t \quad s \text{ and } t > -1.$$

In this case, the mean and variance are given by

$$\mu = ((t + 1)min + (s + 1)max)/(s + t + 2)$$

$$\sigma^2 = (max - min)^2(s + 1)(t + 1)/((s + t + 2)^2(s + t + 3)).$$

For large values of s and t the distribution is symmetrically distributed about the mean and is approximately normal. As s becomes negative and approaches -1, the distribution shrinks to the minimum, but has a standard deviation which is much bigger than the difference between the mean and the minimum. A similar result applies when t approaches -1, in which case the distribution shrinks onto the maximum. Again, this can be a useful property.

THE WEIBULL DISTRIBUTION

We have already noted that the Poisson process describes events which happen at a constant rate. A generalisation of this is events which happen at a changing rate, either increasing or decreasing. Where this rate is power law with time, the resulting distribution of time until failure is called a Weibull distribution.

With a failure rate equal to at^{b-1} the probability density function of time to failure is

$$p(t) = abt^{b-1}\exp(-at^b).$$

The mean and variance of this is provided in the distribution gallery, Table 12.1.

THE LOGNORMAL DISTRIBUTION

If X is a random variable with a normal distribution then $Y = e^X$ is a random variable with a lognormal distribution. This is important if Y is the product of a number of random variables, all of which are themselves lognormal. The properties of the sums of normal random variables can be applied to this. We shall describe this later.

The mean and variance are as follows:

$$\mu_L = \exp(\mu + \sigma^2/2)$$

$$\sigma_L^2 = \exp(2\mu + \sigma^2)(\exp(\sigma^2) - 1) = \mu_L^2(\exp(\sigma^2) - 1).$$

Obviously you need to concentrate on dimensions as X, and hence μ and σ, should be dimensionless.

MIXED RANDOM VARIABLES

Finally, risk modelling sometimes throws up circumstances where a risk may occur or not and, if it does, the consequence is uncertain. This can be decomposed into two random variables:

$$\mathrm{pr}(X = 0) = 1 - p$$

$$\mathrm{pr}(X = Y) = p$$

where Y has its own probability distribution. Thus a project may be considered to overrun with probability P and, if it does, the additional time might be considered to have a triangular distribution of some kind. The mean and variance of this distribution is shown in Table 12.1.

It is worth thinking about the reality of such modelling given that it produces unusual looking curves. The probability density function has a delta function peak at zero and then a standard triangle separated from it. The S-curve shows a jump followed by a traditional S. Ask yourself if this is really what you want and whether at least a fully skewed triangle might be more appropriate.

Figure 12.3 illustrates a jump in the S-curve. The chance of a risk materialising is 50 per cent. The dark line shows the S-curve for the case where the distribution of the impact is a triangular distribution between one and two. The lighter curve is an alternative of a fully skewed distribution between zero and two. For many types of risk this is inherently more plausible than the alternative. This is essentially the case where the risk represents some uncertainty: is the discontinuity really realistic? In neither case can the density function be drawn, as it is infinite at zero.

Multiple events, conditional probabilities and independence

In defining probabilities we used the concept of the 'stabilised relative frequency' of an outcome or event. We did not discuss the nature of the outcome or event in any detail. However, for most 'repeated experiments' the possible events have a much richer structure than we have implied up to now.

For example, if the repeated experiment is waking up in the morning and measuring where I am and whether it is raining, then the events could be 'Manchester', 'raining' or 'dry in Bali', to name a few. The probability of these events will be structured according to the way these events interact with one another. For example, the probability of rain could depend on whether I am in Manchester or London. To deal with this it is useful to define *conditional probabilities*. For example:

$$\mathrm{pr}(\text{rain}|\text{Manchester}) = \mathrm{pr}(\text{it is raining if I wake up in Manchester}).$$

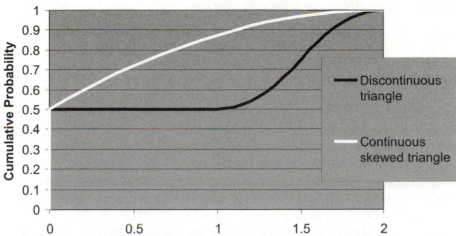

Figure 12.3   Use of triangle distributions in a 50 per cent probability risk

It is pretty obvious (and in fact axiomatic) that for any experiment and two events A and B

$$\text{pr(both } A \text{ and } B) = \text{pr}(A|B)\text{pr}(B)$$

so the probability of waking up to rainy Manchester is the probability that I am in Manchester, multiplied by pr(rain|Manchester) as above.

Two things come out of this. Firstly, if the chance of A does not depend on B then

$$\text{pr(both } A \text{ and } B) = \text{pr}(A)\text{pr}(B).$$

In this case A and B are said to be independent, and this is a necessary and sufficient condition for independence. Independence (or not) of risk events is a key concept in risk modelling.

Secondly, the symmetry in the expression pr(both A and B) means that:

$$\text{pr}(A|B)\text{pr}(B) = \text{pr}(B|A)\text{pr}(A)$$

or

$$\text{pr}(B|A) = \text{pr}(A|B)\text{pr}(B)\,/\,\text{pr}(A).$$

This apparently innocuous result is the celebrated Bayes theorem; it is both intriguing and useful. The key point is the reversal of A and B in the conditional probabilities.

I can imagine waking up not knowing where I am. What does the fact that it is raining tell me? Bayes theorem says:

$$\text{pr(Manchester|rain)} = \text{pr(rain|Manchester)pr(Manchester)}\,/\,\text{pr(rain)}$$

I already know pr(rain|Manchester) and I know the fraction of time I am in Manchester: pr(Manchester). I also know the probability of rain. It is:

$$\text{pr(rain)} = \sum_{\{\text{places I could be}\}} \text{pr(rain|place)pr(place)}.$$

But actually I do not need to know this, as it is location independent. Thus Bayes theorem can use the fact that it is raining to update my underlying probability of waking up in Manchester. To make this concrete, consider Table 12.2 which assumes I wake up only in Manchester or London (I was just getting my hopes up with Bali).

Table 12.2   Conditional probabilities for rain

	Prob	Dry	Rain	Total
London	0.2	0.6	0.4	1
Manchester	0.8	0.3	0.7	1
Total		0.36	0.64	1

Using the numbers in Table 12.2, the chance that I am in Manchester has increased from 80 per cent with no information about the weather to 87.5 per cent (that is, 0.8 × 0.7 / 0.64) with the knowledge that it is raining.

You may not find this very impressive, but using this approach enables doctors to refine diagnoses in the light of new evidence, as well as having many other applications. In Chapter 15 we use it in a decision problem.

It is also used where the A events refer to emerging data, as here, but the B events are essentially the truth of hypotheses about a statistical model: the probabilities become the degree of belief in the hypothesis. This technique gives rise to Bayesian methods in statistical inference.

Joint probability distributions and correlation

Following from this discussion of the structure of events, there are corresponding concepts for random variables.

We could convert our early morning location and weather measurements into random variables, but going back to our repeated experiments gives us better examples of multiple outputs. For instance, the measurement of component failure might include both the time of failure and the temperature at that time. Throwing a pair of dice would result in the score shown by each of them. The relative frequency concepts we used before can be applied just as well to define the probability distribution. This time we will refer to it as a joint probability distribution, to emphasise that it is several random variables being jointly described.

The joint distribution might be discrete (as for the dice), continuous (as for the time and temperature at failure) or might even represent a mixture of both types of random variable (as for the project overrun previously discussed under Mixed Random Variables):

$$p_{mn} = \mathrm{pr}(X = x_m \text{ and } Y = y_n)$$

$$\int_{x_1}^{x_2} \int_{y_1}^{y_2} p(x, y)dxdy = \mathrm{pr}(x_1 < x < x_2 \text{ and } y_1 < y < y_2).$$

We can use a joint probability distribution to determine the marginal distributions of the constituent random variables:

$$p_m^X = \sum_n p_{mn}$$

$$p^X(x) = \int_{-\infty}^{\infty} p(x, y)dy.$$

Note that the joint distribution can be used to determine the marginal distributions, but not vice versa.

Our core concern in risk modelling is to understand the distribution of functions of multiple random variables. That is, if we have a model which defines output random variables in terms of input random variables, we want to know how the output distribution depends on (a) the input distributions and (b) the functions in the model.

A key factor in determining this is whether the input random variables are independent or not. By definition X and Y are independent random variables if and only if the joint distribution is the product of their marginal distributions:

$$p_{mn} = p^X_{m}p^Y_{n}$$

$$p(x,y) = p^X(x)p^Y(y).$$

This implies that whatever the value of Y, the distribution of X is the same and equal to the marginal distribution. The same applies the other way around. It is entirely reasonable that if random variables are independent, then their distributions are not affected by each other. Equally, if their distributions do not affect each other, then there is no measurable dependency.

CORRELATION

As we have seen in earlier sections, risk models invariably contain dependencies. Whilst the outcome of each dice throw is effectively independent (although you could think of things which affect each), we can certainly expect that component failure will be dependent on temperature. So, the next question is how to measure dependence.

One answer is to define the correlation coefficient between two random variables:

$$\rho_{XY} = (E(XY) - \mu_X\mu_Y) / \sigma_X\sigma_Y.$$

$E(XY)$ stands for the expected value of the product XY. We shall show below that if X and Y are independent $E(XY) = \mu_X\mu_Y$ and the correlation coefficient is zero.

It can be shown that the correlation coefficient lies between -1 and 1 and that if it takes either of the values -1 or 1 the relationship between X and Y is linear. The focus of the correlation coefficient is the linearity of any relationship between X and Y and effectively ignores other aspects of any relationship or dependency. Thus, a correlation coefficient of zero does not mean the two random variables are independent.

As an example, consider $Y = X^2$ where X is normally distributed with a mean of 0 and a standard deviation of 1.

$$p(x,y) = (2\pi)^{-1/2}\exp(-x^2 / 2)\delta(y - x^2).$$

The marginal distribution of Y is a Gamma function (for the reason mentioned previously in connection with the chi-square distribution), so the joint distribution function does not satisfy the conditions for independence. But the correlation coefficient is clearly zero (as $E(XY)$ $= \mu_X = 0$).

There are two key points to remember:

1. Independence implies the joint distribution function is separable into the marginals, and a separable marginal implies independence.
2. Independence implies zero correlation, but zero correlation does not imply independence.

Putting dependence and correlation into risk models is discussed in other parts of this book, but as a final comment here, we know the output of risk models is dependent on the input, so we expect correlation between inputs and outputs. We can guess that the more the correlation, the more important the input is for the output. We return to this in the next chapter.

Functions of several random variables

We keep stressing that a risk model is just a set of input random variables and some functions providing the output(s). Some of this is quite simple and we now discuss some basic aspects of functions of random variables.

SUMS OF RANDOM VARIABLES

The most fundamental of these aspects is the case where the function is a sum of random variables. In this case the expected value of the sum is the sum of the expected values. To see this we have by definition that if $X = X_1 + X_2$, then:

$$E(X) = \iint (x_1 + x_2)p(x_1,x_2)\, dx_1 dx_2$$

$$= \iint x_1 p(x_1,x_2)\, dx_1 dx_2 + \iint x_2 p(x_1,x_2)\, dx_1 dx_2$$

$$= E(X_1) + E(X_2).$$

This applies whether X_1 and X_2 are independent or not and can be extended to any number of random variables.

Furthermore, the variance of a sum of random variables can be written in terms of the individual variances and the correlation coefficient:

$$\sigma^2(X) = E(X^2) - E^2(X)$$

$$= E(X_1^2) + 2E(X_1X_2) + E(X_2^2) - E^2(X_1) - 2E(X_1)E(X_2) - E^2(X_2)$$

$$= \sigma^2(X_1) + \sigma^2(X_2) + 2\sigma(X_1)\sigma(X_2)\rho(X_1,X_2).$$

As a special case, if the variables are independent, the variance of the sum is the sum of the variances since the correlation coefficient is zero.

As another special case, if $\rho = 1$ (full correlation implying a positive linear relationship between X_1 and X_2) then

$$\sigma^2(X) = (\sigma(X_1) + \sigma(X_2))^2.$$

There is a corresponding formula for the case that $\rho = -1$ and the relationship is negative:

$$\sigma^2(X) = (\sigma(X_1) - \sigma(X_2))^2.$$

These formulae are useful because summing random variables happens a lot in business risk modelling for the reason that money is always additive.

PRODUCTS OF RANDOM VARIABLES

If X_1 and X_2 are independent and a third random variable X is their product, then the expected value of X is the product of the expected value of X_1 and X_2. To see this, if $X = X_1X_2$ then:

$$E(X) = \iint x_1 x_2 p(x_1, x_2)\, dx_1 dx_2$$

$$= \iint x_1 x_2 p_1(x_1) p_2(x_2)\, dx_1 dx_2$$

$$= \int x_1 p_1(x_1)\, dx_1 \times \int x_2 p_2(x_2)\, dx_2$$

$$= E(X_1)E(X_2).$$

Finally, there is an analogous formula for the variance of the product of independent random variables:

$$\sigma^2(X) = \iint x_1^2 x_2^2 p(x_1, x_2) dx_1 dx_2 - E^2(X_1)E^2(X_2)$$

$$= \iint x_1^2 x_2^2 p_1(x_1) p_2(x_2) dx_1 dx_2 - \mu^2(X_1)\mu^2(X_2)$$

$$= \int x_1^2 p_1(x_1) dx_1 \times \int x_2^2 p_2(x_2) dx_2 - \mu^2(X_1)\mu^2(X_2)$$

$$= (\sigma^2(X_1) + \mu^2(X_1))(\sigma^2(X_2) + \mu^2(X_2)) - \mu^2(X_1)\mu^2(X_2)$$

$$= \sigma^2(X_1)\sigma^2(X_2) + \mu^2(X_2)\sigma^2(X_1) + \mu^2(X_1)\sigma^2(X_2).$$

These formulas can be combined to estimate the mean and variance of the output of a risk model formed of a sum of products where individual random variables are independent.

Some approximations

The final area of probability theory discussed in this chapter covers a number of approximations which are useful both to produce ballpark results and to provide an understanding of what is going on when more exact results are calculated.

CHEBYSHEV'S INEQUALITY

Whilst the mean and standard deviation are only two parameters of a probability distribution, they convey a lot of information. This is perhaps best summed up by Chebyshev's inequality: a simple result which says that a random variable cannot stray too many standard deviations from the mean. Or more precisely, that the probability of this is low. This is obvious in a way: if there were a decent probability of being some way from its mean, the standard deviation would be higher. The beauty of this result is that it is distribution independent.

$$\sigma^2 = \int_{-\infty}^{\infty} (x-\mu)^2\, p(x)dx$$

$$= \int_{-\infty}^{\mu-k\sigma} (x-\mu)^2\, p(x)dx + \int_{\mu-k\sigma}^{\mu+k\sigma} (x-\mu)^2\, p(x)dx + \int_{\mu+k\sigma}^{\infty} (x-\mu)^2\, p(x)dx$$

$$\leq \int_{-\infty}^{\mu-k\sigma} (x-\mu)^2\, p(x)dx + \int_{\mu+k\sigma}^{\infty} (x-\mu)^2\, p(x)dx$$

$$\leq k^2\sigma^2 \mathrm{pr}(X \leq \mu - k\sigma) + k^2\sigma^2 \mathrm{pr}(X \geq \mu + k\sigma)$$

$$= k^2\sigma^2 \mathrm{pr}(|X - \mu| \geq k\sigma)$$

so that

$$\mathrm{pr}(|X - \mu| \geq k\sigma) \leq 1/k^2 \text{ for any } k > 0$$

although it is not much use unless $k > 1$, since probabilities must always be less than one.

The inequalities we have applied during the proof are pretty drastic. First we dropped the central term in the integral and secondly we reduced the integrand in the outer wings. Figure 12.4 shows the overall effect for the case of a normal distribution and $k = 1.6$.

The inequality amounts to approximating the integrand for the standard deviation integral with the heavy black line. The correct integrand is the bimodal lighter line. This is clearly not a good approximation, at least for the normal. Its impact for different distributions is shown in Figure 12.5.

Taking the normal as an example we might try to estimate the P20 and P80 from Chebyshev. The required probability is 40 per cent and this suggests $k = 1.6$, as marked. The actual probability in a normal distribution outside 1.6σ is 11 per cent. (1.6 is the inverse square root of 0.4). Alternatively, we saw earlier that the exact k is 0.84. This suggests that the inequality is not of great practical use for estimating percentiles. However, Chebyshev remains an interesting result, which we build on in the next section.

THE LAW OF LARGE NUMBERS

At the start of this chapter we made progress by asserting the statistical regularity of the results of repeated experiments. This allowed us to define probability as the stable value of a relative frequency. We can now use Chebyshev's inequality to demonstrate statistical regularity. Consider an event which has probability p. The experiment is repeated N times and the relative frequency f is a random variable defined to be n/N where n is the number of times the event occurs. n has a binomial distribution with mean Np and variance $Np(1 - p)$, so f has mean p and variance $p(1 - p)/N$. Applying Chebyshev gives us:

$$\text{pr}(\,|f-p|\geq k\sigma) \leq 1 / k^2$$

or with $q = k\sigma$

$$\text{pr}(|f-p|\geq q) \leq \sigma^2/q^2 = p(1 - p) / (q^2 N).$$

As we can see, the probability that the relative frequency lies outside a defined range about its stable value, in this case of width $2q$, can be made small by making N sufficiently large.

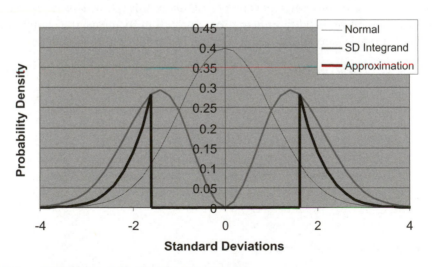

Figure 12.4   Principle of Chebyshev's inequality

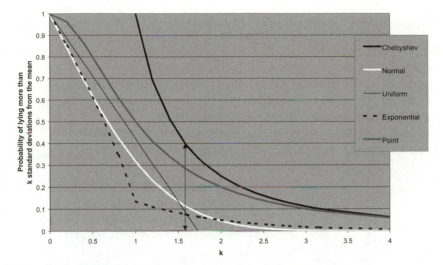

Figure 12.5   Using Chebyshev's inequality as an approximation

Perhaps of more direct relevance is to note that the standard deviation of the relative frequency decreases proportionally to $N^{-1/2}$ as N becomes larger. This is a key result for calculating risk models as the next chapter will show.

THE CENTRAL LIMIT THEOREM

The final piece of mathematics in this chapter is perhaps the most important, and perhaps even the most impressive, of all. It relates to the situation where a random variable is the sum of other random variables and these are independent. Recall that in these circumstances the mean is the sum of the means and the variance is the sum of the variances, so we know the mean and variance of the result. The Central Limit Theorem goes one step further and tells us that the sum has a distribution that is approximately normal. How come?

The brief answer is that as more and more random variables are added to the sum, the individual details are lost. The amount of information goes down and the normal distribution is the minimally informative among all distributions with a specified mean and standard deviation. The information referred to here is analogous to definitions used in statistical mechanical treatments of thermodynamics and it is for the same reason that the distribution of molecular speeds in a perfect gas is normal.

To provide a concrete example, consider a sum of random variables, each of which is a fully skewed triangle. Figure 12.6 shows the distribution of one, then two, then three of these. Even with two distributions the result is quite rounded and the most likely value has shifted to a central point not far off the mean. The normal distributions with the same characteristics are also shown. The greatest deviation is clearly at the margins as you would expect. But it is not long before the Central Limit Theorem takes over even for quite peculiar distributions. You will see the Central Limit Theorem demonstrated at several other points in this book.

A proper proof of the Central Limit Theorem is very complex. In developing the proof, the conditions under which it is true and the sense in which the distribution is approximately normal emerge. In broad terms, these are that no single distribution dominates or, very crudely, that all the individual standard deviations are small compared with the total standard deviation. This is not too surprising.

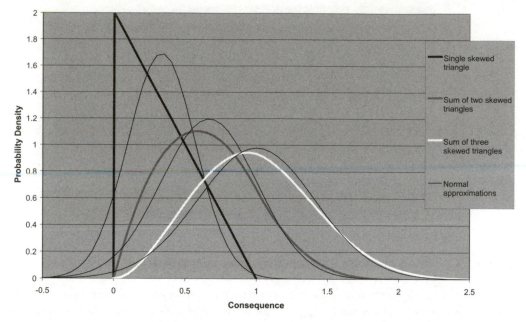

Figure 12.6   Demonstration of Central Limit Theorem for skewed triangles

Is probability relevant?

This chapter has provided a superficial overview of some elements of probability theory which are useful to carry out and understand risk modelling. The starting point for defining probability is the concept of repeatable experiments which demonstrate statistical regularity. Out of this we can develop a rich theory which explains the outcome of various specific types of experiments.

So what? How can this have any relevance to risk modelling in organisations where there can be no concept of a repeatable experiment? Business life only happens once and we cannot try again, even if we wanted. More fundamentally, the idea that the outcome of what we do is random is clearly wrong. We have underlined a number of times the point that life is human error, filled with an exciting mixture of grand plans, incompetence, flashes of brilliance, computer crashes, trend-following consumers, personal grudges and so on.

The answer is, firstly, that the existence of probabilities and their behaviour is not dependent on repeatable experiments. It can just as well be developed as a mathematical construct from a series of axioms (which mirror the common sense aspects of statistical regularity). Secondly, you can choose to adopt probabilities as a way of expressing your beliefs about the likelihood of different future outcomes. Having done this, you can use the theory just as if the future were a repeatable experiment.

In fact, the idea of probabilities as subjective degrees of belief as opposed to stable relative frequencies is one that has been hotly debated over many decades by mathematicians and statisticians. It can be argued that there is no such thing as an objectively definable probability, and this position certainly leads to a clear and coherent philosophy. Some people find this hard to swallow in the context of tossing fair coins and so on. This does not matter: you do not need to believe that all probabilities are subjective to accept that using subjective probabilities is a good idea.

There are a number of points which arise from this.

Firstly, this is not very useful to the average manager. They will not want to think that the validity of their risk model, on which they are making important decisions, is dependent on the outcome of a titanic struggle between two warring camps of academically minded people, subjectivists and frequentists. Do not allow them to worry about such things.

Secondly, though, you have to recognise and embrace subjectivity. There is no right answer, just many reasonable ones from which you need to select one (preferably). Again, this is difficult for managers who put their careers on the line when they make decisions and have unrealistic hopes that a bit of analysis will tell them what to do. The idea of an organisation's subjective probability is a difficult one. But consensus is needed on:

• the input distributions;
• how the model will derive the outputs from the inputs;
• the principle that it is a good idea to build a probabilistic model.

The decision team and their expert support need to work on achieving this consensus. In particular, they need to recognise that achieving consensus on subjective numbers is very difficult. But they need to do it anyway.

Thirdly, these three elements of consensus have failed to highlight perhaps the biggest potential pitfall in risk modelling: independence. The approximations in the previous section and other aspects of probability theory underline the point that probabilistic systems tend to exhibit behaviour which is centred on the average rather than spread over all possible values. It is dependence – correlation – which guards against unrealistic narrowing of ranges.

A familiar practical aspect of this is the idea of diversifying risk in a portfolio of equities. If you put all your money into one equity, then you are exposed to the full risk (standard deviation) of that equity. It you split it between several and their values vary independently of each other, your risk is reduced as the inverse square root of the number of equities. And if you could find equities which are negatively correlated (you won't) you might do even better. Investors use independence to reduce their risk as far as possible (for more on this see Chapter 10); businesses need to recognise their risk is increased by correlation.

This is the most common failing of risk models; that their outputs are too narrow because dependencies between the inputs are not recognised. So we extend the first bullet point above to include that consensus is also needed on:

• the input distributions and the dependence between them.

In general, this is much more important than the precise details of the marginal distributions themselves. Just remember how the typical elements of a risk model – for example, the duration of each task in a schedule – are affected by 'grand plans, incompetence, flashes of brilliance, computer crashes, trend-following consumers, personal grudges and so on'.

13 *Monte Carlo*

We now come to the most important and useful technique in risk modelling. Indeed some people refer to risk modelling as 'doing a Monte Carlo'.

The Monte Carlo concept

The probability theory in the previous chapter was pretty useless for calculating risk models. The short section on functions of random variables looked at sums and products and even this was hedged around with assumptions of independence. The exact calculation of a percentile of a random variable – which is a complex, non-linear function of a set of probabilistic inputs – is impossible almost all of the time. What we need is an approximate method, preferably an easy one, and luckily one exists.

It is nothing more than our old friend the repeatable experiment. We just use a computer to simulate the various versions of the future which are allowed by the model, then collect and analyse the results. More precisely we:

- take a sample from each of the input distributions (recognising dependence as necessary);
- work out the output(s) from the set of inputs;
- do this as many times as needed or we can stomach;
- turn the set of outputs we have into a distribution and estimate the properties we need, such as mean, variance, percentiles and so on.

At this point we could embark on a complex justification for doing this. But it is so obviously a good idea that more discussion of statistical regularity and the law of large numbers seems superfluous. Basically we are just simulating the possible futures we have postulated. What could be more relevant and direct?

Monte Carlo depends on computers, and started as a technique when electronic calculating machines started to become available in the late 1940s and onwards. It was first used to calculate difficult integrals which were needed as part of the atomic weapons programme at that time. If the integral could be written as

$$\int f(x)p(x)\,dx$$

where $p(x)$ is a probability density function (and in some sense it always can be), then the integral is the expected value of the 'random variable' $f(x)$. This can be estimated approximately by sampling from p a large number of times and taking the resulting mean value of f. It was called Monte Carlo simply because of the association of probability with gambling, and the association of gambling with the casinos at Monte Carlo. These days it would have been called the partypoker.com method.

As a simple example, imagine counting the number of rain drops falling on a square paving stone with a circle inscribed on it. The fraction of drops which fall in the circle should reflect the relative area of the circle, $\pi/4$. This is a way of estimating the value of π, equivalent to working out the integral

$$\int_0^1 (1-x^2)^{1/2}\,dx = \pi/4.$$

Because computing resources were still scarce, a lot of effort was put into making the technique as effective as possible. This meant choosing combinations where the variance of the estimate was as small as possible, using so-called variance reduction techniques. Some of this work is still used, but is largely misplaced in risk modelling, not only because computing resources are much larger, but also because risk modelling is done to gain an appreciation of the spread in the future, not to estimate the expected value with great accuracy.

The great strength of Monte Carlo is that if you want a better answer, you can just take more samples. The great frustration is that you need a lot more samples. If, for example, you are interested in the expected value of the total project cost, you can take the mean of the values obtained from each simulation. After N simulations you have

$$\sum_i c_i/N.$$

Because the c_i are independent (there is no dependence between simulations), this has an expected value equal to the expected value of the cost. E is a random variable which is an estimator for the expected value of the cost. The variance of E is proportional to $1/N$, and hence its 'accuracy' is $N^{-1/2}$. To get an answer 10 times more accurate you have to do 100 times more simulations. The variance reduction techniques are needed to live with this truth. It soon makes a demand on computing resources and there are some quantities which are very difficult to estimate with any accuracy at all. However, looking on the bright side, the inverse of this problem is that you do not have to do many simulations to get a rough and ready answer.

THE MONTE CARLO PROCESS

It is worth briefly describing the process in order to identify both the straightforward areas and the difficulties we can anticipate.

Take a sample from each of the input distributions (recognising dependence as necessary)

Spreadsheets contain random number generators. They are based on the idea of dividing a very large number by a smaller, but still large number in order to use the remainder. Once you have a random number, uniformly distributed between 0 and 1, you can use the cumulative distribution function of the input distribution (or an approximation from a reference book) to get the sample. Spreadsheet functions help with this. They quite often include inverse cumulative probability distribution functions. What is a lot more difficult is to model dependence between the input distributions. We shall come to ways of doing this shortly, but it is a really good idea to avoid the problem by modelling dependence explicitly.

Work out the output(s) from the set of inputs

This may be simple or complicated. Sometimes it is just a matter of adding some costs together; sometimes you may need the rate of return of a time series of costs; sometimes it may be necessary to model the ordering of tasks within a project plan. But in general a spreadsheet, again perhaps with specialised functions, will be able to help. You may have an issue with importing from a database (for example, the planning system) into the spreadsheet.

Do this as many times as needed or we can stomach

No problem in principle, although the obvious constraints are time and the ability to store all of the data.

Turn the set of outputs we have into a distribution and estimate the properties we need, such as mean, variance, percentiles and so on

This is not necessarily as simple as it looks. It is fairly easy to order a set of outputs and draw an S-curve. It is surprisingly more difficult to turn this into a graph of the probability density function. It is straightforward to estimate means and variances: we use the sample mean and sample variance without even thinking about it (this is discussed in some detail later in the chapter), and the properties of these are well understood. Percentiles can be estimated straightforwardly too, although their properties are less well known.

More fundamentally, there is an issue of 'so what?'. Most S-curves look the same, but it is useful to try to get inside the model and see what is driving it and what factors are immaterial. All of this will be discussed in what follows.

How to do Monte Carlo simulations

There should now be no doubt that the spreadsheet environment is appropriate for Monte Carlo, just as it is for other calculations. The description has also shown that Monte Carlo can be supported by specialist tools and, accordingly, there are proprietary toolkits for Monte Carlo which act as spreadsheet add-ons. These carry out tasks such as:

- generating (correlated) samples for input functions;
- controlling the running of the simulations;
- collecting the output samples;
- drawing pictures;
- using the output data to produce estimates of means, standard deviations, percentiles and the like;
- providing diagnostics on the working of the model.

One such tool kit is @RISK from Palisade Corporation. This is what I have used to derive the results presented in the following examples. I have no reason to think it is better than any other tool kit, but it is used by many people. If you do not have £600 but do have a bit of time and some programming skills, it is not too difficult to write your own routines. You should also be aware that it is not the intention of this book to be an @RISK user guide.

Let us try a simple example. Recall how we illustrated the Central Limit Theorem discussion through a series of fully skewed triangular distributions. We can use @RISK to reproduce the results. First, we define a number of inputs using the risk distribution functions supplied with @ RISK, in this case RiskTriang(0,0,1) which gives the fully skewed triangle distribution. We then define a series of output functions as the first, the sum of the first and the second, the sum of the first three, and so on. Lastly, we define a set of outputs to be RiskNormal(0.333,0.236) and so on, normal distributions with the appropriate means and standard deviations to match the Central Limit Theorem approximations.

The results are shown in Figure 13.1 for 10 000 samples; even with this many simulations it only takes a few seconds to run. The thick lines are the estimated probability density functions for the sums of one, two and three of the triangular distributions. Thin lines denote the approximating normals.

The input functions, the single triangle and the normals, are relatively smooth. This is an artefact of the default sampling method which chooses one value from each of the 10 000 equiprobability boxes which the input distributions can be partitioned into. This form of sampling (called Latin Hypercube) is a carry over from the days when variance reduction was a key driver in Monte Carlo techniques. It reduces the variance of the estimate of the mean. It generally does not help much with most business risk model outputs.

The functions which combine variables, the sum of two and three triangles, are jagged. This happens because it is difficult to draw a probability density function from a sample without excessive smoothing. You can experiment with this in @RISK.

You can see from Figure 13.2 that the S-curves are very boring, and that Monte Carlo gives much better results for these cumulative probabilities. You can also see that the normal approximation from the Central Limit Theorem is very accurate, except for extreme percentiles.

Modelling dependence

We have already said, if you can model dependence explicitly, do. Inflation in the cost of specialist skills depends on general inflation and the impact of local effects such as the perennial 'shortage of electricians in the south east' and management determination to control costs. Model these separately.

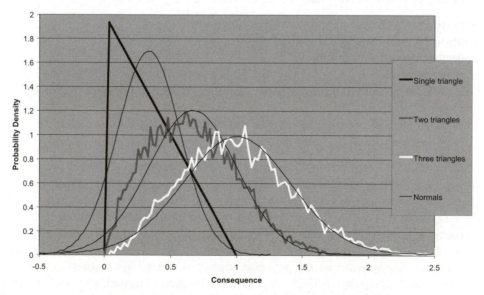

Figure 13.1   Summing triangle distributions – probability density

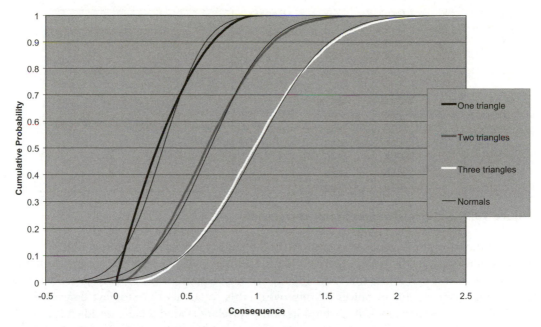

Figure 13.2   Summing triangle distributions – S-curves

Sometimes we know something is correlated, but do not have an underlying model which can be quantified by independent random variables. In this case, the Monte Carlo tool kit provides a tool which enables you to inject some correlation, and therefore dependence, into the relationship between two dependent variables.

It is actually quite difficult to define a sample from two distributions which has a specific correlation coefficient. What is much easier is to set up samples with a specified *rank* correlation coefficient. The rank coefficient is just the correlation coefficient of the rank, or order, of the members of the sample. Consider a simple case where we have four samples of X and Y as shown in Figure 13.3.

The graph shows clearly that X and Y are negatively correlated, but that there is still some scatter. The correlation coefficient is –0.86. However, the points are correlated enough to have retained their order and the rank correlation coefficient is correspondingly –1.

It is easier for software to inject rank correlation coefficients into samples. In fact, you can set up a rank correlation matrix in which the rank correlation between any pair of the input variables can be specified, subject to certain restrictions. This method also has the advantage that the rank correlation coefficient is one for any pair of variables which have an exact monotonic relationship between them. As we noted earlier the same is true for the correlation coefficient only if this relationship is linear.

It may not be immediately obvious that the rank correlation coefficient between two dependent random variables is independent of sample size. However, this is indeed the case, and hence there is a relationship between the correlation coefficient and rank correlation coefficient for particular distributions, and for a particular nature of the dependence. You can use @RISK, for example, to look at the two correlation coefficients where an output is the sum of two normal inputs. You will find that the rank correlation coefficient is slightly less than the correlation coefficient, by 4 per cent at most. You need about 100 000 samples to see this with any accuracy!

No	X	Rank(X)	Y	Rank(Y)
1	7	2	2	3
2	1	4	7	1
3	9	1	1	4
4	6	3	6	2

	Values	Ranks
E(XY)	16.50	5.00
E(X)	5.75	2.50
E(Y)	4.00	2.50
E(X^2)	41.75	7.50
E(Y^2)	22.50	7.50
CC	-0.86	-1.00

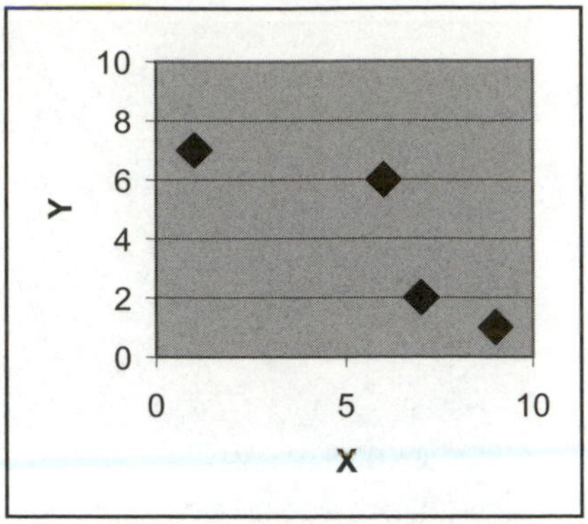

Figure 13.3   Correlation and rank correlation

The question for the analyst is what rank correlation coefficient to choose. Since it must be a number between 0 and 1, otherwise the modelling would be explicit, an answer many people arrive at is 0.5. While this lacks any kind of justification, it is probably as good as any other number in the circumstances. To improve on this you either have to have data available for analysis, or you must look at scatterplots of the correlated variables and decide if they look right. Figure 13.4 shows scatterplots derived using normal distributions. Each of these pictures has 1000 points.

Now you see that modelling dependence explicitly really is a good idea.

Visualisation and importance

Now we come to look at the guts of a Monte Carlo model, so we can understand what is going on. Not only do we need to satisfy ourselves that it is working as intended; we also must be able to explain it to others, including our customers and managers, with confidence. It is surprising how often a risk model will throw out an unexpected result and you need to establish whether it is an error or an unanticipated feature of the model.

SIMPLE COST RISK MODEL

Let us start with a simple case, the model is simply a sum of costs. A really useful chart to draw is simply a four point column chart of the contributing costs. Table 13.1 and Figure 13.5 show the input model and the four point chart which shows the minimum, P20, P80 and maximum of each risk, as determined from the Monte Carlo calculations.

In Microsoft Excel the chart shown in Figure 13.5 is called Open-High-Low-Close in the Stock category. You can add a central point (mean or P50) by using the five point variant, but it is not as attractive. We shall refer to it as the sensitivity chart. We shall refer to the thin lines joining the minimum to the P20 and the P80 to the maximum as 'whiskers'.

Because the output is the direct sum of the input, you can see at a glance how each input contributes. As well as gaining an appreciation of the general size and spread of the distributions, you can see how some of them are skewed and what the impact is of the mixed distributions; that is, those that are non-zero only some of the time (Risk 6 for example). An important point to notice is that some of the costs contribute not only to the spread of the

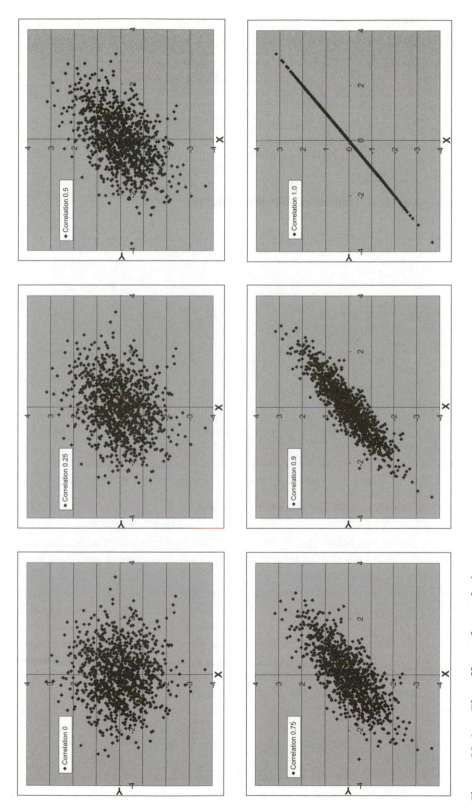

Figure 13.4   The effect of correlation on scatter

Table 13.1   **Simple risk model**

	Prob	Impact	Value	
Risk 1	1.00	0.67	0.67	Triangular (-1,0,3)
Risk 2	0.20	3.33	0.00	Fully skewed triangular (0,0,10)
Risk 3	1.00	2.00	2.00	Normal (2,1)
Risk 4	1.00	6.67	6.67	Triangular (0,5,15)
Risk 5	1.00	1.67	1.67	Fully skewed triangular (0,0,5)
Risk 6	0.05	20.00	0.00	Fixed consequence (20)
		Result	**11.00**	

Min, P20, P80, Max Diagram

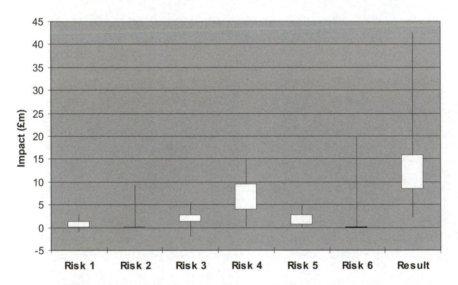

Figure 13.5   **Sensitivity chart for simple risk model**

result, but also to the central value. This is obvious, but easily forgotten in what follows. The same chart can also contain the output cost, marked Result in this case, so again you have an opportunity to see a good general picture.

This works because all the risks are measured on the same scale and the result is simply a sum. What if the inputs to the model are all of different units? In this case it would make sense to draw everything on an output scale. One approach is to keep all the inputs except one at a typical value, say the mean, and vary the remaining one over minimum, P20, P80, maximum range. This provides Figure 13.6, which is similar to Figure 13.5, except that the overall effect of each risk on the result has been lost: you cannot see what is driving the output cost to its central value (of around £13 million). We refer to this as a *variation* sensitivity chart.

What Figure 13.6 does show is that the spread in the result is largely driven by the spread in Risk 4 and that in Risk 6. The others are relatively unimportant. A good way to get a better idea of this is to draw scatter charts showing how the result depends on the risks. These are presented in Figure 13.7.

Inspection of these diagrams tells you most of what you want to know about the inputs and their effect on the output. However, if you want a single measure of the impact, you can

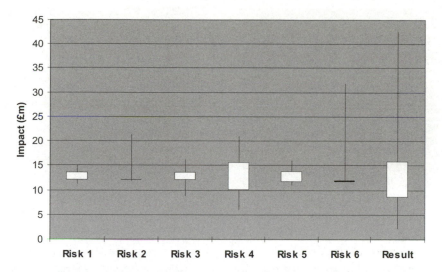

Min, P20, P80, Max Output Diagram

Figure 13.6   Variation sensitivity chart for simple risk model

calculate the correlation coefficient between each input and the output. Where the correlation coefficient is high, the input is having a big effect on the output; where it is low, it is having little impact. You can calculate either the correlation coefficient or the rank correlation coefficient. Figure 13.8 shows the correlation coefficient (easily obtained from the Microsoft Excel spreadsheet function CORREL).

As expected, the correlation chart shows the largest effect from Risks 4 and 6 and the smallest from Risk 1. Similarily, @RISK can draw you something called a tornado chart. This is the correlation chart on its side and ordered by correlation (see Figure 13.9). You can choose to have the correlation coefficient (somewhat confusingly called 'regression' in @RISK) or the rank correlation coefficient (called 'correlation' in @RISK).

A tornado chart is not a bad idea, but be careful. What @RISK will do is correlate outputs (that is, anything marked as such in the spreadsheet) with inputs (that is, any of the defined probability distribution functions). In practice a risk such as Risk 2, which combines the chance of something happening with the probability distribution of its consequence, will be regarded as an output in @RISK and will not feature on the tornado chart. That is why the data for the chart was exported and drawn separately.

SIMPLE PROJECT RISK MODEL

Let us see how this works through for a slightly different example where the output is not the sum of inputs. The input shown in Table 13.2 represents a very simple schedule risk assessment where a construction project has three tasks: obtaining planning permission, site clearance and construction itself. Construction cannot begin until the other two tasks are complete. This is the single schedule dependency in the model.

The duration of the project is therefore the sum of the construction time and the maximum of the permission and clearance times. The big risk for clearance is considered to be the number

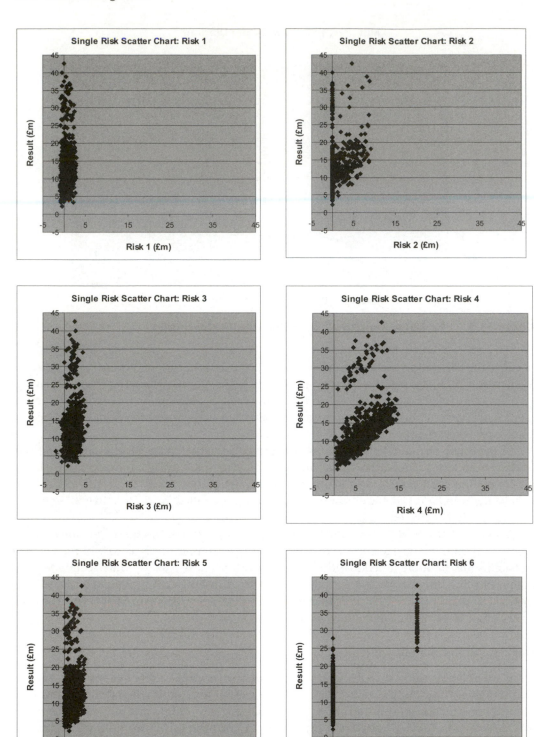

Figure 13.7   Scatter charts for individual risks

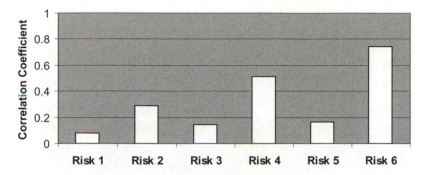

Figure 13.8   Correlation chart for simple risk model

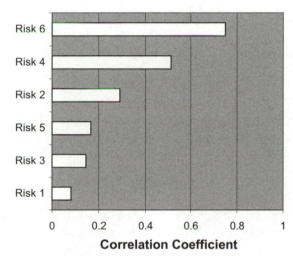

Figure 13.9   Tornado chart for simple risk model

Table 13.2   Project risk model

	Impact	Value	
Planning permission	8.67	8.67	Triangular (6, 8,12) weeks
Site clearance workforce	15.00	15.00	Uniform (10,20) workers
Construction	11.67	11.67	Fully skewed triangular (10,10,15) weeks
	Duration	**21.67**	Permission and clearance (150 work-weeks) complete before construction

of workers available and so this is modelled as a risk. The clearance time is then modelled as the work-weeks required (150 in this case) divided by the number of workers available.

This example has been chosen because you cannot draw the number of workers on the same graph as the project duration. (Also, the recognition that resources are a significant project constraint is important but not a natural feature of many schedule risk analysis which apply distributions to task durations in a formulaic way.) Of course we could have modelled the duration of clearance with some distribution between 7.5 and 15 weeks. But what if the workforce were shared with some other task? This is discussed further in Chapter 7.

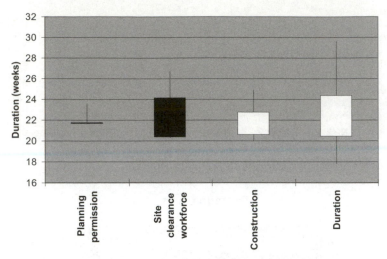

Figure 13.10   Variation sensitivity chart for project risk model

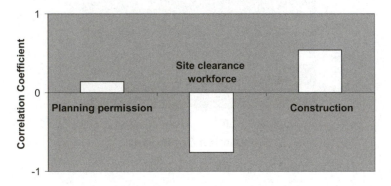

Figure 13.11   Correlation chart for project risk model

The output sensitivity chart is shown in Figure 13.10. Again, each input but the one being illustrated is held at its mean value. Figure 13.10 shows:

- that the overall project duration lies between 18 and 30 weeks, with a most likely range of 21 to 25 weeks;
- that in most simulations it is clearance that affects duration, rather than the time spent on gaining planning permission (in fact with resourcing at its mean value of 15, there is a probability of 17 per cent that duration will be determined by planning permission, hence the inverted T; when both vary this rises to 26 per cent);
- there is no lower whisker on clearance (that is, the P20 is also the minimum) which means that with permission at its mean (8.67 weeks), having clearance resources at their P80 (18 workers) is enough to complete clearance more quickly (that is, in 8.33 weeks) – it is this sort of thing which can get confusing, but provides good insights;
- that clearance looks to have a bigger effect on project duration than construction.

These results are confirmed by the correlation chart shown in Figure 13.11. Obviously, the availability of resources is negatively correlated with duration, something which is also shown on the previous chart by the black shading which Microsoft Excel conveniently adds. There is a clear message that to reduce project risk you need to sort out the site clearance resources!

Finally, further insight into all this can be obtained from the scatter charts, drawn in Figure 13.12.

These scatter charts show the circumstances in which each task is limiting and how this affects the overall project duration. For example, the first chart, being a fairly scattered scatter chart, indicates that the duration is not highly dependent on obtaining planning permission. Only in the long duration tail of its distribution is the scatter pattern distorted at the lower right-hand side. Conversely, the second diagram shows that there is good (negative) correlation between workforce size and project duration. Only when the workforce is near its maximum at the right-hand side is the scatter greater, as gaining planning permission takes a larger role in the model.

These diagrams are invaluable. Draw as many as you can and make sure you understand what they tell you (so you can tell your client).

Sampling and estimation

Up to now we have blissfully pursued the philosophy that the main point of Monte Carlo is to replicate multiple futures so that we can just stand back and admire the results. The emphasis has been on modelling and pictures, rather than mathematics. Obviously this could not last and we now come to how we can use Monte Carlo to estimate quantities such as expected values, standard deviations, percentiles and so on. We particularly want to know how accurate these estimates will be.

SOME IDEAS IN STATISTICAL INFERENCE

Statistical inference is about using the outcomes of repeatable experiments to draw conclusions about the properties of the underlying random phenomena. This is obviously what we want to do when we have done some Monte Carlo modelling and we have a wealth of data to draw on. If there is not enough data, we can generate some more.

What we need is a function of outputs which will be a good approximation to the quantity we are trying to estimate. This might be the mean, standard deviation, or P20 of one of the outputs, or even each a point on the S-curve.

Such a function is called an *estimator*. An estimator is a random variable, which is a function of other random variables. To understand how good an approximation it is we need to understand its probabilistic behaviour; for example, we need to identify its mean and standard deviation. This can get confusing as, unsurprisingly, the estimator for the mean of a distribution is the mean of a sample drawn from the distribution. We shall try to keep this distinction clear.

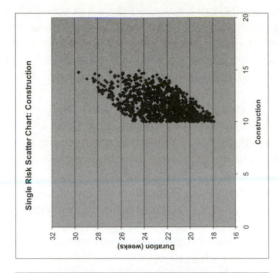

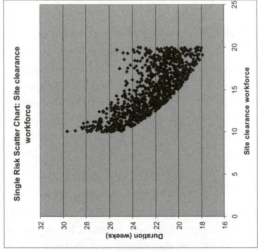

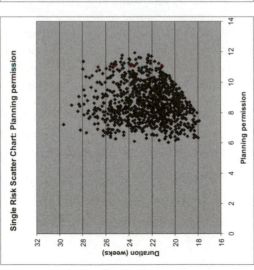

Figure 13.12   Scatter chart for project risk model

ESTIMATING THE MEAN

It is pretty obvious, as we have already said, that a good estimator for the mean of a random variable is to find the mean of a sample drawn from the distribution. So if we have done a Monte Carlo simulation of the project cost, we just take all N costs, add them up and divide them by N. The estimator, M, is the sample mean:

$$M = \sum_i x_i/N.$$

Because it is a sum of random variables, its expected value is the sum of expected values so:

$$E(M) = NE(X)/N = E(X) = \mu.$$

This shows that the expected value of the estimator of the mean is equal to the mean. An estimator with this property is said to be *unbiased*.

Because the estimator is a sum of *independent* random variables, its variance is the sum of variances:

$$\text{var}(M) = N\,\text{var}(X)/N^2 = \sigma^2/N.$$

Thus, the larger the number of samples, the smaller the standard deviation of the estimator of the mean. It gets smaller in a way that is proportional to the inverse square root of N, as we would expect.

A tool kit such as @RISK gives you an estimate of the mean worked out this way and, with experience, you will find that it is generally pretty accurate and does not cause you any trouble.

ESTIMATING THE VARIANCE AND STANDARD DEVIATION

Obviously, to estimate the variance or standard deviation of an output the obvious thing to try is the sample variance or standard deviation. The function

$$S^2 = \sum_i (x_i - M)^2/N$$

is the variance of the output in the sample generated. This expression can be expanded out carefully, remembering that there is an element of each x_i in the M term (the estimator of the mean above). Because of this

$$E(S^2) = (N - 1)\,\sigma^2/N$$

so S^2 is not an unbiased estimator of the variance, but $NS^2/(N - 1)$ is. Whilst statisticians get excited about unbiased estimators, it is really immaterial whether you use S^2 or $NS^2/(N - 1)$, as the difference, being of order $1/N$, is small compared with the error of order $1/N^{1/2}$. Either way S is a good estimator of the standard deviation, but is certainly not unbiased, whichever version you choose.

An algebra masochist can go on to calculate the variance of the estimator, S^2. You need to keep account of all the terms where any x_i is repeated 2, 3 or 4 times. The result is:

$$\text{var}(S^2) = ((N - 1)^2/N^3)(M_{m4} - \sigma^4 + 2\sigma^4/(N - 1))$$

$$\approx (\beta - 1)\,\sigma^4/N.$$

M_{m4} is the fourth moment about the mean and β is the kurtosis. The primary conclusion we draw from this is that the standard deviation of the estimators for the variance and standard deviation, like the standard deviation of the estimator for μ, will be proportional to $1/N^{1/2}$ for large N.

However, on a more practical basis you will find it quite frustrating trying to use Monte Carlo to estimate the standard deviations of outputs. Compared with estimators of the mean, S is considerably more volatile and difficult to pin down if you do not have the resources to do thousands and thousands of simulations.

ESTIMATING PERCENTILES

The final quantity we shall aim to estimate is percentiles. We have seen how they are sometimes used in pricing risk, so it is quite important to get this right or at least to have some appreciation of how wrong they can be. It is quite embarrassing to have to tell a client that when you did the Monte Carlo again, you realised the price should be £37 million not £36 million. Mathematically, the difference may be insignificant, but people do worry about the odd £1 million.

It is pretty obvious that if you have 1000 samples, a good estimate of the P80 should be the 800th ranked value. So we define the estimator R_n:

$$R_n = x^r_n$$

where x^r represents the ranked results, so that R_n is the nth ranked value out of N in total. We expect that n will be about PN where P is the desired probability, that is, for P80, $P = 0.8$. What is the distribution of this estimator R_n? We now hit some of the trickiest mathematics in the book (whilst still remaining profoundly informal), so you might want to go straight to the answer.

At any point x, its probability density distribution $q(x)$ is related to a binomial:

$$q(x) = N!P^{n-1}(x)(1 - P(x))^{N-n}p(x)/((n-1)!(N-n)!).$$

Here, $p(x)$ is the probability density of the output we are trying to estimate the percentiles of and $P(x)$ is its cumulative probability distribution. This represents the probability that $n - 1$ of the points fall below x and the nth falls precisely at x. You can check that this has the characteristics of a probability density function by integration and changing the dependent variable from x to P:

$$\int q(x)\, dx = \int_0^1 N!P^{n-1}(1 - P)^{N-n}\, dP/((n-1)!(N-n)!) = 1.$$

In P-space this is just a Beta distribution, a fact that enables us to find the mean and variance of R_n:

$$E(R_n) = \int q(x)x\, dx = \int_0^1 N!P^{n-1}(1 - P)^{N-n}x(P)\, dP/((n-1)!(N-n)!)$$

$$E(R_n^2) = \int q(x)x^2\, dx = \int_0^1 N!P^{n-1}(1 - P)^{N-n}x^2(P)\, dP/((n-1)!(N-n)!).$$

Here $x(P)$ is the inverse cumulative probability distribution, that is for each P, P is the probability that the random variable is less than x. In other words $x(P)$ is the percentile: its graph is the S-curve turned on its side.

For large N the Beta distribution is approximately normal with mean n/N and variance $n(N - n)/N^3$. This shows that its standard deviation is small and we are zooming in on the required percentile where $P = n/N$, thus justifying its use as the estimator:

$$E(R_n) \approx n/N = P_0.$$

This is approximate – you can fiddle around with terms of order $1/N$ to make it unbiased.

If you expand $x(P)$ about $P = P_0$ you can find the approximate value of the variance of R_n for large N. Without going into details:

$$\text{var}(R_n) \approx \sigma^2 \, (dx/dP)^2 = P_0(1 - P_0) / (Np^2(x_0))$$

where:

$$P(x_0) = P_0.$$

Here σ is the standard deviation of the Beta distribution and dx/dP can be inverted to give $dP/dx = p(x)$ the probability density function evaluated at the percentile estimate. So at last we have something useful. The standard deviation of the percentile estimator becomes small as the number of samples becomes large in the usual way. But it is inversely proportional to the probability density function at that point. So if you are trying to get percentiles far out in the wings of distributions, they are likely to be not very accurate. The fact that P_0 or $1-P_0$ get small at the edge does not compensate unless you have a strongly bounded distribution. You have been warned.

Figure 13.13 shows the size of error you can expect. For example, if you have 1000 samples and are looking for the P80, the error is about 5 per cent of the standard deviation.

ESTIMATING PROBABILITY DENSITY FUNCTIONS

This brings us nicely to the issue of the probability density function. This book strongly recommends that you do not show them to clients (see Chapter 3), but we have just seen how they affect the accuracy of percentile estimates. We noted earlier that it is tricky to invert the Monte Carlo data to get a probability density function. The tool kits do not make a very good job of it; they just sort the data into bins and draw histograms. The trick is to apply the right amount of smoothing to the data without overdoing it. You will find a Monte Carlo tool on my website (www.riskagenda.com) which incorporates my best attempt at this problem to date.

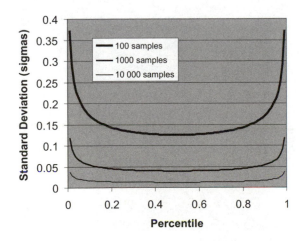

Figure 13.13   Standard deviation of percentile estimators

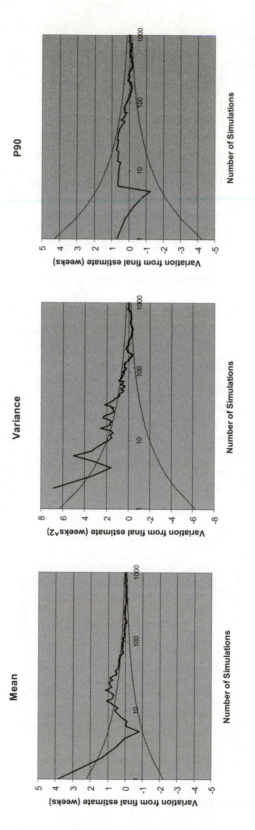

Figure 13.14　Convergence of estimators

PUTTING THIS TO USE

We conclude this section by providing an example of how you can use these estimators. We will apply them to the same project example.

Figure 13.14 shows the mean, variance and P90 of project duration as it is estimated after each simulation of 1000. The estimates, which are the jagged lines, converge to zero (by definition). The two curves on each chart show the standard deviation of the estimator, as calculated using the methods above. They all decrease like the inverse square root of N and have been drawn each side of the x-axis. Broadly this gives an idea of the spread you might expect in the estimates. The spread in the P90 estimator is clearly larger than that of the mean, as expected. On the whole, though, these are a fairly well behaved set of estimates.

I would still repeat the warning that standard deviation and percentile estimates are significantly more volatile than those of means and care is needed.

Summary

The main messages from this chapter have been:

- Monte Carlo is an elegant, powerful, yet simple technique. Anyone can do it.
- However, there are dangers in not knowing what you are doing.
- It is essential that Monte Carlo simulations, just like all risk modelling, recognises dependence.
- It is worth putting a lot of effort into visualisation and explanation of the results. Recommended tools include sensitivity charts showing the maximum, minimum P20 and P80 values, correlation charts and scatter charts. These all help to verify the results and make them more comprehensible.
- Monte Carlo works out some quantities more effectively than others. It can estimate mean values very accurately, but is less useful at estimating standard deviations and percentiles, especially out in the wings. It is possible to find situations where it is virtually impossible to find reasonable answers.

14 *Other Methods*

We said at the start of the previous chapter that Monte Carlo is one approximate method for calculating risk models. So the obvious question is: what else is there? The answer is: not much. That is why 'doing a Monte Carlo' is synonymous with working with quantitative risk models in some people's minds. It is important to bear in mind though that Monte Carlo is not an end in itself and that is why this chapter has been added to cover risk modelling outside of Monte Carlo.

Exact methods

The first question to ask is whether there is any non-randomised way (that is, other than Monte Carlo) to work out the probability distribution of outputs in a risk model. This is a hopeless task in general, as you can see from the following mathematical formulation:

$$P_f(x) = \int_{\{\text{all } x_i \text{ such that } f(x_i) \le x\}} p(x_1, x_2, \dots, x_N) \, dx_1 dx_2 \dots dx_N$$

which just says that the cumulative probability distribution of an output function f of N random variables $x_1, \dots x_N$ is found by integrating over parts of the N dimensional space in which f is less than some number. Obvious, but also impossible in general.

Of course there are some special cases. We have already discussed sums of random variables. The sum of two independent random variables has a distribution given by:

$$p(x) = \int p_1(x_1) p_2(x - x_1) dx_1 .$$

The most important case of this is where p_1 and p_2 are normal, in which case their sum is also normal. If this were not the case the Central Limit Theorem would not be true. Also, if p_1 and p_2 are exponential, then so is p. But in general this integral is hard to work out. This reminds us that Monte Carlo started as a way of doing difficult integrals.

Another interesting case is when f is the maximum of the x_i. This models the situation in a schedule risk analysis when a third task cannot start until two initial tasks have been completed. If the tasks are independent then:

$$P(x) = \pi_i P_i(x) .$$

To see this, for example in the case that $N = 2$, we need to find the region of a chart with axes x_1 and x_2 in which the maximum of x_1 and x_2 is x. This region is defined by $x_1 \le x$ and $x_2 \le x$. If x_1 and x_2 are both positive, this is the square $0 \le x_1 \le x$, $0 \le x_2 \le x$ and the integral separates:

$$P(x) = \int_{\{\max(x_1, x_2) \le x\}} p_1(x_1) p_2(x_2) \, dx_1 dx_2$$

$$= \int_0^x p_1(x_1) \, dx_1 \times \int_0^x p_2(x_2) \, dx_2$$

$$= P_1(x) P_2(x).$$

As an example, Figure 14.1 shows the pre-construction stages of the project risk example outlined in Chapter 13. A simple spreadsheet has been used to generate the S-curves for the planning permission and site clearance tasks. They can be multiplied to provide the S-curve for the event representing completion of both tasks. It can be seen to have the appropriate properties: the curve is very close to the site clearance S-curve and equal to it once planning permission has been completed with certainty after 12 weeks. (Of course you might want to revise your inputs after that statement.)

This example can be taken to the next stage as well. Finding the exact distribution for the total project duration is simple in principle; but very complicated in practice, needing different integrations for about 15 separate zones.

What is potentially more useful is the ability to work with means and standard deviations. These can be calculated from the cumulative distributions by integrating the formulas by parts:

$$\mu = \int_L^U xp(x)dx = [xP(x)]_L^U - \int_L^U P(x)dx$$

$$= U - \int_L^U p(x)dx \text{ or } L + \int_L^U Q(x)dx$$

$$\sigma^2 = \int_L^U x^2 p(x)dx = [x^2 P(x)]_L^U - 2\int_L^U xP(x)dx - \mu^2$$

$$= U^2 - 2\int_L^U xP(x)dx - \mu^2 \text{ or } L^2 + \int_L^U xQ(x)dx - \mu^2 .$$

Here L and U are the assumed lower and upper bounds of the distribution. This allows the integrals to converge. Also, $Q(x) = 1 - P(x)$ is the descending cumulative with $Q(L) = 1$ and $Q(U) = 0$. The idea is that these integrals can be calculated using a simple numerical scheme in a spreadsheet to give the mean, variance and standard deviation.

In the construction project example, the mean and the standard deviation of first stage completion can be calculated at 10.71 and 1.89 weeks respectively, using a fairly coarse interval of 0.2. These figures can be used with the corresponding ones for the final project

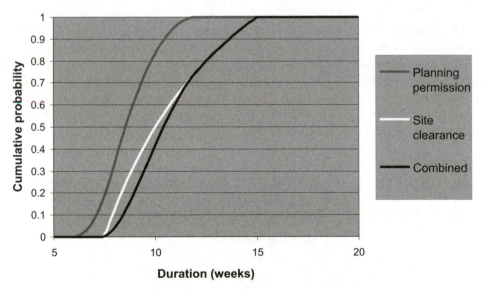

Figure 14.1   Distribution of time to completion

task to estimate the mean and standard deviation of the project overall (22.37 and 2.25 weeks, respectively).

I am not seriously suggesting that these methods should be used as a matter of routine. There are at least three good reasons for this:

- many models are too complicated to get very far;
- they are time consuming;
- it is not worth the bother when Monte Carlo is so quick and effective.

However, it useful when unanticipated results are found, or when you want to understand the model better, to be able to look into what is going on in more detail. Alternative methods can be helpful for this.

The direct method

One method which is very useful is the so-called direct method. This can be used when the output is the sum of random variables and these variables are independent. We know that:

- the mean is the sum of the means;
- the variance is the sum of the variances;
- the output distribution is approximately normal.

It is easy to develop a spreadsheet which lists the risks (or inputs), their means and their variances. The risks are added to get the mean and variance of the output. You can then put in the normal distribution function to draw the approximate S-curve.

We should note that the mean is exact, whether the inputs are independent or not. This finding is very useful because it is independent of the normal assumption. It follows from the fact that the mean of a sum of random variables is the sum of their means, as we demonstrated in Chapter 12.

Although the variance is exact only if the inputs are independent, you can in fact model correlation by manipulating the formulae. For example, if two inputs are fully, positively correlated, you can add the standard deviation instead of the variances; and for a full negative correlation you can subtract them:

$$\sigma = \sigma_1 \pm \sigma_2$$

instead of

$$\sigma = (\sigma_1^2 + \sigma_2^2)^{1/2}.$$

In fact, in general:

$$\sigma^2 = \sigma_1^2 + \sigma_2^2 + 2\sigma_1\sigma_2\rho_{12}$$

so that if you know, or assume, the correlation coefficient between two variables, you can work out the variance of the sum. This can be generalised further:

$$\sigma^2 = \sum_i \sum_j \sigma_i \sigma_j \rho_{ij}$$

where ρ_{ij} is the complete correlation matrix.

Although you can draw the normal as an approximation, what is most important is to know the mean and standard deviation. As we noted in Chapter 2, for most business risk assessment all that is needed is a central value and an idea of spread. I have seen elaborate assessments based on risk register and Monte Carlo, and all the black box aspects that this implies, when all that was needed was to add up the means. The direct method would have given a much more accessible output.

The method still works when the risk is a mixed one, that is, it has a probability of happening and a distribution of the impact if it does. Recall that if:

$Y = X$ with probability p

$\quad = 0$ with probability $1 - p$

then

$$\mu_Y = E(Y) = pE(X) = p\mu_X$$

$$\sigma_X^2 = \text{var}(Y) = p\,\text{var}(X) + (1 - p)\,E^2(X) = p\sigma_X^2 + p(1 - p)\mu_X^2$$

where X is the random variable representing the distribution of the consequence if the risk materialises. The method works well even for this type of distribution, even where X has a single value, providing the whole analysis is not dominated by this single risk.

It is useful to look at an example of this. Table 14.1 shows four such risks with various probabilities and impacts. It also shows the columns added to apply the direct method to calculate mean and variance.

Figure 14.2 shows the normal approximation and the 'exact' result obtained from Monte Carlo (from 1000 samples). The most likely values are 3 and 13 as would be expected (they each have a probability of 28.8 per cent). However, the normal is still a reasonable approximation.

Finally, the direct method is a very good method to use if you do not have £600 for the software or, more relevantly, do not want to go to the trouble of learning how to use yet another computer package. The direct method allows you to focus on the problem in hand rather than become another Monte Carlo nerd.

Discrete probability distributions and Bayesian networks

Another obvious way to calculate risk models is to discretise the probability distributions. Such an approximation should become more accurate as the distribution is represented on a finer and finer mesh. This is analogous to the finite element and finite difference methods used in fluid and solid mechanics. However, discrete probability calculations are very difficult and will not be described here.

Table 14.1   Simple point risk model for the direct method

	Prob	Impact	Value	Mean	Variance
Risk 1	0.50	10.00	10.00	5.00	25.00
Risk 2	0.20	8.00	0.00	1.60	10.24
Risk 3	0.10	4.00	0.00	0.40	1.44
Risk 4	0.80	3.00	3.00	2.40	1.44
		Result	**13.00**	**9.40**	**38.12**
				SD	**6.17**

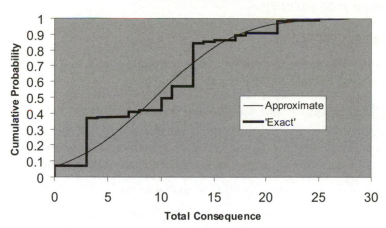

Figure 14.2   Results of the direct method for point risks

There are a number of tools which can do this using proprietary calculation techniques. Generally these are based around so-called Bayesian networks. The idea is you can set up a model, perhaps using influence diagrams such as the decision example in Chapter 8. The model can be quantified and the efficient calculation algorithms enable the network to be easily recalculated. It is then possible to explore the impact of new information as it becomes available. The work can be carried out using graphical computer tools based around the influence diagrams. This is all based on the conditional probabilities and Bayes theorem described in Chapter 12.

You can find a review of the technique and some examples in *Enabling a Powerful Marine and Offshore Decision-Support Solution Through Bayesian Network Technique* by Eleye-Datubo,*et al.* (in *Risk Analysis*, 26: 3, June 2006, 695–721).

When Monte Carlo does not work

Despite its very general philosophy, there are some cases where Monte Carlo does not work. This can be the case when the sampling process does not adequately look into the feature which the output requires. Two examples come to mind:

1. A contract is priced at P80. A variation order is then issued to allow an additional task to be done. It is desired to keep the price at P80. What should the value of the variation order be? The way to do this is to run Monte Carlo both with and without the extra task, and look at the difference in the P80s. Because of the sampling errors in the P80 estimates, however, it is difficult to calculate this difference with any accuracy. Of course, you can explain to the client that this does not really matter if you embrace the Monte Carlo approach – it is just a matter of living with probabilistic prices. On the other hand, you may prefer to be able to do an accurate estimate.
2. You are doing a system reliability analysis where a component has an unreliability of 10^{-4}. You are using 1000 samples but realise the event will not happen. So you do 100 000 simulations and the event happens about 10 times. But another part of the system – considered to be independent – has an unreliability of 10^{-2}. But, you still don't see it. So you do 10 000 000 samples – which takes a week and you still do not have a very accurate

sample. When you do some more samples, you run out of memory. Monte Carlo is simply not suitable for small probabilities.

CHANGES IN PERCENTILES

If you make a small increment to a random variable and want to know what the change in a percentile is you need to evaluate the integral:

$$P_1(x) = \int P(x - y)q(y) \, dy.$$

Here P_1 is the augmented cumulative distribution and P is the original cumulative distribution. $q(y)$ is the probability density distribution of the small increment. You can expand $P(x)$ in the neighbourhood of some point x_0, which is taken to be the required percentile:

$$P(x) = P_0 + (x - x_0)P'_0 + (x - x_0)^2 P''_0/2 + \text{smaller terms}$$

where $P_0 = P(x_0)$, $P'_0 = dP/dx$ at x_0 and is therefore $p(x_0)$ and $P''_0 = d^2P/dx^2$ at x_0 and is therefore dp/dx at x_0. Putting this into the integral gives:

$$P_1(x) \approx \int (P_0 + (x - y - x_0)P'_0 + (x - y - x_0)^2 P''_0/2)q(y) \, dy$$

$$= P_0 + (x - x_0)P'_0 - \mu P'_0 + (x - x_0)^2 P''_0/2 - \mu(x - x_0)P''_0 + (\sigma^2 + \mu^2)P''_0/2$$

where μ and σ are the mean and standard deviation of the additional distribution q. We are trying to find x such that $P_1(x) = P_0$, that is, the point at which the incremented distribution has the same percentile as the original at x_0. Since q is small, x is close to x_0 and we can look first at terms proportional to $(x - x_0)$ and find:

$$x - x_0 = \mu$$

so that the percentile is increased by the mean of the additional random variable, as you might expect. Including terms proportional to $(x - x_0)^2$ gives us:

$$x - x_0 = \mu - \sigma^2 P''_0/(2P'_0) = \mu - (\sigma^2/2)d\ln p/dx \text{ at } x_0.$$

The second term represents the risk premium given that dp/dx will usually be negative for large percentiles.

You can now see why Monte Carlo is so poor at calculating these changes in percentiles. We have already pointed out that the probability density function is difficult to evaluate from a Monte Carlo, let alone its derivative. The risk premium is dependent on the global behaviour of the overall distribution and could only be found by taking the Monte Carlo distribution and applying some heavy smoothing, or curve fitting. One approximate way to find the risk premium is to assume the underlying distribution, p, is normal.

SMALL PROBABILITIES

Traditional Monte Carlo had a technique called importance sampling to ensure that low probability areas were explored. This essentially oversampled the unlikely areas, but gave them a reduced weight. Monte Carlo as applied to risk modelling generally assigns equal weight to each sample, or simulation.

In the illustrative example we gave at the start of this section, we discussed the occurrence of two events, one with probability 10^{-4} and the other with probability 10^{-2}, so that the probability of both events occurring is 10^{-6}.

We could have calculated this probability in Monte Carlo by setting the probability of the first event at 50 per cent, but giving the events where it occurred a weight of 2×10^{-4}. Similarly, the second event could also be given a probability of 50 per cent, and their weight would be 0.02 (and the weight of the events where it does not occur would be 1.98). The $N/4$ samples where both events occurred would have weight 4×10^{-6}, so normalising would give a probability of 10^{-6}. Obviously this is very contrived, but could be useful in some circumstances.

The usual way to calculate reliabilities, especially where they are high, is to use *cut set analysis*. The idea behind this is that you identify all the combinations of events which would result in the system failing. Each such combination of events is called a cut set and has a probability. One way to get at this is to use the fault tree technique described in Chapter 5. If system failure does not result when you remove any event from the cut set, it is called a minimal cut set, and you can calculate its probability. If you have a complete set of minimal cut sets, you can define system failure. There is just one snag. You cannot in general easily work out the probability of all the cut sets together. You cannot add them up because it would double count those combinations of circumstances which are common to more than one minimal cut set. This is a trickier problem than you might at first sight think. It results in a series of approximations.

The first, and most obvious approximation, is to add them up anyway. If all the probabilities are small, the probability of the overlapping terms is very small. For example, if the system fails if A fails or B fails, and A and B both have a probability of 0.01, the approximate result is 0.02. The correct result is 0.0199. To see this just itemise the possibilities:

A and B fail	$0.01 \times 0.01 = 0.0001$
A fails, B does not	$0.01 \times 0.99 = 0.0099$
A does not fail, B does	$0.99 \times 0.01 = 0.0099$
Neither A nor B fails	$0.99 \times 0.99 = 0.9801$

So the total is 1 and the sum of the first three items, which comprise all the members of this complete and mutually exclusive list which represent either A failing or B failing, is 0.0199. This is less than 0.02 by 0.0001, the probability of both failing, which is double counted when you add the probability of A failing to that of B failing.

This immediately suggests another approximation based on success logic. The system will succeed if none of the cut sets occurs. So multiply the complements of the cut set probabilities and take the complement. This works both in the above example, and in the case where both A and B have to fail. But inevitably it does not work in more complicated cases because it does not correctly recognise common areas. However, this approximation is never worse than the first one.

There are other approximations which can be used that are built into reliability software. However, there are no exact solutions to the general problem. This is because for reasonably complicated problems there are a huge number of possibilities. For example, with N components there are 2^N possible states, each of which in principle has to be accounted for in the quantification.

So, in cases where the approximations have larger errors there is a case to try a Monte Carlo analysis, possibly with the importance weighting suggested above. It is straightforward to turn the system logic into a spreadsheet model, and this can be simulated in the usual way.

Summary

The main messages from this chapter can be summarised as:

*   Monte Carlo is by far the best way to quantify risk models because of its ease of use and reasonable accuracy.
*   For simple models, the direct method is very useful. This simply adds means and variances and uses a normal approximation. It can serve as a useful check on the main result of a more complex model.
*   A technique in which there is growing interest is Bayesian networks. This combines powerful mathematical techniques with graphical interfaces to enable risk models to be built and calculated in intuitive ways. However, this remains a technique for the specialist practitioner.

15 *Decision Analysis*

Risk management is about making decisions about what to do in the face of future uncertainty and seeing them through. Risk analysis supports the decisions by providing different versions of the uncertain future accompanied by probabilistic information about the likelihood of each one. The next question for us is to ask how this information can be used.

To answer this we provide a description of standard decision theory. We then discuss the limitations of this, which in turn will provide a background for the account in Part III of the way people actually take decisions.

Decision theory

Suppose you have two courses of action. The results of the risk analysis are expressed as the two S-curves in Figure 15.1.

Option B has the higher mean, but also has more spread, resulting in an appreciable probability of loss. It has a higher reward, but also a higher risk. Does this mean we should not select it?

To find a possible answer we quote from the preface of D.V. Lindley's book *Making Decisions* (Second Edition, 1985, Wiley, vii):

> *The main conclusion is that there is essentially only one way to reach a decision sensibly. First, the uncertainties present in the situation must be quantified in terms of values called probabilities. Second, the various consequences of the courses of actions must be similarly described in terms of utilities. Third, the decision must be taken which is expected – on the basis of the calculated probabilities – to give the greatest utility. The force of 'must', used in three places there, is simply that any deviation from the precepts is liable to lead the decision maker into procedures which are demonstrably absurd – or as we shall say, incoherent.*

This statement does not leave much room for doubt: make decisions this way or suffer the fate of being labelled incoherent. But when we have understood what 'this way' entails, we shall have to challenge it.

The first point in Lindley's prescription is the use of probability, just as we have defined and used it throughout this book. We have also mentioned the concept of *utility*, which we will now discuss at greater length. This is a measure of the preference of some outcomes over others. When we have defined the utility of each outcome, we select the option which has the maximum expected utility. This is the expected value of utility regarding it as a random variable.

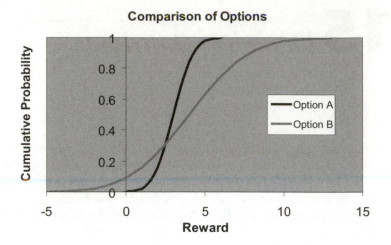

Figure 15.1   Comparison of two options

SIMPLE EXAMPLE

Thus, suppose we have a risk which occurs with probability p and leads to a loss L. We can spend some money, C, to reduce the probability of the risk materialising to $p/2$. We can also spend some more money, D, on reducing the loss to $L/2$. We can spend C, D, neither or both, so there are 4 options. Assuming for the moment that the utility of losses is simply their financial value, we can develop the following table, Table 15.1.

Evidently the optimal solution depends on the values. The option 'C only' is worth doing if $C < pL/2$, and similarly for D only. However you would only add the second one if $C + D$ is less than $3pL/4$. The preferred options are indicated in Figure 15.2 which shows (C,D) space.

Of course this is nothing but a standard cost–benefit calculation, with risk thrown in as part of the benefit evaluation.

NON-LINEAR UTILITY

Returning to the initial question, we can see straightaway that this prescription of maximising expected utility might validate the selection of Option A over Option B in the example. Although the expected *reward* of Option B is greater, if the *utility* of making a loss were disproportionately lower, we might find that Option A became preferred. For example, if the

Table 15.1   Decision table for simple example

Option	Probability	Certain Loss	Risk Consequence	Expected Utility
Neither	p	0	L	$-pL$
C only	$p/2$	C	L	$-C - pL/2$
D only	p	D	$L/2$	$-D - pL/2$
Both	$p/2$	$C + D$	$L/2$	$-C - D - pL/4$

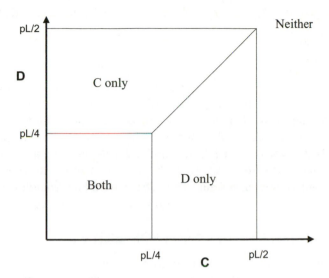

Figure 15.2   Decision chart for simple decision

area where the reward becomes negative represents bankruptcy, we might regard this as far worse than could be compensated by any profit. In this case we might set the utility function $u(x)$ to be:

$u(x) = 0$ where $x < 0$

$= 1$ where $x \geq 0$.

In this case, by inspection of the chart and understanding that the expected utility is just the probability of a positive reward, the expected utility of Option A is 1 and of Option B is about 0.9. Option A is now preferred.

DEFINING UTILITY

We said that utility is a measure of the preference for one outcome over another. We assume we can order preferences so that if C_1 is preferred to C_2 and C_2 is preferred to C_3 then C_1 is preferred to C_3. If this were not the case we would be incoherent. What this means is that if we had C_1 we would pay to swap it for C_3, since it is preferred, we would then pay again to swap C_3 for C_2 and pay a third time to swap C_2 for C_1. We would have made three payments and be back where we were.

Resuming the story, however, consider a choice between C_2 and a random process which results in C_3 with probability $1 - p$ and C_1 with probability p. If $p = 1$, the random process gives C_1 and we would prefer it. Conversely if $p = 0$ the random process gives C_3 and we prefer the certainty of C_2. There must, the argument runs, be a value of p between 0 and 1 where we would be indifferent to the certainty of C_2 compared with the random process (usually called a gamble) giving C_1 or C_3. If C_2 is only slightly preferred to C_3 then p is close to zero; if C_2 is only slightly less preferred than C_1, p will be close to one.

More generally, if C_w is the worst possible outcome and C_b is the best, then the utility of all other outcomes can be defined in this way with a number between 0 and 1 (inclusive). In the example we said that any loss is as bad as the worst loss ($u = 0$) and any gain is as good as the highest gain ($u = 1$). This is incoherent, but might in some cases be a reasonable approximation.

SUBJECTIVE UTILITY

Utility is defined as a probability. We have already discussed the subjective nature of probability at some length and this must now apply to utility too. All the questions about 'whose probability?' are now supplemented with questions about 'whose utility?' The manager of a company choosing between A and B might try to avoid loss at all costs: perhaps to avoid bankruptcy or maybe to protect their job. A shareholder in the company has a portfolio to deal with risk and might wish the manager to be less risk averse. The shareholder's utility might simply be reward as plotted in Figure 15.1. The shareholder would expect the manager to choose Option B, independent of their aversion to loss or bankruptcy.

ELICITING PREFERENCES, UTILITIES AND PROBABILITIES

Even more fundamentally, the process of utility formulation depends on forcing through the process of making someone accept that there must be an indifference probability. The logic is impeccable, but in practice people may not accept it, however incoherent you brand them. 'You cannot put a value on human life,' and so on. This is important not only for utility, but also for eliciting probabilities. We did not discuss this in Chapter 12, but one way to find a person's subjective estimate of the probability of an event is to explore their preferences between the future uncertainty and a random process which delivers the event with known probability. For example, if you offer someone the choice between £5 if planning permission is achieved in 3 months and participation in a game. The game is to select a random number using the Microsoft Excel random number generator (to avoid traditional balls, urns and the like). If the random number is less than p you win the same £5; if greater you do not. If p is close to one, the subject will accept the game; if p is close to zero they await planning permission. There must be a value of p, you argue, at which the person is indifferent to the choices. That is their subjective probability that planning permission will be obtained in 3 months.

This is fine if the subject plays ball, but if not then you have a problem. The problem is not just that you cannot obtain the probabilities and utilities to feed into a calculation, but that the subject has refused to participate in the one-and-only coherent approach to decision making. Most likely it is seen as too subjective and unreasonable in its insistence on valuing consequences which are complex, difficult to predict and, in some cases, raise moral issues.

The subject will feel vindicated when he hears that the maximising expected utility approach, whilst fine for individuals, has no analogue for collective decision making. Most famously, Arrow's impossibility theorem proves there is no procedure for obtaining a social ordering of options from those of the individuals in the society which satisfies certain requirements. Especially, one might retort, if individuals refuse to disclose theirs. This was discussed more extensively in specific contexts in Part III.

UTILITY RANGES

Although we have defined utility to be between 0 and 1, this is not really important and any linear function of utility defined this way can be used. To see this, if:

$$u_1(C) = au(C) + b \text{ for all C}$$

then the indifference probability of C_2 compared with the (C_1, C_3) random process is given by:

$$u_1(C_2) = pu_1(C_1) + (1 - p)u_1(C_3)$$

so

$$p = (u_1(C_2) - u_1(C_3)) / (u_1(C_1) - u_1(C_3))$$
$$= (u(C_2) - u(C_3)) / (u(C_1) - u(C_3)) = u(C_2)$$

since

$$u(C_3) = 0 \text{ and } u(C_1) = 1.$$

RISK AVERSION, RISK SEEKING AND RISK PREMIUMS

The extent to which utility is a non-linear function of reward is considered to reflect risk aversion or risk seeking attitudes. For most people it can be assumed that the slope of the utility function decreases at higher values: your second million is not as valuable as your first. This is known as a risk averse utility function. The utility function we used for the manager avoiding losses at all costs is one example. Conversely, a utility function for which the slope increases at higher amounts is said to reflect risk seeking behaviour.

How is this reflected as risk premiums? Suppose we have a utility function $u(x)$ and our current wealth is X. Then near X:

$$u(x) = u|_X + (x - X)u'|_X + (x - X)^2 u''|_X / 2 + O((x - X)^3).$$

If a project, deal, bet or any other proposition has expected outcome μ and standard deviation σ, the expected utility is:

$$E(u) \approx u|_X + \mu u'|_X + (\mu^2 + \sigma^2)u''|_X / 2$$

$$\approx u(X + \mu + R)$$

where R, the risk premium, is given by

$$R = (\sigma^2 / 2)u''|_X / u'|_X = (\sigma^2 / 2)(\ln u')'|_X.$$

Thus, for risk averse utility functions, for which $u'' < 0$, the risk premium is negative. This is the amount we would pay to avoid the risk associated with the proposition. For example, if the utility function is logarithmic, a form which is consistent with many people's revealed preferences, then $R = -\sigma^2 / (2X)$ where X is your current wealth.

There are a number of interrelated comments to be made:

- the risk premium is not large in general; if the standard deviation is 10 per cent of the project cost and the project cost is 10 per cent of your wealth, the risk premium is 0.005 per cent of your wealth or 0.05 per cent of the project cost;
- only if you are betting the farm is the risk premium comparable to the value of the bet;
- the risk premium is proportional to variance, not standard deviation, contrary to what most people might expect and contrary, for example, to the supposed expectations of investors as modelled in the CAPM (see Chapter 9);
- and in any case, surely risk aversion is about our attitude to uncertainty; not our view on the different outcomes per se.

These all combine to suggest that our view of risk, and hence the way we make decisions involving risk, is affected by the spread, and not just expected values. This is a key insight, but not one that reflects Lindsey's advice at the start of the chapter. People do not act coherently.

In Chapter 9 we sought a way around this for investors by explicitly building probability into the utility function in the form of the 'worry' occasioned by non-performing portfolios. It is interesting to speculate whether this is coherent or not. To the extent we are putting probability into the utility function, it is not; to the extent that worry is an outcome, especially if it leads to ulcers, for example, it is.

Leaving this on one side, according to decision theory you can make money out of people who do not act coherently, so let us see how we might do this with a construction contractor who prices at P80. You have a portfolio of construction risks with a mean of £100 million and standard deviation of £10 million. The contractor offers to build your project for £108.4 million (leaving profit out of it for the time being for the sake of making the point). As it happens, your portfolio of risks can be split into two (independent) portfolios, each with a mean of £50 million and standard deviations of £8 million and £6 million respectively. So you offer to buy the first portfolio back for £56.7 million (what he would have charged you). 'All right,' he says. You then offer to buy the second lot back for £55.0 million, and he agrees to this too. Well, now you have the same risks you started with but also have £3.3 million you did not have before. Go through this 30 times and you can get your building for nothing.

The discerning reader has probably spotted the flaw in this. It is a bit like going to the travel agent and saying that because they will sell you 1.35 euros for £1 they ought to give you £100 for the 136 euros you have in your pocket (being generous). Pricing at P80 gives the contractor an additional margin for accepting risk; it is nothing to do with their utility of money. A better analogy is a car dealer who does not think in terms of portfolios, but aims to make a profit on every car passing through. A contractor will aim very hard not make a loss on an individual job, independently of its size. It is also likely that the contractor will seek this margin because of his suspicion that the risk analysis is not right: that it neglects some risks or dependencies.

To summarise: people and organisations are more concerned about downside risk than decision theory says they should be. They seek rewards to reflect this concern. This does not make them money-making machines because they will refuse to engage in the externally-driven deal swapping which this requires (even if you tell them they ought to because it is in line with their revealed preferences).

This discussion of decision theory has been brief, but covers the main points. For the purpose of this book the most important point is that, leaving risk averse or risk seeking utility functions on one side, the theoretically best approach to decisions is to maximise expected reward, or minimise expected cost. As we noted, this is just cost–benefit analysis. There are problems with this, but the idea still forms a good starting point. There is a tendency for worrying about the problems to lead to different starting points. The most important point for now is to understand better how to do this when there are different types of outcome than cost.

Multi-attribute decisions

In Chapter 2 we emphasised that the consequences of risk materialising could be of many different types: environmental impacts, death or injury, reputational damage and so on. One aspect of decision theory is to rank outputs which have several dimensions or attributes, independently of the probability with which they arise.

Of course, the utility theory we have just examined provides a formulation: we just elicit the utility of each outcome. But to break the problem down, it is useful to separate the different attributes. The obvious way to do this is to write the utility as the sum of individual utilities, or values of each attribute:

$$u(x_1, x_2, \ldots , x_N) = v_1(x_1) + v_2(x_2) + \ldots + v_N(x_N)$$

where there are N attributes and the functions $v_i(x_i)$ represent the value of each attribute x_i.

This kind of formulation underlies a common scheme for supporting decisions where each aspect of a prospective holiday or a vendor bid is scored. The scores are multiplied by a set of weights then added and the holiday or vendor with the highest score wins. The total score is a linear function:

$$S = \sum_i w_i s_i$$

where the w_i are the weights and the s_i are the scores of the attributes. The attributes will generally tend to be difficult to value financially: a room with a view versus the number of local restaurants; a 10 hour flight versus a 1 degree higher average temperature. By using the weights (high, medium, low) and the scores (from one to five) we can create the illusion we are not putting cash against the attributes. But of course we are; it is just a bit less obvious. Paradoxically it is the price which is often left out of a supplier evaluation and considered separately.

Whilst these schemes are good in principle, they do tend to suffer from two problems:

1. The weights are not properly evaluated in the light of the scores (which are often normalised in some way). The way the weights are defined is what determines the difficult tradeoffs and throwing weights in without proper thought is a good way to abdicate from the real issues in a decision.
2. The method often acquires too many attributes, with the result that the Central Limit Theorem kicks in, the standard deviation of the scores is quite narrow and all of the options seem to score the same.

Sometimes it is not obvious that this kind of exercise has added much value. It is better to be clear what the constraints are and what the two or three key attributes are, than to have a scoring scheme for 50 of them. This creates an illusion of rigour, whilst actually allowing us to get away having avoided coming to terms with the stark approach required by utility theory.

However this is tangential to this book, as it is nothing to do with risk per se. What is important for risk analysis is to consider how to find the value functions for the range of consequences we commonly deal with in business risk management.

A good starting point is to look at the organisational objectives. As we emphasised back in Chapter 2, the only risks of interest are those that that affect the attainment of the objectives. A popular management fad for setting strategy, developing and communicating objectives and measuring performance is the balanced scorecard. This will generally cover a number of objectives in four areas: financial, customer, internal and growth. The purpose of the balanced scorecard is to help managers find a way of looking at issues which will eventually feed through into the performance (effectively the financial performance) of the organisation.

As such, the balanced scorecard idea is more of a prompt (similar to the prompts often used in risk workshop) for financial issues than a way of adding additional dimensions to finance. The issue is not trading off customer satisfaction (or safety, or the environment) against operating costs, but instead understanding the impact over time of customer satisfaction (or safety, or environmental performance) on profit, survival and shareholder value.

For most organisations the challenge is to gain an understanding of linkages; to build models of the business if you like. Trading off competing objectives along the lines suggested by multi-attribute theory should not be an issue.

This is where reputational risk analysis comes in. It is concerned with the long-term and hard-to-predict consequences of risk. We have to accept that things will come along and hit us that we did not expect, and simply did not and could not imagine. This should not stop us from trying, though; like the not-so-gullible contractor we discussed, making some provision for robustness in the face of unforeseen risks materialising.

Decision trees

We conclude this chapter with a discussion on a common technique in decision analysis which is closely tied in with risk. This has to do with the decision-making process rather than the decision itself, when conditions such as these apply:

- you may not have to make the decision now;
- you may want to collect more information;
- the decision you make now may be affected by the decisions you are going to make later.

Figure 15.3 shows a *decision tree* representing a situation where a developer is contemplating buying a piece of land for development. It is a brown field site and the developer is concerned that the land remediation costs may be prohibitive.

The diagram is fairly self explanatory. It is similar to an event tree (see Chapter 5) but contains two types of nodes. Decision nodes are marked by squares and followed by bold labels. These represent choices the developer can make. Event nodes, the same as event tree nodes, represent different outcomes. The assessed probability of each outcome is also indicated and at the end of each branch, the payoff is marked in italics.

The developer has an initial choice between buying, walking away or carrying out a site investigation (at a cost of I). If he buys straight away he thinks there is a chance of 30 per cent that high remediation costs H, will be required and his payoff is the development gain G, less these costs. Conversely there is a 70 per cent probability that they are low L, and the payoff is $G - L$.

If the developer commissions the site investigation the structure is similar, but the probabilities have shifted. If the outcome of the survey is positive, the probability of low costs has increased to 90 per cent; if negative, that of high costs is increased to 80 per cent. The payoffs are the same, except that they recognise the cost of the site investigation.

You can see that the probability of the outcome of the site survey has also been included in the diagram. It is important to realise that the probabilities on a decision tree have to satisfy certain coherence requirements. In this case, the site investigation probabilities are related to the probability improvements, noted above, that the survey brings. This is discussed further

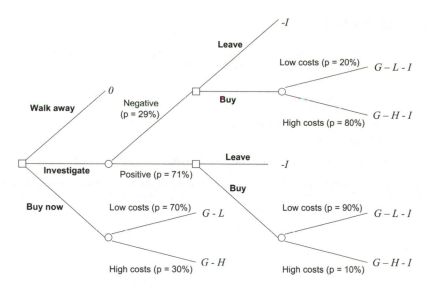

Figure 15.3   Decision tree for site development

in the Reliability of Oracles box. Suffice it to say these probabilities are coherent and we pass straight to analysing the decision tree.

The way to do this is to work backwards, starting from the last decision. The developer is of course as rich as Croesus so his utility of the sums involved is linear. So looking at the top right decision, the expected utility of the buy and leave decisions respectively are:

$$u_{buy} = 0.8(G - H - I) + 0.2(G - L - I) = G - I - 0.8H - 0.2L$$

$$u_{leave} = -I.$$

The developer buys if $G > (0.8H + 0.2L)$. Since this decision node occurs when the site investigation gives a negative outcome, it is unclear why he would have done the investigation if he is going to buy even with a poor result. We can assume that $G < (0.8H + 0.2L)$ and that he will walk away if the investigation is negative.

Applying the corresponding treatment to the node where the site investigation has a positive outcome, the same logic would suggest he always buys, in which case $G > (0.1H + 0.9L)$.

To avoid tedious nomenclature, we normalise in terms of the remediation costs as follows:

$$g = (G - L)/(H - L)$$

$$i = I/(H - L).$$

Thus, if $g > 0.8$ it is always worth buying and if $g < 0.1$ he should always walk away (with these assessed probabilities).

Turning to the first decision, we see that the expected utility of the three options is as follows:

$$u_{walk\ away} = 0$$

$$u_{investigate} = p_{positive}(G - I - 0.1H - 0.9L) + p_{negative}(-I)$$

$$= (H - L)(p_{positive}(g - 0.1) - i)$$

$$u_{buy} = 0.7 \times (G - L) + 0.3 \times (G - H) = (H - L)(g - 0.3).$$

Reliability of Oracles

How, exactly, does commissioning the site investigation improve the probabilities? The usual way to think about this is to model the investigation in terms of the probabilities of getting it wrong:

$$p^o_1 = \text{pr(positive|high)}$$

$$= \text{pr(positive outcome) when remediation costs will actually be high}$$

$$p^o_2 = \text{pr(negative|low)}$$

$$= \text{pr(negative outcome) when the remediation costs will actually be low.}$$

This is what we might call modelling the oracle: we think about the chance that the expert company doing the site survey will turn out to be wrong, when the actual state of the site is eventually revealed through clean up costs.

But what we want for the decision tree is actually the opposite probabilities:

$$p^y_1 = \text{pr(high|positive)}$$

$$p^y_2 = \text{pr(low|negative).}$$

These are the probabilities that the eventual costs are not in line with the expert's forecasts. We are not modelling the expert so much as thinking holistically about the site and expert techniques together. If you like, p^o is the probability of the expert oracle getting it wrong; p^y is the probability of you getting it wrong, having listened to the expert.

Luckily, as we noted in Chapter 12, Bayes theorem allows us to move from one to the other, for example:

$$\text{pr(high|positive)} = \text{pr(positive|high)pr(high)} / \text{pr(positive)}$$

where

$$\text{pr(positive)} = \text{pr(positive|high)pr(high)} + \text{pr(positive|low)pr(low).}$$

Since we assume we have estimates for pr(high) and pr(low) (0.7 and 0.3 in the example) we can go ahead and calculate the p^y_1 and p^y_2, using p^o_1 and p^o_2.

This process is called Bayesian updating because what we are doing is taking a prior estimate of the probability distribution of remediation cost (pr(high) and pr(low)) and working out what our updated values, the posterior distributions, would be in the light of each of the two results of the investigation and our model of the oracle p^o_1 and p^o_2. Bayesian methods are very powerful for using information to update subjective probabilities. This assumes you are coherent in terms of using your prior probabilities and your model of the expert.

Of course in putting the example together I cheated. I knew what values of p^y_1 and p^y_2 I wanted and worked out p^o_1 and p^o_2 to get them. From this I could work out pr(positive) and pr(negative) as on the decision tree. That is why they are not round numbers. Try it.

Decision tree analysis can get unnecessarily complicated this way. I have to admit I always find it confusing. What is important is to have a coherent set of probabilities. (It was this that meant that all the lines joined at the point in the value of information diagram in Figure 15.4.)

It is not necessarily obvious that p^o_1 and p^o_2 are the best way of modelling an oracle. For example, if you model yourself and the oracle in terms of p^y_1 and p^y_2 and assume values of pr(positive) and pr(negative), you can calculate pr(high) and pr(low) by simple conditional probabilities without complicated Bayes inversion. In the case of the site investigation, p^o_1 is the probability of a positive survey outcome but high costs. This would perhaps equate to the probability of not finding a pollutant. p^o_2, the probability of a negative survey but low eventual cost is harder to imagine: perhaps the pollutant found during the survey is less widespread than thought. On the other hand, p^y_2, the probability of low costs given a negative outcome, might reflect a possible advance in clean up technology (or perhaps just turning a blind eye). It has nothing to do with the oracle, but a valid model nonetheless.

I just repeat: the important thing is to have a coherent set of probabilities which survive a sanity check and careful thinking about what is really going on.

The value of $u_{investigate}$ has been obtained by assuming the buy decision if the outcome is positive and the leave decision if not. Thus, buying is better than investigating if:

$$i > p_{positive}(g - 0.1) - g + 0.3 = 2(0.8 - g)/7$$

because $p_{positive}$ is actually 5/7 as you will have seen from the Reliability of Oracles box. This sets an upper limit on the value of the information of the site survey, and thus what it is worth paying. Note that this goes to zero at $g = 0.8$, the value we identified above as being the point where the developer should buy anyway.

Investigating is better than walking away if:

$$i < p_{positive}(g - 0.1) = 5(g - 0.1)/7.$$

Finally, buying is better than walking away if $g > 0.3$.

The situation is summarised in Figure 15.4, which charts the value of the site investigation information v. The investigation should be commissioned only if $i < v$.

This shows there is only a range of potential gain where it is worth doing a site investigation. Outside this range it is obvious what to do. Within the range it is still only worth spending a certain amount to improve the probability of success. This amount becomes small at the edges of the range as the decision becomes more obvious. The maximum worth spending in this case is 14 per cent of the difference between the low and high site remediation costs.

This analysis is obviously very simplified. Many of the quantities presented as certain would not be. The outcomes are very coarsely categorised and would need to be refined. Trees can quickly become very complicated. However, the example gives a good flavour of how

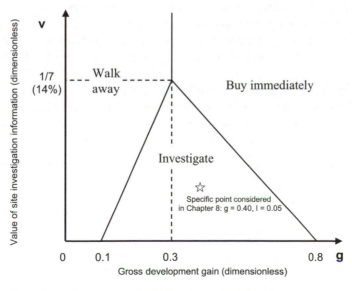

Figure 15.4   Decision chart and the value of information

additional information can be used to improve decisions and how decision making can be structured. Note in particular the need to work backwards in decision trees. This reflects a sad, but fundamental truth: you cannot decide now, without knowing what you would decide later for each circumstance which may arise.

Decision trees are a useful tool for structuring and resolving decision problems. They do depend on maximising expected utility, and so you have to accept this as a premise. They are closely related to influence diagrams which we recommended in Chapter 8 as a way to think about issues prior to building a risk model.

Summary

Classic decision theory provides a very straightforward prescription: maximise expected utility. This is coherence. If you are not coherent in your preferences and you consistently act in accordance with these incoherent preferences when given the chance, you could be caused to lose consistently: in the jargon, you become a money-making machine. Although in principle this leads to the generation of risk premiums, in practice these will be relatively small compared with those that are generally required. Indeed, neither people (although they should), organisations nor societies usually act so as to maximise expected utility. The way they actually make decisions is described in Part III.

On the other hand, decision trees, together with influence diagrams, are useful tools for structuring problems and developing risk models.

One topic this book has not delved into is game theory. Potentially this is an enormous omission. The risk models described are all based on the premise that the future is the outcome of random events, with probabilities that are changed only by our own risk management actions. In fact, the world, and the business world particularly, is characterised by multiple players; each with their own objectives and acting rationally, not randomly, in order to achieve them.

This is precisely the field that game theory tries to analyse. It is concerned with optimising your strategy when your competitors (including your partners – no two people at an organisation have completely aligned objectives) will act in such as way as to optimise theirs. Unfortunately, but hardly surprisingly, this is a much more difficult field. And to the extent that theoretical results have been found they do not appear to explain what people actually do.

The important point is to be aware of this. It is not a reason to avoid developing risk models. Much of the modelling will be concerned with events which are well approximated as the outcome of random processes. But what ABCo should really worry about is the environmental impact assessment of Product B which XYCo has sent to the European Commission.

Index

Figures are indicated by bold type and tables by italic.

A

ABCo
 baseline forecast 47–8
 Basic Risk Model 39
 benefits for of quantitative analysis 49–50
 compared to YZCo 57–60
 complete model 97–8, *98*, **98**
 downside scenario 49
 financial overview 100–2, *101*
 likelihood and consequence categories *22*
 Monte Carlo risk model **102,**
    102–7, *103, 105, 106*
 operational risk model *94*, 94–5
 overhead cost risk model 95–6, *96*, **96, 97**
 Prioritisation Scheme 22
 probability distribution of
    project delay 51
 profit and loss statement and
    balance sheet **50**
 profit spread **39**
 profit spread with dependence **42**
 project plan for production facility
    119, 119–23, **120, 121**
 qualitative risk profile *23*
 risk identification workshop
    output 18–19, *18–19*
 risk model results and meaning 52
 risk prioritisation matrix *22*
 risk provision 99
 risk register *20*
 target financial performance 49
 valuing risk *27*
additive properties in risk models 93
applicability of techniques 89
approximations 189–91, **190, 191, 192**, 221
Arrow, Kenneth xiv, 226
assumptions 89
aversion to risk 227–8

B

BAA 155

bankruptcy in waste management
    PPP **112,** 112–15, **113, 114**
baseline forecasts 47–8
Bayes theorem 185, 232
Bayesian networks 132–4, 135, 218, 222
behaviour and risk models 126–7
bell curves **35**, 35–6, **37**
beta distribution 183
betting the farm 29
bidder perspective of waste
    management PPP 61–2, **63**
binomial distribution 176–7, 179
business risk management 5–6, 130
business risk modelling
    relevance of probability 192–3
    and safety risk modelling 169

C

caps in contracts 109–10, **110**
Central Limit Theorem 191
central values and spread, equations for 40
Chebyshev's inequality 189–91, **190, 191**
chemical industry 160
chi-squared distribution 183
client perspective of waste
    management PPP 73–4
clouds of vagueness xiii, xiv
coin tossing 176
completeness in safety risk modelling 158
component modelling 81–3
conditional probabilities 184–6, *187*
consequences
    and likelihood chart 10, 12–13
    measuring with common scale 19–20
    of a single risk 24
contingency 49, 123–6, **124, 125,** *126*
continuous probability distributions 177–9
corporate risks for waste management PPP 65
correlation 41–2, 187–8, 199–200, **200, 201**
cost models
    additive properties 93
    operational risk *94*, 94–5
    overhead costs 95–6, *96*, **96, 97**
    see also risk modelling

costs and sales 40–3
critical path analysis 118
cryptosporidiosis influence diagram 131, **132**
cut set analysis 221

D
database systems 30–1
decision-making
    decision theory 223–9, **224, 225, 227**
    decision trees **134,** 134–5,
        227, 230–4, **233**
    multi-attribute decisions 229–30
    private sector 149–56
    public sector 139–47
    risk aversion 227–8
    risk premiums 228
    risk seeking 227–8
dependence 40–3, 66, 89–90,
        187–8, 193, 198–200
dice tossing 176
direct method of risk modelling
        217–18, *218,* **219**
discrete probability distributions
        176–77, 218–9
diversity 84–5
downside p-values 43–4

E
Edwards v. The National Coal Board 163
equations for central values and spread 40
estimators 207, 208–13, **211, 212**
event and fault trees 84–91, **85,**
        86, 87, 88, 131
exact methods of risk modelling 215–17, **216**
exponential distribution 178

F
facilitation of risk identification
        workshops 19
fault and event trees 84–91, **85,**
        86, 87, 88, 131
financial management of waste
        management PPP 74–5, **75**
financial model for waste management
        PPP 69–72, **71,** *71*
financial overview of ABCo
        project 100–2, *101*
financial risk modelling 110–11
float 49
fN-curves 158–60
frequencies 90, 158–9

G
gainshare contracts 109
game theory 234
gamma distribution 182–3
Gantt charts 118
government decision-making. *see*
        public sector decision-making
Green Book, The (HMT) 139–43
guidance on risk management 11

H
hard-to-value benefits or disbenefits 141–3
hazards 157
    see also safety; safety risk modelling
HAZOPS 19
health and safety risk 4
    see also safety; safety risk modelling
health benefits, valuing 143
human behaviour and risk models 126–7

I
identification of risks 17–20
independence 184–6, 193
    see also dependence
inflation 66
influence diagrams **131,** 131–4, **132, 133**
information systems 29–31
    see also software

J
joint probability distributions 186–7

K
kitchen sink approach to risk modelling 53
kurtosis 180

L
Layfield, Sir Frank 166
likelihood and consequence
    bands 21–4
    charts 10, 12–13
Lindley, D.V. 223
lognormal distribution 183–4
London Underground PPP 146–7

M
Making Decisions (D.V. Lindley) 223
management
    financial, of waste management
        PPP 74–5, **75**
    knowledge of risk modelling 44–5, 60, 76

as a source of risk 164
stakeholder expectations of **152,**
    152–4
see also risk management
matrices 28
maximin 144
mean 180, *181,* 213
    consequence 28
    estimating 209
    of probability distribution 45
    properties 46
minimax 144
mixed random variables 184, **185**
moments 180
Monte Carlo risk model
    ABCo **102,** 102–7, *103, 105, 106*
    concept and background to 195–6
    correlation 199–200, **200, 201**
    displaying results 200–7
    estimators 207, 209–13, **211, 212**
    mean 209, 213
    modelling dependence 198–200
    operational risk model 95, **96**
    overhead risk model 96, **97**
    percentiles 210–11, **211**
    process for 196–7
    simple cost risk model 200–3,
        202, **202, 203, 204, 205**
    simple project risk model 203,
        204–7, *205,* **206, 208**
    simulations 197–8, **198, 199**
    software for 135–6
    standard deviation 209–10, **211,** 213
    statistical inference 207
    unsuitable occasions for use 219–21
    using @Risk software 197
    variance 209–10, 213
multiple events 184–6

N
National Audit Office (NAO) 146–7
National Coal Board, Edwards v. 163
negotiations, role of risk model during 74
non-financial consequences of risk 28
non-linear utility 224–5
normal distribution 178–9
nuclear industry 157–8, 160, 166

O
objectives, business 10
operational risk model *94,* 94–5
opportunities and threats 10
optimism bias 140

option appraisal 139
Orange Book, The (HMT) 139
overhead cost risk model 95–6, *96,* **96, 97**

P
p-values, downside 43–4
percentage reference table *153*
percentiles 180, **181,** 210–11, **211,** 220
Peterson, Martin 168
PFIs. *see* private finance initiatives (PFIs)
physical risk models 129–30
Poisson processes and frequencies
        82, 159, 176–7, 178
PPPs. *see* public private partnerships (PPPs)
precautionary principle 167–8
private finance initiatives (PFIs) 60
private sector decision-making
    capital asset pricing model (CAPM) 150
    investor expectations 149–50
    stakeholder expectations
        concerning risk **152,** 152–4
    systematic and unique risk 149–50
probabilities 90
    small 220–1
probability 55–6
    approximations 189–91, **190, 191, 192**
    beta distribution 183
    binomial distribution 179
    Central Limit Theorem 191
    Chebyshev's inequality 189–91, **190, 191**
    chi-squared distribution **182,** 183
    conditional probabilities 184–6, *187*
    correlation 187–8
    density function 177
    discrete distributions 218–9
    distribution 36–7, 45, 175–9
    distribution gallery *181*
    gamma distribution **182,** 182–3
    independence 184–6
    joint probability distributions 186–7
    kurtosis 180
    large numbers 190–1
    lognormal distribution 183–4
    management use of 13
    mean 180, *181*
    mixed random variables 184, **185**
    moments 180
    multiple events 184–6
    percentiles 180, **181**
    Poisson process 176, 178
    products of random variables 188–9
    random processes and variables 173–5
    relative frequency 174

relevance to business risk
    modelling 192–3
repeatable experiments 173–5
skewness 180
standard deviation 180
statistical regularity 174
subjectivity of 192–3
sums of random variables 188
triangle distribution 182, **182**
variance 180, *181*
Weibull distribution 183
procurement in the public sector
    144–6, 154–6, *155, 156*
products of random variables 188–9
projects
    funding for contingencies
        123–6, **124, 125,** *126*
    influence diagrams 131
    plans **119,** 119–23, **120, 121, 122**
    and risk 117
    schedule risk analysis 118
    software tools 118
public private partnerships (PPPs) 60
public sector comparator (PSC) 73,
    145–6
public sector decision-making
    The Green Book 139
    investor coherence **151,** 151–2
    option appraisal 139, 143–4
    procurement 144–6, 154–6, *155, 156*
    risk transfer and sharing 144–6
    risk transfer to the private
        sector 154–6, *155, 156*
    treatment of hard-to-value 141–3
    treatment of risk *140,* 140–1
    utility and worry **151,** 151–2

Q
qualitative risk analysis 21–4, *22, 23,* **24**
quantification of fault trees 90–1
quantitative risk analysis
    bell curves **35,** 35–6, **37**
    benefits and drawbacks 55
    benefits for ABCo 49–50
    business risk management 5–6
    compared to qualitative 33
    financial risk 5
    health and safety risk 4
    as part of risk management xiv
    physical risk analysis 5
    reliability analysis 4
    s-curves **36,** 36–7, **37**

R
random processes and variables
    173–5, 184, **185,** 188–9
rank correlation 199–200, **200**
rationality and safety risk modelling 164–6
*Reducing Risk, Protecting People: HSE's
    decision making process* (HSE) 165–6
redundancy 84
regulation (safety), risk based 160, 163–8
relational database systems 30–1
relative frequency 174
reliability analysis 4
reliability modelling
    as a binary system 81
    component modelling 81–3
    use of historical data 83–4
repeatable experiments 173–5
reputation 28
residual risk 15
residual waste disposal risks for waste
    management PPP 64–5
risk
    defined 10–13
    non-financial consequences of 28
    organisational 6
    in projects 117
    residual 15
    treatment of in public sector
        decision-making *140,* 140–1
    as two-dimensional concept 10, 12–12
    unacceptable and tolerable 166–7
    and uncertainty 6
    valuation of 26–8, *27*
risk analysis
    qualitative 21–4, *22, 23,* **24**
    use of in safety risk modelling 168
    waste management PPP 62–6
Risk Analysis (journal) 129–30, 131
risk assessment
    defined 13–14
    identification of risks 17–20
risk aversion 227–8
risk evaluation 24–6
risk management
    basic disciplines of 9
    and context 15
    defined 14–15
    growth and importance of 3–4
    guidance on 11
    importance of communication 15–16
    process of **16,** 16–17
    see also management
risk modelling 38–44

ABCo compared to YZCo 57–60
ABCo results and meaning 52
binary 81 (*see also* reliability modelling)
direct method 217–18, *218*, **219**
exact methods of 215–17, **216**
financial 110–11
and human behaviour 126–7
management knowledge of 44–5
outline process 54
range of possible models 129–30
reflecting risk register 47–54
role during negotiations 74
summary 76–7
waste management PPP 66–9, **67**, *68*, **68**
see also cost models; Monte Carlo risk
     model; safety risk modelling
risk premiums 29, **29**, 77–8, 151–2, 228
risk provision 99
risk register 19, *20*, 47–54
risk seeking 227–8
risk software 135–6, 197
risk transfer and sharing 108–10,
     144–6, 154–6, *155, 156*

S
s-curves **36**, 36–7, **37**
safety 28
     see also health and safety risk;
          safety risk modelling
safety risk modelling
     and business risk modelling 169
     chemical industry 160
     completeness 158
     fN-curves 158–60, **159**
     frequencies 158–9
     good practice 167
     hazards 157
     lack of commitment by regulators 166–8
     need for caution 157
     nuclear industry 157–8, 160, 166
     Poisson process 159
     precautionary principle 167–8
     and rationality 164–6
     risk based regulation 160, 163–8
     safety case 163
     single lead junctions **161**, 161–3, **162**
     unacceptable and tolerable risks 166–7
     uncertainty 164, 165
     use of risk analysis 168
     see also risk modelling
sales and costs 40–3
scenario modelling 50
schedule risk analysis 118

scoring schemes 141–2, *142*
sensitivity chart 67, **67**, 69, **69**
single lead junctions **161**, 161–3, **162**
Sizewell 'B' nuclear reactor 166
skewness 180
software 30–1, 118, 135–6, 197
spreadsheets 30, 31
standard deviation 46, 180, 209–10, **211**,
     213
standards 11
statistical inference 207
statistical regularity 174
subcontractor perspective of waste
     management PPP 72–3
subjectivity
     of probability 13, 38, 192–3
     of utility 226
sums of random variables 188
systematic risk 149–50

T
templates, lack of in business risk
     management 130
time dependence 66
*Tolerability of Risk from Nuclear Power
     Stations, The* (HSE) 166
tolerable and unacceptable risks 166–7
transition risks for waste management PPP
     65
transportation risks for waste
     management PPP 63
treatment of risk 26–9
triangle distribution 182, **185**
Turnbull requirements 18

U
unacceptable and tolerable risks 166–7
uncertainty xiv, 6, 164, 165
uniform distribution 176, 177–8
unique risk 149
utility
     defining 225–6
     eliciting preferences and probabilities
          226
     non-linear 224–5
     ranges 226–7
     subjective 226
     and worry **151**, 151–2

V
Value for Money Assessment (HMT) 145–6
variance 180, *181*, 209–10, 213

W
waste disposal risks for waste
    management PPP 64–5
waste management PPP 61
    bankruptcy **112,** 112–15, **113, 114**
    bidder perspective 61–2, **63**
    client perspective 73–4
    financial management of 74–5, **75**
    financial model 69–72, **71,** *71*
    improving risk profile 68–9, **69, 70**
    influence diagrams 131, **131**
    negotiations 74
    pricing 111–15, **112, 113, 114**
    risk analysis 62–6
    risk model 66–9, **67,** *68,* **68**

    role of public sector comparator (PSC) *73*
    subcontractor perspective *72–3*
waste processing risks for waste
    management PPP 64
weaknesses of project plans 121, 123
Weibull distribution 183
workshops
    for estimating risk 21–2
    risk identification *18,* 18–19, 65–6
worry and utility **151,** 151–2
    see also utility

Y
YZCo 57–60

About the Author

Andy Garlick is in the forefront of risk management professionals. For 25 years, he has provided advice to clients on many different aspects of risk, and has helped to build risk-based consulting businesses. He is now a freelance risk consultant who continues to promote better ways of dealing with risk.

A mathematician by discipline, Andy originally worked on modelling fluid flows, particularly the modelling of interstellar gases, star formations and explosions. During a long period working for the United Kingdom Atomic Energy Authority he started working on the analysis of the safety risk posed by nuclear reactors and other installations. Randomised methods, also called Monte Carlo, became one of his particular interests.

With the privatisation of the UKAEA as AEA Technology, Andy moved into management roles. He became particularly interested in the adaptation of the risk-based approach for other types of plants and beyond, to commercial applications in business. His aim was to make the techniques more relevant and more accessible. His final role with AEA Technology was to help found its management consulting practice, Risk Solutions, which is now a successful independent firm.

As a director of Manex (UK) Limited, Andy's main project was the London Underground public private partnership. Andy then set up his own consulting firm, The Risk Agenda and the idea for this book began to form.

The purpose of The Risk Agenda is to improve the way organisations deal with an uncertain future:

- by contributing to the advancement of good practice;
- by helping organisations adopt this good practice;
- by working with them on their specific risk challenges.

Andy is a member of the Society for Risk Analysis and a Fellow of the Institute of Risk Management. He helps organise the North-West branch of the IRM and its special interest group on PPP/PFI.

You can find out more about Andy and The Risk Agenda by visiting the website www.riskagenda.com. This features RiskBites which tell you more about risk analysis and management. The site also provides tools and other materials for free download, including examples from this book. The Risk Agenda offers courses based on this book or on other risk topics which can be customised for different organisations. If you would like to learn more, you can email Andy at andy.garlick@riskagenda.com.